EDUCATIONAL TRANSACTIONAL ANALYSIS

While there are a small number of titles exploring transactional analysis in specific educational settings, there is no comprehensive account of this practical psychology for learning. *Educational Transactional Analysis* draws together a team of contributors from the international educational TA community, offering perspectives from Europe, India, South Africa, Australia, Japan and the United States to explain and illustrate the practice of this exciting development in education.

Establishing a seminal overview that will make it the 'go-to' text, the book covers four key parts:

- philosophy, politics, principles and educational transactional analysis;
- the identity of the teacher;
- educational transactional analysis and schooling;
- educational transactional analysis: adult learning and community development.

Aimed at educators in all contexts, researchers, students and trainers, this book will be an essential resource for those that wish to deepen their understanding of educational TA or are involved in formal TA training.

Giles Barrow (TSTA-E) began his career as an English teacher in the UK. He has subsequently worked in specialist provision and support services and has written a number of publications on learning, teaching, education and transactional analysis.

Trudi Newton (TSTA-E) discovered transactional analysis around 30 years ago and has since enjoyed introducing others to it through training, supervision and personal connection. She also writes and consults with other educators to enable radical learning and community development.

EDUCATIONAL TRANSACTIONAL ANALYSIS

An international guide to theory and practice

Edited by
Giles Barrow and Trudi Newton

Routledge
Taylor & Francis Group

LONDON AND NEW YORK

First published 2016
by Routledge
2 Park Square, Milton Park, Abingdon, Oxon OX14 4RN

and by Routledge
711 Third Avenue, New York, NY 10017

Routledge is an imprint of the Taylor & Francis Group, an informa business

British Library Cataloguing in Publication Data
A catalogue record for this book is available from the British Library

Library of Congress Cataloging in Publication Data
Barrow, Giles.
  Educational transactional analysis: an international guide to theory and
  practice/edited by Giles Barrow and Trudi Newton.
  pages cm
  Includes bibliographical references and index.
  1. Educational psychology. 2. Learning, Psychology of. 3. Transactional
  analysis. I. Newton, Trudi. II. Title.
  LB1051.B2496 2016
  370.15 – dc23
  2015012731

ISBN: 978-1-138-83237-4 (hbk)
ISBN: 978-1-138-83238-1 (pbk)
ISBN: 978-1-315-68677-6 (ebk)

Typeset in Bembo and Stone Sans
by Florence Production Ltd, Stoodleigh, Devon, UK

CONTENTS

ACKNOWLEDGEMENTS

One of the things we enjoy about the transactional analysis world is the generosity and zest that its members show in working together to develop new projects. Throughout the process of creating this book we have appreciated the willingness, enthusiasm, flexibility and patience of our contributors: Jan Grant and Rhae Hooper in Australia, Karen Pratt in South Africa, Tomoko Abe in Japan, Marina Ragan Joseph in India, Jean Clarke in the USA, Dörte Landmann, Gernot Aich and Nevenka Miljkovic in Germany, Ferdinando Montuschi and Cesare Fregola in Italy, Nicole Pierre and Agnès Le Guernic in France, Jacqueline Goosens in Belgium, Sylvia Schachner in Austria, Evelyne Papaux in Switzerland, Henk Tigchelaar in the Netherlands and Rosemary Napper, Susannah Temple and Pete Shotton in the UK. We thank all of them . . .

We also thank our translators, Evelyne Papaux, Sarah Gornall, Suzanne Lines and Ute Schicha, for their hard work and creativity – as well as enabling us to increase our range of contributions, we learned a lot about the potential and the limits of language – and about the diverse cultures of education and of TA.

Next, we want to thank all those who gave us permission to use their material; thanks to Sage Publications, and to Michelle Binur in particular, for permission to reproduce diagrams from *TAJ*: the CAP model (Barrow 2007), the Script Helix (Summers and Tudor 2000), Spiral Dynamics, Autonomy and Homonomy (Salters 2011), Behavioural Manifestations of Ego-states (Temple 1999), Nine Behavioural Modes (Temple 2004), OK Communication (Pratt and Mbaligontsi 2014). Thanks also to Laurie Hawkes for permission to reproduce her version of the Permission Wheel (Jaoui 1988), to Ian Stewart and Vann Joines for their Symbiosis diagram (2012) and to Helen Davies and For Effect for the illustrations in Chapter 4.

For granting permission to republish written material we thank the following:

- *International Journal of Transactional Analysis Research* and editor Julie Hay for 'Mathematical Calculation Procedures and Drivers in Action in the Learning

Environment' by Cesare Fregola, first published in *The International Journal of Transactional Analysis Research* 1.1: 30–9.

- The Italian TA Journal, for 'La Conquista del Silenzio: Itinerari Educativi' (The Conquest of Silence: Educational Journeys) by Ferdinando Montuschi, published in 16: 59–69.
- ESF éditeur and Sophie Courault, for permission to translate material from Nicole Pierre's book *Pratique de l'Analyse Transactionelle dans la Classe*, (2002: 60–76).

In bringing it all together and creating the final manuscript, appreciative thanks to David Newton for creating the diagrams, for preparing and organizing the typescript, and for unfailing support from the beginning and throughout; and to Bruce Roberts and Sarah Richardson who have given us all the encouragement, counsel and practical help we could ask for. And sincere thanks also to our reviewers, Ruth MacConville and Anna Sierpinska, who believed in the idea of the book and made excellent and inspiring suggestions which enabled us to re-shape our original proposal and create a more substantial work, more expressive of current thinking in educational TA.

And finally – thanks to all our colleagues, mentors, TA friends worldwide, trainees and workshop members, who have discussed the ideas, shared their responses and helped us to get to here.

CONTRIBUTORS

Tomoko Abe TSTA-E became the second TSTA in Education in Japan in 2014. She and her course participants enjoy humanistic and radical training experiences, which are very new to their society. It is a privilege, she believes, to be with people when they start realizing that learning is fun.

Dr Gernot Aich PTSTA-E teaches at the University of Education, Schwäbisch Gmünd, and researches negotiation skills and teachers' ability to solve conflicts. He developed the Gmünd Model for Teacher–Parent Conferences. He also leads a TA training group, works as trainer for academies and schools and has published several books and articles on communication.

Jean Illsley Clarke PhD, CFLE, TSTA-E, author and parent educator, received the Eric Berne Memorial Award for applied transactional analysis in education in 1995. The award was primarily for her book *Self-Esteem: A family affair*. Her most recent book is *How Much is Too Much?*

Cesare Fregola PTSTA-E is Professor of Didactics of Mathematics for the Integration in the Primary Education Faculty at L'Aquila University. He leads the Experimental Pedagogy Laboratory at the Università Roma Tre. Cesare is a researcher, educator and expert advisor on learning environments for lifelong learning.

Jacqueline Goosens TSTA-E loves teaching as her way of integrating the tools she has learned. She has practised and taught TA for over 30 years and practised with family constellations for fifteen. She likes the giving and receiving of her businesses, as trainer, supervisor and therapist; she also loves to sing.

Jan Grant, BEd, MEd (Adult Ed) is a Teaching and Supervising Transactional Analyst (Education and Counselling) and a Certified Imago Relationship Therapist. Jan lives and works in Sydney and divides her time between her private practice and her teaching and supervising at the Australian College of Applied Psychology.

Rhae Hooper is a speech and drama teacher, a CTA, PTSTA and a trainer, facilitator, coach, mentor and supervisor providing coaching and group training for the corporate and private sector. She has held senior management roles in the International Corporate sector and has been a trainer for over 35 years.

Marina Rajan Joseph is a PTSTA-E and a professor of public health in India. A deeply spiritual person, her passion is to integrate TA theory into methods of education and supervision across disciplines of education and health care, empowering health care providers, educators and learners for 'Abundant Living'.

Dörte Landmann TSTA-E was for many years a teacher and school counsellor for teachers and socially insecure children with behavioural difficulties. It is important to her that people develop skills and mindfulness to achieve satisfaction in their own lives. She led the pedagogy and adult education part of the TA association in Germany and was on the Ethics Committee.

Agnès Le Guernic is a TSTA-E who works as a supervisor and life coach in Paris. She is the author of several articles and books about TA. She is also the author of the blog analyste-transactionnelle.fr.

Nevenka Miljkovic PTSTA-E works with trainers and in training coaches and counsellors. Her special focus is to support educators with TA so that they feel safe in their work and enjoy their teaching and training.

Ferdinando Montuschi is Emeritus Professor of Special Education at the Università Roma Tre, psychologist, psychotherapist and TSTA-E.

Rosemary Napper MA(Ed), TSTA-E has a zest for learning and a curiosity about how adults learn. As a result she relishes training trainers and has written a number of books and chapters on adult learning. Centred in Oxford UK, she also works regularly in Brazil, India and Japan.

Evelyne Papaux TSTA-E has for years been relating with children and their families, children with special needs, children in multicultural environments and in homecare. Her enthusiasm for educational TA comes from her conviction that TA is an effective means of prevention in children's education.

Nicole Pierre TSTA-E has been a high school teacher and a trainer of educators. She is an education consultant, a specialist in mental management and learning strategies, and an NLP practitioner.

Karen Pratt is a South African Teaching Transactional Analyst in Education. She works as a coach and facilitator with individuals and communities wanting to grow and change. She is particularly curious about the spaces within and between people, and how those can become ever-more authentic and enlivening – impacting human systems.

Dr Sylvia Schachner PTSTA-E has over twenty-five years' experience teaching in primary schools, and for fifteen of them she has been using TA. She is now an education consultant and Specialized Education and School Development Manager in Vienna.

Pete Shotton BEd, CTA-E, CTA-P, TSTA-E has worked in education settings with young people and adults since 1978. He is a TA trainer and supervisor working with educators and psychotherapists, and also works as an education advisor for social workers, foster carers and looked-after children in a social care agency.

Susannah Temple PhD has been an educator all her life in one way or another, passionate about supporting the quality of the dynamics between teachers and learners where the inspirations and growth are mutually offered and mutually rewarding.

Henk Tigchelaar, PTSTA-E, worked for over 40 years as a teacher in primary and secondary schools and universities. He is also a musician. He uses TA to invite people from an OK–OK attitude to find their own autonomy. He is a director and trainer at the TA Academy in the Netherlands.

ABBREVIATIONS

The following abbreviations are used throughout the text:

TA	Transactional analysis
CTA	Certified Transactional Analyst
TSTA	Teaching and Supervising Transactional Analyst
PTSTA	Provisional Teaching and Supervising Transactional Analyst
C	Counselling
E	Educational
O	Organizational
P	Psychotherapy
EATA	European Association for Transactional Analysis
ITAA	International Transactional Analysis Association
TAJ	*Transactional Analysis Journal*
P	Parent ego-state
A	Adult ego-state
C	Child ego-state

} fields of application in TA

Note to readers: This book is many things, but it is not a TA primer. We suggest *TA Today* (Stewart and Joines 2012) or *Working It Out at Work* (Hay 1996) as good sources for learning more about TA ideas. There are also useful overviews on itaaworld.org and eatanews.org.

INTRODUCTION

Giles Barrow and Trudi Newton, UK

> One child, one teacher, one pen and one book can change the world. Education is the only solution. Education first.
>
> (Malala Yousafzai, UN Assembly, July 2012)

Education involves an act of faith. When we gather in the education endeavour, teachers and students step into unknown territory; a creative process that has potential to change, renew and transform. Ultimately, education is a way through which humankind expresses an enduring capacity to thrive. In turn, educational transactional analysis provides a psychological framework for explaining what happens in learning, how teacher and student roles interact, and illuminates why educational processes are, as Yousafzai claims, 'the only solution' to how individuals act to change the world.

This publication is the first comprehensive account of educational transactional analysis. The intention is neither to fix nor prescribe what it entails, nor to claim that what follows is the only way of making sense of educational transactional analysis. What we want to do is breathe further life into an educational psychology that has been gradually emerging since its early days in the 1960s and has gathered pace over the past ten years or so. In addition to providing a psychological frame-work, we also present educational transactional analysis as a distinct theory of teaching and learning. In other words, educational transactional analysis is as much about an educational theory, with a robust purpose and method, as it is an approach for illuminating the psychological dimension of the educational process.

This book is partly about the relational aspects of teaching and learning. It is also concerned with integrity in education, both that of the teacher and in theoretical terms. Mostly, though, we are setting out a comprehensive account of educational transactional analysis as a combined pedagogical theory and educational psychology. This is neither a book about just education, nor one solely focused on transactional analysis. For readers familiar with either of these topics, there will be newness here. For those coming from outside the TA professional community, perhaps with some general background in TA concepts, our intention is to encourage a re-framing of what TA might have meant for you in the past. For readers familiar with mainstream debates about learning theory, we invite you to consider a pedagogical perspective rooted in a psychological framework.

In many respects our work has an introductory intention because, despite having been around for several decades, educational transactional analysis has remained elusive and well camouflaged. Positioned between the world of educational theory and practice, and the psychotherapeutic domain from which transactional analysis originated, educational transactional analysis has escaped a distinct identity. This book aims to declare the purposes, applications, principles and philosophy of educational transactional analysis. It presents a comprehensive account of how educational transactional analysis has developed, how it is practised, and the distinctive perspective it offers to educators.

In establishing this position we have sought contributions from a richly diverse group of experienced TA educators. The diversity extends across different dimensions. We have the voices of those who were at the very beginning of educational TA, in some respects before it even existed – Jean Illsley Clarke writes a retrospective account about these earliest days – and other contributors who represent the subsequent three generational phases of senior practitioners, along with a handful of contributions from some of the most recently qualified Teaching and Supervising Transactional Analysts in the field. We have also gathered voices from all of those areas in the world where educational transactional analysis is practised: colleagues from Japan, India, South Africa, Australia, mainland Europe, the United Kingdom and the States, all present perspectives drawn from their respective cultural contexts.

There are a couple of other ways in which our contributors differ significantly: Educational TA is practised wherever learning takes place, so there are stories from a range of educational contexts. In the past, 'TA in education' has occasionally been regarded by some as an activity that a handful of TA practitioners 'do' with children in schools. Our intention here is to do away with this misunderstanding: educational transactional analysis has always been about the educational endeavour wherever that takes place. So, readers will come across accounts from adult education, the corporate world, professional development and training, community projects, higher education, vocational training, parent and family support, specialist and mainstream schooling, Early Years, primary and secondary education, as well as teacher training and personal growth programmes. This is the first time a publication has offered such a comprehensive overview of where educational TA is practised, both worldwide and in terms of contexts.

Educational transactional analysis: a weak concept

There is a final dimension of diversity at work throughout the contributions. We want to account for both pedagogy and practice, and highlight linkage with associated non-TA models. We want to ensure a wide coverage of TA concepts and reference material. What we have not done is to synthesize or assimilate the voices of the contributors into a homogeneous whole. Each author speaks from their own condition, their personal sense of self as an educator. What this means is that readers may find themselves keenly resonating with the approach in one chapter, only to be disappointed or irritated by another. Our intention is that the reader's experience of each contribution will illuminate something about the educational partnership. Maybe the reader senses a 'wise sage' emerging in a chapter, or a 'patient guide'; perhaps, instead, there is a meandering explorative experience or a clear straightforward introduction to new content. Each of these accounts may connect differently to the reader/student. And each may frustrate – the sage may provoke insubordination, the guide become cloying, the meandering explorer simply confuse, and the teacher of new material indicate arrogance. All of these responses tell us something more about the purpose of learning, the role of student and the intention of the educator. Educational transactional analysis is ultimately about who you are as an educator – and only then about what you do. Each chapter is an expression of how each contributor steps up and into being an educational transactional analyst. Readers can make their own decision about how the experiences contribute to their own professional development narrative. As ever, the student makes meaning from the relationship.

We suggest that educational transactional analysis can be described as a *weak* concept. In defining it as such, we are drawing on the work of Biesta (2014), who discusses weakness in relation to education generally. For us, this notion of weakness captures a distinctive quality of how we experience being and doing educational transactional analysis:

> education only works through weak connections of communication and interpretation, of interruption and response, and [. . .] this weakness matters if our educational endeavors are informed by a concern for those we educate to be subjects of their own actions – which is as much about being the author and originator of one's actions as it is about being responsible for what one's actions bring about.
>
> (Biesta 2014: 4)

So our work is essentially dialogic, a process of to-and-fro in which the individual ascribed as 'learner' or – in our relationship right here with you – as 'reader', has the responsibility and potential to determine what's useful, meaningful, or of value in some other way. Crucially, this co-creative partnership involves the 'teacher' in preparing themselves to teach.

Biesta continues by cautioning against a simplistic understanding of a dialogic educational method in which there is a blurring of teaching and learning into a single entity:

> This has indeed become a popular and even fashionable idea in contem-
> porary educational discourse and practice, as can be seen in such notions as

'communities of practice' and 'learning communities'. But to think of education in these terms runs the risk of eradicating what I see as essential for education, which is the presence of a teacher, not just as a fellow learner or a facilitator of learning, but as someone who, in the most general terms, has to bring something to the educational situation that was not there already.

(2014: 6)

Each contributor brings an expertise to this collection, rooted in a specific educational context; and, in our bringing these perspectives together, we are aware of 'bringing something to the situation that was not there already'. This 'situation', in our view, refers partly to the transactional analysis community – and also to a wider educational audience. While we know that what we have to share is worthwhile, *how* it is of value to readers is less certain. And it is this uncertainty that lies at the heart of Biesta's notion of 'weakness'. Strong concepts, on the other hand, reduce uncertainty and, in the case of education, become subject to prescription, preemption, systematizing and reductionism. The role of the educator in educational transactional analysis is more akin to that of a midwife or cultivator, in which a key quality is to exercise *creative indifference*, a term drawn from gestalt practice:

It is based on the idea that [the educator] does not have a vested interest in any particular outcome. It is another way of facing the existential uncertainty of the unknown – not a simple task. . . . [The educator] is willing to accept whatever 'is and becomes'. This model of growth is easy to see in the physical world where a gardener provides the right conditions of light, warmth and water, clears away the weeds and protects against disease or insect attack. The flowers will then grow naturally and mature into their full 'flowerness'. The gardener is not trying to impose his will or 'make' the flower other than it naturally is. . . . It means [the educator] is free to engage wholeheartedly in whichever path [the learner] chooses. . . . It is trust in the healthiness of organismic self-regulation and in the deeper wisdom that lies in us all.

(Joyce and Sills 2009: 40)

So, our intention throughout this work is to remain open-minded as to how practitioners respond *in their own right* to our collection of invitations, provocations and observations. We have resisted inclinations to define and categorize, or to prescribe and capture, what educational transactional analysis is – and is not. And what we bring has emerged from our joint experience as educators, which we believe is more than useful in opening this broader consideration of the purpose and practice of educational transactional analysis.

A joint endeavour

We have thought it useful to say a little about how this writing project came about. To do so gives an insight into what motivates us personally as educators and editors

– while also sharing additional general thoughts on educational transactional analysis practice. In most respects our joint working arose from a 'weak' process. As leader of a behaviour support team in south London, I was interested in expanding the range of theoretical models the team used in working with students, families and professionals. Members of the team participated in all sorts of professional development, returning with thoughts on how helpful particular methods might be. One member of the team recalled someone – Trudi – in her home village who knew about an approach called TA, and thought maybe it would be worthwhile considering. We arranged a training event that would prove to be instrumental in the development of a whole-system approach to running a local authority support service – and a long-standing friendship.

That training session involved teachers, social workers *and* students based in what would now be referred to in the UK as 'a pupil referral unit'. This was a centre for students aged 14–16 years who had been excluded from school, with some being at risk of custody. The aim was for Trudi to introduce transactional analysis, and then for staff to consider how useful it might be. Suffice to say, it was a defining moment and, for individual students, an epiphany. At one stage Trudi was explaining the Adult ego-state, having covered the functional Child and Parent states. All of a sudden, one of the young men in the group rushed up and grabbed the pen; he began marking the flipchart and explained – with massive energy – his anger at being regarded as rebellious when pointing out inconsistencies in teacher-behaviour. This, he believed, was demonstrating Adult awareness. Trudi and I realized at this point that, whatever TA might be, it had the potential to be far more than merely 'useful'.

A second defining episode was in 2005, at an international TA conference in Edinburgh. We had been exploring two related ideas. On the one hand, Trudi had begun to construct a model for connecting TA concepts to form a unique, health-orientated design. On the other hand, I had been experimenting with inverting the 'Parent-Adult-Child' metaphor. The conference gave us a first opportunity to test out our thinking with others. Following a series of workshops, we revised our ideas to form the basis of two subsequent articles in the *Transactional Analysis Journal* (Barrow 2007; Newton 2007). In most respects, the papers represent the core of our mutual interest in educational transactional analysis; they provide a framework for encouraging the human desire to thrive, and a philosophy of resilience, renewal and hope. Since those earlier days, we have wanted to create an archive of material – theoretical, technical and practical – to specifically support TA practitioners in education and educators generally interested in the relational aspects of teaching and learning. This present book represents our most comprehensive contribution to that project.

A third experience to share at this point was the culmination of a long period of work in developing an introductory TA course for children and young people. The programme is featured in more detail in Part 3, but the point in raising it here is that it links to a final important introductory observation. Initiated in east London, a model of teaching TA to children had been trialled and led to an awarding of certificates to all the children who had taken part. At the very first award ceremony twenty or so students a gathered to share the work they had done in learning about TA models and applying them in their day-to-day life at school. As the children arrived they set out their project work and we were struck by the wonderful inventiveness, creativity and sheer energy that the children had invested in their learning. It was really moving to hear individual pupils talk about the impact the material had had on their sense of motivation, confidence and achievement, both within and outside the context of the classroom. In the video of the event Trudi gives a brief speech to the pupils and teachers and in doing so makes a comment, almost to herself. 'When we started out on this journey we had no idea that it would end in this wonderful way. Or perhaps, maybe we did.'

It is this last phrase which connects to the purpose of sharing this story – and indeed all the stories – in this collection. We want to offer a note of caution with particular regard to what we claim as educational transactional analysts. In the spirit of commitment to emergent process we are less interested in claiming causality for what TA 'does' to people. In many respects this reflects cautiousness about the increase in evidence-based practice in education. Attractive though this paradigm may be it has limitations in the field of teaching and learning. Drawn from particular initiatives in medicine, the preoccupation with proving what works in relation to changing specific conditions in individuals has become part of a 'common sense' approach to professional development and practice. As educational transactional analysts we carry some reservations about the efficacy of this way of framing the educational partnership when we arrive at the process with a commitment to support healthy growth. In referring to the assumptions of evidence-based practice, Biesta comments;

> While both assumptions may be valid in the field of medicine . . . I do not think that they can easily be transposed to the field of education. To begin with the role of causality: apart from the obvious fact that the condition of being a student is quite different from that of being a patient – being a student is not an illness just as teaching is not a cure – the most important argument against the idea that education is a causal process lies in the fact that education is not a process of physical interaction but a process of *symbolic* or *symbolically mediated* interaction.
>
> (Biesta 2010: 34)

So by all means enjoy our stories, we intend that they serve to illustrate a particular aspect of theory or process. However, we encourage readers to hold back a little from imagining too simplistic a connection between what educators do and what happens next.

PART 1

Philosophy, politics, principles and educational transactional analysis

INTRODUCING PART 1

Giles Barrow, UK

Our opening part comprises a series of short chapters providing an initial statement of intent, and an over-arching framework for the contributions that follow through the rest of the book. The relational method and pedagogical objective of educational transactional analysis is *freedom*, whether it is the freedom from life-script that comes through the educational partnership, or the freeing up of power, options and creativity generated because of the learning endeavour. This intrinsic renewal, gifted by and through educational processes, is the focus of our opening chapter on *philosophy, assumptions and principles*, in which I share some observations on what Parker Palmer describes as 'the integration of soul and role' (Palmer 1998), and how that underpins professional identity and educational practice.

My intention is to take hold of the spirit that some identify in educational transactional analysis; to explain an aspect of what is often *experienced* in the process. By drawing on the concepts of *liminality*, *natality* and *regeneration*, the chapter explores the sense of awakening embodied in the potential of a teaching and learning relationship. In doing so, options as to the purpose of educational transactional analysis emerge, and my objective is not to oblige readers or trainees to adopt my views, but to consider how, as individual educators, we create encounters in learning.

The idea of 'encounter' runs across each of our three opening chapters: Pete Shotton considers the political and power implications of educational partnerships. Those familiar with his work will not be disappointed in Shotton's close scrutiny of how power unfolds between those charged with the role of teacher and others as learners. He introduces a subtle revision of the totemic TA reference to 'OK-ness', and ventures into contextualizing the learning relationship. One of the limitations in some of early TA literature was the emphasis on individual autonomy, with the consequent risk of separating off from belonging to the collective whole. Tied in with this was a tendency to discount the impact of the political perspective – the complex issues of social, cultural and economic power – as well as its influence on the capacity for, and engagement in, personal autonomy. Running alongside this theme in early TA were the efforts of many practitioners who pursued social activism, promoted radical psychiatry and community empowerment. Shotton revisits this territory from the perspective of the classroom, and opens a theme that is implicit in many of the contributions to subsequent parts.

The third chapter, by Trudi, is an essential contribution for those interested in understanding how educators do something additional in establishing educational transactional analysis. If my opening chapter speaks to the spirit of the encounter, and Shotton explores its power dynamic, Trudi explains its theoretical framework. Extending her previous work on the importance of metaphor, this chapter situates educational transactional analysis as being both distinct and familiar within the broader context of TA theory and practice. It is in many respects a demonstration of what Shotton describes as 'we count – you count – context counts', in the sense that both the clinical and educational perspectives of TA have significant value within their respective contexts of application. TA practitioners are often more familiar with the former, and here Trudi expands on the latter.

In reading her account of the importance of *symbolic metaphors*, I am reminded of an incident a few years ago: I was training nursery practitioners in the same south London area where Trudi and I first met in the 1990s; it was the second day of training on supporting good practice in Early Years provision. Most of the group were living and working locally. At some point, I introduced the ego-state model and drew on the board the three-stacked circles. As I did so, one of the women in the group – Cheryl – immediately called out that she had come across the image in the past. She explained that she had attended a local secondary school when she was younger, very troubled by her home circumstances, and also very troublesome at school. She was frequently at risk of being excluded and was eventually referred for additional support.

Cheryl went on to talk about a woman called Lesley who would meet with her, help her make sense of her experiences, and explore ways in which she might be able to settle at school, continue with her education and take her exams. During one of these meetings, Lesley drew the ego-state stacked circles diagram, and Cheryl began to connect its meaning with what was going on, both at home and in the classroom. Needless to say, Cheryl managed to keep her place at school, sit her exams, and was successful enough to open her own nursery.

A nice tale in itself; but what made it more so was that, over a decade beforehand, Lesley had been one of the first members of my staff team to attend basic TA training with Trudi. Unbeknown to me, Cheryl had been one of the young people Lesley had supported during that period; and here I was, hearing the impact of that encounter, fifteen years afterwards.

Educators rarely witness the full implications of their joint efforts with the learner.

> We cannot organize the educational event in advance. Certainly we can plan and prepare, but we cannot characterize it until we are in it and the students themselves have brought their own contributions. And there is a point beyond

which our tendency to characterize becomes inimical to experience, inimical to teaching ... yet this tendency to characterize and to elevate the gratifications of the profession – the status of expertise, the pleasures of jargon, the pride of method – is composed of two things, both inescapably human and hard to transcend: anxiety and vanity; here again, a difficult spiritual task.

(Dennison 1969: 258)

As educational transactional analysts, we step into the arena uncertain of (and also reluctant to 'fix') what happens next. It is, at its best, an act of faith.

1

EDUCATIONAL TRANSACTIONAL ANALYSIS

Underpinning assumptions, principles and philosophy

Giles Barrow, UK

This chapter offers a personal theoretical perspective on educational transactional analysis, bringing together a series of related themes and concepts. The objective is to establish a position from which educational transactional analysts might choose to ground their practice, principles and philosophy. For readers at the outset of their training, the discussion will indicate the kind of theoretical territory worthwhile considering when developing a sense of professional identity. Those readers further engaged in training as educational transactional analysts, and those close to certification – they may find the material illustrative of how philosophy, theory and practice can be integrated to form a coherent model of education.

The discussion pursues a path that begins with the concept of natality and its links with the function of education. By exploring the work of Hannah Arendt and others, I propose that learning is an essential component of individual experience and collective human endeavour. The second part of the discussion leads to considering the role of the educator in a natality-orientated learning process. To explore this I draw attention to the role of imaginal cells in the process of metamorphosis and the idea of liminality. The discussion concludes with an account of how the educator might increase a sense of groundedness in undertaking their role. This aspect is expanded through considering the work of Parker J. Palmer and the integration of soul and role in the teaching and learning process.

Natality and education

The concept of 'natality' is relatively unfamiliar, despite its relevance to every single living organism. Referring to both the physical and metaphorical act of birth and the subsequent processes of becoming, beginning and belonging, natality is an idea that has significant potential for educators, much of which is yet to be realized. In the limited range of material available on natality, Hannah Arendt is one of the first and significant thinkers. Arendt formed several theses about society and human purpose. For the focus of this discussion, it is her essay 'Crisis in Education', in the collected work *Between Past and Future* (Arendt 1961) that warrants most attention. Arendt presents the purpose of education as establishing a cross-generational transaction through which the old world is renewed by the becoming generation. The 'essence of education is natality, the fact that human beings are born into the world' (Arendt 1961: 174). This reflects a different emphasis on a human-liberalist view of education that prizes the dissemination of information as crucial to learners' liberation from ignorance. Instead it is the promise presented by the existence of a new generation that underwrites the need to share knowledge and understanding. The role of the educator in this model is to take care and ensure the safe passage of what is already known, and which will fuel new development by the next generation.

Arendt's focus in her essay was the schooling of children and young people. At the time, she expressed concerns of the failure to honour the promise and potency of a new generation. Specifically, her observation was that by discounting the significance of this learning transaction, new generations were left stranded, at risk of infantilization, and at the mercy of totalitarianism. Her personal experience as a Jew in Nazi Germany had convinced her of the need of effective, good quality education as a means of combating a tendency to fundamentalism. Arguably, her approach to a natality-based model of learning applies to adult learning processes as well as children's, where individuals regardless of age are coming fresh to new arenas of experience and learning. This might be in regard to specific skills: craftwork, technical or administrative tasks; or professional training, for example in becoming a transactional analyst.

Importantly, natality is crucial in terms of combating a natural tendency to decline and entropy, which results in death and is ultimately expressed in the concept of mortality. All living things eventually decay and die. The purpose of birth is to ensure continual renewal. The process of learning is one way in which this act of renewal is carried out at a collective, societal level. In TA terms, the desire to grow and renew is represented by 'physis' (Berne 1957), and this in turn is at the heart of educational transactional analysis. The educator is essentially attending to, and accounting for, the physis of the learner and the collective physis of the learning community – which is carried out as part of humanity's push for growth.

There are clearly links to other learning models that amplify and elaborate the natal core of Arendt's initial work. The radical pedagogy of Jack Mezirow's transformational learning, for example, describes a process in which adult learners experience a 'new birth' through a systematic shift in their personal frame of reference in which empowerment and insight are key objectives (Mezirow 1991). 'De-schooling' advocates seek to free learners from archaic and utilitarian mass-schooling entrapment (Holt 1976; Illich 1972). However, it is Arendt's work that explicitly connects the purpose of learning with natality.

My objective is to position educational TA within a theoretical base that combines radical theory with the flourishing that is inherent in natality. I suggest that the concept of cultivation best describes the natal influence on radical learning theory. I have written elsewhere of the links between cultivation and the role of the educator (Barrow 2011), and my purpose in re-introducing the idea here is to foreground the process of cultivating the physis of the learner as fundamental to educational transactional analysis. In my view, this extends the desire for social change – and especially in terms of re-focusing personal power – advocated by radical theorists. I see the emphasis on cultivation as referring to the further beauty and blossom that is realized through radical learning. Educational TA is about more than instigating social change; it is in support of the renewing human spirit fulfilling itself beyond what it has so far accomplished. Each step made by individuals towards greater insight, closeness and achievement contributes to collective cultivation.

The imaginal cell, metamorphosis and liminality

The role of the educator in this landscape combines both privilege and challenge. To explore this duality I want to draw on a metaphor based on the biological process of metamorphosis. Biologists have known for many years that organisms subject to metamorphosis have a peculiar feature; the imaginal cell. Present from the very beginning of the process, the imaginal cells present a fascinating illustration of agents of change. While the organism is in the form of pupa, these cells are few in number and have no apparent function. As the organism grows into the familiar shape of a caterpillar the quantity of imaginal cells increases. At the point when metamorphosis begins the organism in effect collapses within the carapace of the chrysalis into a 'gloop', an unstructured mass, but with the imaginal cells intact. This is a point of significant vulnerability for the organism, as any young child knows who has been warned not to break the chrysalis shell.

It is at this stage of total collapse that the function of the imaginal cells becomes clear. Within the gloop, the cells that have been the source of such resistance and inertia are revealed as the blueprint for the constituent elements of the butterfly. From the earliest stages of metamorphosis these cells 'held' the form that was not possible to envisage at the beginning. As the cells continue to multiply and connect, so the butterfly takes shape and eventually emerges from the encasement; metamorphosis is compete and the organism is renewed. I have found this process a powerful metaphor for exploring the roles of the educator, learner and purpose of education.

Transformational learning provides a liminal experience. Developed by Victor Turner (1974), liminality refers to the 'in-between' spaces, phases and experiences that we come across throughout our lifetime. Whether it is the universal periods of weaning, adolescence and ageing, or specific rites of passage, Turner proposes that the individual crosses a threshold (limen) from one concrete state and into a period of ambiguity. During this phase a previous sense of identity, social position, frame of reference and personal narrative undergo disintegration. Talking of liminality and rites of passage, Turner explains its potential:

I meant by it not a structural reversal [. . .] but the liberation of human capacities of cognition, affect, volition, creativity etc., from the normative constraints incumbent upon occupying a sequence of social statuses, enacting a multiplicity of social roles.

(Turner 1974: 75)

Liminal phases offer a dynamic opportunity, despite the internal experience of collapse and overwhelm generated by the separating from the normative constraints. In TA terms, Turner describes a shift from script towards autonomy, a loosening of the frame of reference.

I suggest that training to become an educational transactional analyst involves, for many individuals, a liminal phase. Recently, in sharing ideas about radical education theory and its emphasis on co-creative learning, a participant said with an incredulous expression; 'I cannot imagine such a way of learning'. His frame of reference of learning had been entirely formed on the basis of schooling. This is such a common contamination: that schooling is synonymous with education. I have discussed this elsewhere (Barrow 2009), and it is not my intention to re-visit the process of schooling and its links with personal script. My point here is that the TA training experience invites trainees into a deep reflection on how they have constructed a sense of professional identity as an educator – often limited to the image of a schoolteacher – and have yet to fully understand the implications of this in terms of transactional analysis practice and principles. Consequently, for many educational trainees, recreating a professional identity involves an encounter with confusion and upset as old frames are deconstructed. In this phase, the role of the trainer/supervisor is to contain the liminal space, to provide the chrysalis, while the regeneration takes place.

The inner landscape

In profiling the importance of natality in framing learning, and its impact on defining the purpose of education, I have used the concept of metamorphosis and liminality to explore the learner's experience. In this final part I want to focus on the internal experience of the educator. Little is written on this theme; most professional development for teachers is focused on improving what content is taught and how best to deliver the curriculum. Occasionally – and, increasingly, only in academic arenas – is the purpose of education considered. Rarely is the question asked: 'Who is the teacher?'

Teaching, like any truly human activity, emerges from one's inwardness – for better or worse. As I teach, I project the condition of my soul onto my students, my subject and our way of being together. The entanglements I experience in the classroom are often no more or less than the convolutions of my inner life. Viewed from this angle, teaching holds a mirror to the soul. If I am willing to look in that mirror, and not run from what I see, I have a chance to gain self-knowledge – and 'knowing myself' is as crucial to good teaching as knowing my students and my subject.

(Palmer 1998: 2)

Parker J. Palmer is arguably one of the best – and few – contemporary educators focusing on the inner landscape of the teacher. His work describes the integration of 'soul' and 'role' as a way of achieving a high quality of authenticity. For Palmer, the congruence of personal values and core identity – soul – in the learning relationship is paramount. Warning against a pious potential in this claim, Palmer continues, 'Identity and integrity have as much to do with our shadows and limits, our wounds and fears, as with our strengths and potentials' (1998: 13).

I have found Palmer's writing especially important in guiding my outward journey in leading learning groups, as well as an internal exploration of what it means for me to be a teacher. There is much in his approach that can support a consideration of the educational transactional analyst training process. Just as those training in the clinical fields undergo their own psychotherapy, educational TA practitioners need to engage in deep reflection on what it is to inhabit the role of educator. What ghosts must be exorcized? What qualities and aspirations might need rejuvenation? What must be let go of, and what needs to be welcomed? For trainees coming from the position of a schoolteacher, the process can be both humbling and a relief: a shift from 'needing to know it all' towards embracing uncertainty. Others may come from a shaming experience of being schooled, and here the challenge is to re-consider learning as transformational and to experience a new sense of belonging and personal agency in education.

The exploration of this inner landscape is in itself a parallel, liminal stage in the formation of the educational transactional analyst and is to be acknowledged, celebrated and supported. In becoming familiar with an emerging sense of vocation, Palmer offers a series of paradoxes that are present in the learning environment and which are summarized below:

The space should be bounded and open. Limits enable learning in terms of creating focus, even in exploratory work. Yet there needs to be an openness as to the many paths that can be taken.

The space should be hospitable and 'charged'. The process needs to give opportunity to rest and recuperate. Yet if it's too safe then things can remain superficial so by becoming charged we recognize the risks in going deeper.

The space should invite the voice of the individual and the voice of the group. Individuals need to be able to express thoughts and feelings and groups can create a common voice about concerns and passions.

The space should honour the 'little' stories of those involved and the 'big' stories of the disciplines and traditions. People's experience must be heard and connected to the larger themes that run across human experience and understanding.

The space should support solitude and surround it with the resources of community. There should be time for individual reflection and self-absorption which can focus the struggle that sometimes comes with learning. And there needs to be opportunity to call upon others so that our introspection can be challenged and affirmed.

The space should welcome both silence and speech. Silence can give rise to deeper levels of insight, relationship and connection with the world. And by putting it into words we may test and increase our understanding; to make concrete what is drawn from the silence.

(Adapted from Palmer 1988: 74–7)

Educational caritas

Arguably, at the heart of the work of the educational transactional analyst is a love for learning. Nel Noddings writes extensively on the ethics of care in education and, in her work with Shore, identifies the notion of educational caritas:

> we assert that love in education, or educational caritas, is something very real. It is a force that can be the most powerful agent in the classroom, leave the most lasting impressions, and touch lives most deeply.
> . . . it is a desire to come into direct, undiluted contact with the human partner of the educational enterprise, to go beyond superficialities and become involved with the other person . . . Educational caritas may also involve a deep interest and even passionate commitment to the subject matter being taught . . . Linked to this passion for the material being taught, but probably more importantly, is love of the acts of teaching and learning.
> (Noddings and Shore 1984)

I suggest that, when we are at our most effective as teachers, we demonstrate this love for what we do, for the learner and the notion of learning for learning's sake. Clearly this is not a constant state, and I associate this with the features of elusive and oscillating autonomy – awareness, spontaneity and intimacy. Palmer describes something similar:

> If we dare to move through our fear, to practice knowing as a form of love, we might abandon our illusion of control and enter a partnership with the otherness of the world . . . This relational way of knowing – in which love takes away fear and co-creation replaces control – is a way of knowing that can help us reclaim the capacity for connectedness on which good teaching depends.
> (Palmer 1998: 56)

In many respects this reference to 'love in learning' brings us back to the beginning – natality. Expressing a desire to teach and learn is drawn out of and fuelled by the fact of our being alive. Physis drives the insistence both to learn and to demand teaching from others. Alongside this desire is the disruption caused by a 'disorientating' dilemma and the consequent challenges of a renewing liminal process. Containing this process, the educator must combine both knowing themselves and the subject, yet being completely open to what might happen next; the paradox of knowing and not knowing.

Conclusion

I have described a personal philosophy that can underpin an educational TA perspective. The intention is not to persuade readers to adopt this as a professional creed or preferenced position. My purpose is to provoke reflections about professional identity and practice for the reader to create their own; to encourage a robust scrutiny of 'who we think we are' when we step up and into the role of educator. How do we reconcile our personal experience of schooling with our intentions as a TA practitioner? What are the resources and role models we draw from as we begin a group learning process? What values are expressed when we are our better selves in the learning partnership? Do we hold out hope when learners may have lost sight of its possibility in their learning? Do we play our part in demonstrating educational caritas?

In responding to these questions, it is possible to reach beyond the familiar topics of planning lessons and workshops – or being preoccupied with whether we 'know it all' or 'know enough' about a specific theme. While these are important in establishing communities of learning, such technical aspects are given spirit, or soul, because of the internal work of the educator. So many of the teachers I have worked with talk about their early intentions to change the world through their work. And so many express a sense of fatigue and disappointment as their initial enthusiasm has waned. It is such a bold aspiration, to change the world. It can become so quickly de-railed or overwhelming – there is such a lot of world to change! So, we must begin again – accounting for the apprehension in both ourselves and others; open, with a commitment to start with what is in the moment, accompanied by a love for learning. We change the world, transaction by transaction, through what happens now between the educator, the subject, the learner and our collective desire for renewal.

2

WE ALL COUNT

Addressing the problem of power in education

Pete Shotton, UK

> The first proposition that I advance – and the most basic one – is that there is nothing like neutral education. Education is a political act. It is impossible to analyze education without analyzing the problem of power.
>
> (Freire 1971: 25)

> Education either functions as an instrument which is used to facilitate the integration of generations into the logic of the present system and bring about conformity to it, or it becomes the 'practice of freedom', the means by which men and women deal critically and creatively with reality and discover how to participate in the transformation of their world.
>
> (Shaull, in Freire 1984: 15)

Across the world education has become inextricably linked with politics and power. In these opening quotations from Freire and Shaull our attention is drawn to a tension which runs through education systems and process, a tension which invites those of us who consider ourselves to be educators to question our motivation and purpose. Why do we choose to educate? And, having chosen to be educators, where and how do we pursue our vocation? We often join the available groups or systems such as schools, training programmes or universities in order to practise, and at this point we are usually required to adapt to the social and political context in which these bodies are located.

Shaull presents this process of adaptation as a stark choice, promoting either integration and conformity or freedom and transformation. Harber suggests that there are:

> three main ways of looking at the relationship between formal education, individuals and society:

- that education improves society;
- that education reproduces society exactly as it is;
- that education makes society worse and harms individuals.

(Harber 2004: i)

The first two of these perspectives are often written about and discussed in the media, and education is generally viewed as a positive and beneficial enterprise; yet in my experience it is the third observation that often occupies and challenges educators, especially when seen through the prism of Shaull's opposing functions. In *Dumbing Us Down* (Gatto 1992), a skilled and inspirational educator and teacher, describes how he gave up working in schools because he could not come to terms with the 'fatally flawed' system:

> Mass education cannot work to produce a fair society because its daily practice is practice in rigged competition, suppression, and intimidation. The schools we've allowed to develop can't work to teach nonmaterial values, the values which give meaning to everyone's life, rich or poor.
>
> (Gatto 1992: 69)

As a student, teacher, trainer and supervisor, I have been involved in many existential discussions with fellow learners and educators about our role and purpose with regard to individuals and society. In this chapter I will examine the political pressures that impact on the process of education and will use transactional analysis as a method for working with the often-conflicting demands that educators encounter.

Transactional analysis, politics and education

Transactional analysis was described by Eric Berne in the subtitle to his book *Transactional Analysis in Psychotherapy* (1961) as 'a systematic individual and social psychiatry'. Berne himself rarely mentioned politics explicitly, despite his observation in his early writing that 'Psychiatrists . . . should and must concern themselves with political affairs.' (Berne 1947: 292). However Moiso (1998) argues that ideological and political involvement is crucial for transactional analysts to foster Berne's idea of TA as a social psychiatry:

> Alongside Berne's attention to the psychosocial dimension, we must place a psycho-political dimension. Given the widespread and pervasive sense of malaise in contemporary life, we cannot reasonably entertain the possibility of curing an individual without considering and addressing the broader social context.
>
> (Moiso 1998: 3)

If we replace the word 'curing' with 'educating,' then Moiso is drawing our attention to the importance of social context to learning and making a connection to the fundamental philosophical roots of TA; that people are OK, that everyone has the capacity to think, and that people decide their own destiny (and that these decisions can be changed). Hobbes and Tudor point out that these principles 'are generally viewed as reflecting existential thinking, attributable to the influence on Berne of Virginia Satir, who coined the phrase, "I count. You count. Context counts"' (Dryden 2002: 258).

I believe that, because of the political, economic and social forces that come into play whenever and wherever education becomes an organized pursuit, it is crucial that we pay attention to the importance of context, and that we develop methods for reflecting upon, understanding and engaging with contextual forces and conditions. In doing this we need to consider:

- The political and social context. Does the system require and reinforce particular roles for particular groups and what part does education play in maintaining this?
- The organizational demands placed on educators. How much are they negotiated? How much are they imposed? What is the requirement to comply?
- Our purpose as educators. Does it need to be the 'either/or' proposed by Freire and Shaull or could it be both social integration and the development of individual autonomy?

I have discussed these factors in many training and workshop settings and use a variation of the OK Corral (Ernst 1971) as a way to promote and facilitate discussion, with the lines crossing diagonally, see Figure 2.1. Rather than using Berne's 'OK' terminology I revert to the original language of Satir, namely 'I count, you count'. To me, this places a more considered and objective value on people in relationship to each other than the implicit warmth and positivity of OK-ness, which in my experience can feel forced and incongruent.

By positioning the model in this way we create a level connecting the I+U– and I–U+ positions, which I draw as a line showing an ongoing communication between the two. This interchange and exchange was an idea that I first developed with a group of 15-year-old boys who were using the OK Corral to describe their everyday experiences in school. They identified some teachers as appearing to operate from an I+U– position in trying to maintain control in the classroom in order to cover what they were really feeling, which the boys identified as I–U+. I set the model out on the floor and the boys acted out what they were describing by walking between the two positions. They then started to realize that this was a dynamic that they could expect to encounter in peer-group relationships as well.

The model as presented in this way seemed applicable to many aspects of school life and I realized how often in organizational structures we are invited to compare ourselves to, and compete with, others in order to maintain hierarchical 'order', and are required to place ourselves in one or other of these two positions in many of our working relationships. I therefore represent the line between the two positions as a consensual and symbiotic status quo, and it is here that we can map educational processes which 'facilitate the integration of generations into the logic of the present

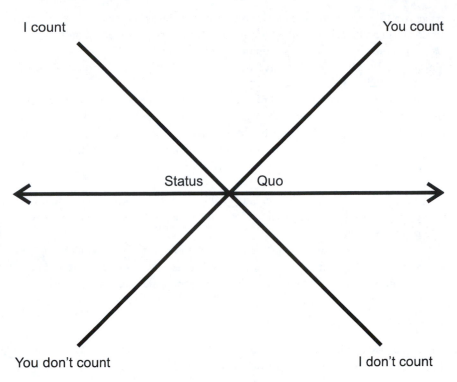

I count
You count
Status Quo
You don't count
I don't count

FIGURE 2.1 Life position map (adapted from Ernst 1971)

system and bring about conformity to it' (Shaull 1984: 15). In mapping these processes I use the concepts of *hegemony* to describe the political and social context
and *compliance* to describe organizational governance and protocols.

Hegemony

The term *hegemony* is long established in describing systems of leadership and rules
which are supported by an implicit or explicit threat of force and use of power.
In the early twentieth century, the Italian Marxist philosopher Antonio Gramsci
(1977) developed the concept in understanding the development and maintenance
of social class systems. He examined the ways in which the ruling class developed
societal structures and norms which reinforced their dominance and position in
order to maintain a political, social and economic status quo. What becomes implicit
in this system is the idea that this status quo is somehow fundamental and beneficial
to all social classes. The role that education and schooling play in maintaining this
order is described by Davies:

> We are not totally controlled or brainwashed, but are subject to attempted
> limitations on freedom of thought or intellectual mobility. [. . .] Education

is, of course, central to this hegemony, as ideological legitimations of class are both conveyed and (re)constructed on a daily basis, through use and limitations of our cultural capital.

(Davies 2004: 49)

Formal education, and its accompanying schooling systems, is now an accepted human activity across the globe, and as such it is inevitably integrated into political and governmental thinking and structures. The potential power of this integration is brutally and succinctly summed up in the following quote from Joseph Stalin: 'Education is a weapon, whose effects depend on who holds it in his hand and at who it is aimed' (quoted in Meighan 1994: 4).

The politicization of education and schooling can be traced back to the development of formal schooling systems in western Europe and the United States in the nineteenth century, a period of rapidly developing industrial and economic revolution and expansion. Green (1990: 80) highlights the 'conforming' purpose of these systems, suggesting that in the nineteenth century the education system came to assume a primary responsibility for the moral, cultural and political development of the nation, like a secular church, assimilating immigrant cultures, promoting religious norms, spreading a standardized language, to forge a national identity and culture, above all, to indoctrinate in the political and economic creeds of the dominant classes.

This highlights the significance of formal schooling of children, an accepted and widespread practice across the world. Schooling is imposed at crucial developmental stages in the lives of children and young people and is therefore likely, in transactional analysis terms, to play a major part in the formation of personal and cultural scripts. The way that schools operate is often studied and analysed, but the hegemonic purpose that is fundamental to their existence is not widely debated.

In a global study of formal education, Harber states, 'the dominant or hegemonic model globally [. . .] is authoritarian rather than democratic'. He does point out exceptions, and goes on to say that,

> while the degree of harshness and despotism within authoritarian schools varies from context to context and from institution to institution, in the majority of schools power over what is taught and learned [and how, when and where it is taught and learned] is not in the hands of pupils. Government officials, head teachers and teachers decide, not learners.

(Harber 2004: 24)

The hegemonic tradition of formal education, laid down in childhood, can also have a strong influence on adult education programmes, in that both students and trainers often have expectations of the learning situation and programme which are based on their experience of school. As a trainer of educators and psychotherapists, I often encounter adult learners who have contaminated and limited beliefs about the transformative possibilities of education and often about their own learning abilities. These beliefs are rooted in the hegemonic learning script, with its enforced components of an externally prescribed curriculum, standardized and limited universal assessment systems, didactic teaching and learning methodology, and success criteria based on marking and grades. These elements promote a situation where the teacher, administrator or politician controls and rations knowledge and learning and holds power over the learner. Hegemony demands that, whether they agree with it or not, educators and learners are bound into systems that reinforce this power dynamic.

Rogers, in *Freedom to Learn* (1969: 5), noted that 'it is not because of any inner depravity that educators follow such a self-defeating system. It is quite literally because they do not know any feasible alternative'. The system is so pervasive that it is easy for educators to be drawn into a bystander role. They may not agree with the structures and regulations that govern their work and at the same time their employment opportunities and professional credibility are governed by a requirement to conform to the hegemonic norm.

Hegemony is maintained by way of the interchange between the I+U– and I–U+ positions and, using this model, can be easily identified in systems and schools. When mapped on the model, see Figure 2.2, the co-dependent nature of the two positions becomes clear.

Within this system the intentions of both positions are not necessarily negative, but the ongoing exchange between the two is Parent–Child, rather than the Adult–Adult negotiation and problem solving of the I+U+ position.

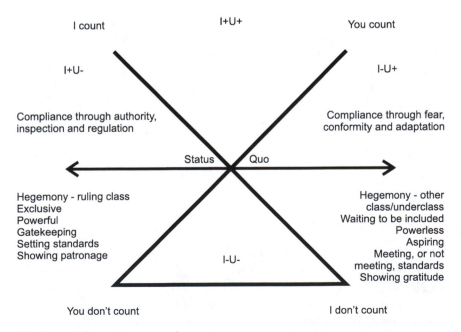

FIGURE 2.2 Life position map – hegemony

In the diagram, I have sealed the I–U– position. I do this to emphasize the lack of options in that position. Systems, schools and people who are occupying that place are stuck – usually – by some form of poverty within the overall system. Changing the situation for them will require support and input. Drego reframes the 'rescuer' label, that is used in transactional analysis to describe a position in a psychological game, as an opportunity to encourage 'altruistic caring and social protection' (2006: 100). For this to happen in a healthy way the 'rescue' will come from the I+U+ position. Example:

> In England and Wales in the 1990s and early 2000s there were a number of high profile cases of children dying through cruelty and neglect. After the death of Victoria Climbié in 2000, the government of the time, responding to societal reaction and the resulting public enquiries and reports, imple-mented the *Every Child Matters* agenda and reforms. This was an overarching approach, bringing together all those agencies who worked with children and enabling them to work together to meet the needs of all children. The Department for Education became the 'Department for Children, Schools and Families'.
>
> When the government changed in 2010, the new coalition government abandoned the Every Child Matters framework and replaced it with *Help Children Achieve More*. The Department for Education was reinstated. A colleague summed it up as children's value to society moving from 'being' to 'doing'. Using the model, we can argue that at this point an I+U+ solution to the needs of those in the I–U– group was replaced by a hegemonic I+U– solution.

The hegemonic state can be found throughout education systems, programmes and schools. It is maintained by a framework of regulations and structures which can be grouped under the heading of compliance.

Compliance

Compliance means conforming to rules and standardized requirements or protocols within organizations. What this can mean in practice is that rules replace values. The more rigid the rules and the structure, the easier it is to comply, leading to a minimalist attitude. In education, compliance is often enforced by standardized curriculum content, examination and assessment targets, and inspection regimes. This is partly attributable to the development of an education market, where schools and other education organizations compete with each other to recruit and retain students in order to maintain, or increase their reputation and revenue. This leads to a limited set of criteria which become the socially acceptable markers of success. In working within the confines of these criteria a climate and language can develop which is target focused and risk averse. What this means is that qualities such as creativity, spontaneity, ambiguity and flexibility are not welcome. These are autonomous integrating Adult qualities, threatening the inflexible structured Parent of the compliance culture, where change is implemented through the content of regulation rather than the process of growth.

I see this in practice on a daily basis in my role as a manager of a team of education workers supporting the needs of children and young people who are looked after by the state. My team helps young people to make sense of the trauma they have experienced while at the same time supporting them in accessing and achieving in school. Mutually respectful relationships are vital to this work. Young people and their foster carers are enthusiastic and positive about the support and the outcomes that they see. However, when it comes to judging how successful and effective we are, this affirmation is not recognized. The criteria we are judged on are attendance, number of exclusions from school and tertiary exam results. This is a familiar pattern across the education spectrum. In the UK, the *Guardian* newspaper reported that 60 head teachers had left their posts in the two years 2012 to 2014 due to poor inspection results (Lepkowska 2014). Changes to inspection criteria had resulted in schools previously judged to be good or outstanding now being deemed as requiring improvement, and the accepted method for addressing this has now become to change the management. This is the extreme end of the hegemony/compliance education system. The educators have continued to educate, but the political ideology and the compliance criteria by which they are judged have changed. There are a range of responses to situations like this. It is very easy to be drawn into the Drama Triangle in roles of Victim or Persecutor, and the might of the hierarchy can appear overwhelming, inviting resignation and cynicism.

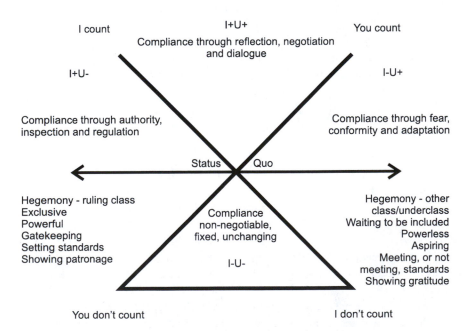

FIGURE 2.3 Life position map – hegemony and compliance

However, key components of education are the concepts of change, development and transformation and our power as individuals and in groups lies in speaking up and accounting for our work and engaging in dialogue with all parts of the system.

When I have discussed the model in workshops, there has often been a debate about whether the term *compliance* should be included in the I+U+ quadrant, in that it is seen as inherently parental, inevitably maintaining hegemony. It has been suggested that it is replaced with cooperation. I welcome the debate, and I believe that it is in the spirit of the model to aim for negotiated, agreed, values-based compliance structures, see Figure 2.3.

Conclusion

Education systems are so inextricably linked to political and economic frameworks that to question their validity or purpose can feel risky, negative and futile. The maintenance of the hegemonic system can appear to be more important than transforming lives through learning, leading to Freire's 'problem of power' (1975: 17).

My quest as an educator is to be curious, to explore life's possibilities, to question: Why this curriculum? This subject? This method? This setting? Who benefits from these teaching and learning structures? Who loses out? My attitude has occasionally been described as anarchic. This is usually meant as a pejorative. However, when I look at the derivation of anarchy it means 'without rulers'. If I translate this into transactional analysis language and concepts, I could interpret it as meaning 'without (archaic) Parent'. And, if I then reframe it in a positive way, I can say 'with Adult'. What this can mean is summed up in the following passage from Moiso:

> Let us remember that in transactional analysis, the healthy relationship is one in which two individuals put themselves on equal terms and base their negotiations on the specific characteristics of autonomy of the Adult: awareness, as the capacity to know how to distinguish self from other; spontaneity, as the capacity to act on one's motivations in the first person; and intimacy, as the capacity to open oneself to another in an authentic exchange of experience and feelings.
>
> We can thus define the quality of life as the result of three factors: belonging, being and becoming. Belonging involves the individual's having a place within the environment and with others; being concerns who and how a person is as an individual; and becoming relates to what a person does to attain individual aims and aspirations. Belonging provides the foundation for being and becoming.
>
> (Moiso 1998: 4)

This passage informs us as to the content of the 'I count, you count' quadrant presented in Figure 2.4, providing an alternative to the hegemonic status quo.

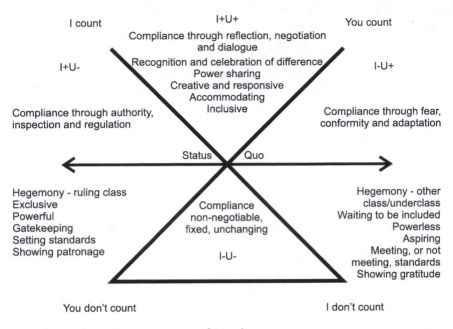

I count

I+U+
Compliance through reflection, negotiation
and dialogue
Recognition and celebration of difference
Power sharing
Creative and responsive
Accommodating
Inclusive

You count

I+U-

I-U+

Compliance through authority,
inspection and regulation

Compliance through fear,
conformity and adaptation

Status Quo

Hegemony - ruling class
Exclusive
Powerful
Gatekeeping
Setting standards
Showing patronage

Compliance
non-negotiable,
fixed, unchanging

I-U-

Hegemony - other
class/underclass
Waiting to be included
Powerless
Aspiring
Meeting, or not
meeting, standards
Showing gratitude

You don't count

I don't count

FIGURE 2.4 Life position map – a way forward

The I+U+ relationship, when applied to education, offers a forum and a model where roles can be negotiated and systems developed which allow for both social cohesion and individual growth and development, enabling belonging, being and becoming.

This is an idea that can be applied at every level in education systems. Skilled educators operate on an Adult–Adult level with learners, regardless of differences in age or hierarchical status and role. They respect and encourage learners' autonomy. They talk, they listen and they understand.

The problem of politics in education is a wide ranging one, with hegemonic beliefs and imposed compliance structures applying constraints to creativity, growth and autonomy for both educators and learners. Many effective practitioners work successfully within, or possibly despite, these constraints. Their achievement is to nourish the critical and creative growth of learners and to transform lives, while working within a societal framework where success is judged by crude generalized attainment targets meeting the limited requirements of politically determined criteria. As educators it is vital that we pay attention to, analyse, and engage with the political forces that aim to have power over the work that we do.

3

TURNING TO RESILIENCE AND POWER

Metaphor and meaning in relational learning

Trudi Newton, UK

'I love the Parent ego-state!' I heard this startling statement, slightly shocking to me as a new TA trainee, made by Jean Illsley Clarke in a workshop in Brussels 25 years ago. The shock was because most TA people at the time decried the Parent as the source of problems, script issues, limitations on the sacred freedom of the Child. Jean wanted to turn this around and 'talk up' the Parent as the well-spring of care, structure and support. I was hooked.

This was a beginning (or another beginning), for me, of looking at how accepted ideas could be re-examined to bring back into them 'what lies behind' – the beliefs and values, the stories that grew out of them, and the ongoing narrative that we all take part in.

In this chapter, I will examine how we create systems which then constrain us, and consider what we can do about it; how we get back to an informing philosophy and make changes, not just for ourselves but through the discourse we engage in. First, I will introduce some of my own recent encounters with writers from different fields beyond education, who have influenced my thinking about learning – and then go on to explore the dialogue between these ideas, TA, and education.

Constructing stories

'Ideas grow from encounters' – in this short sentence, Valeria Ugazio sums up a whole world of philosophy (Ugazio 2013: xi). Encounters between people in direct contact, as in my example with Jean Clarke, but also at a distance between writer and reader; discourse of any kind builds social structures. Sometimes, the encounter may be from well outside our own familiar domain – but we make a connection and new vistas open up.

Ugazio is a family therapist and clinician. She writes, in her amazing book *Semantic Polarities: Permitted and forbidden stories* (2013), of the detailed way that we construct meaning through language, in our families and other interpersonal contexts. These polarities are explored in stories of family members who she meets in therapy, but also through explorations of families in literature – for example, *Sons and Lovers* or *Brothers Karamazov*. Polarities are not just found in families – conversation 'in every group with a history' is organized, she says (2013: 21), around opposing meanings such as 'just/unjust' or 'closed/open'. Ugazio takes four such polarities – good/bad, free/dependent, winning/losing, belonging/excluded – and describes case-histories where these are linked to psychological disorder. She notes that in other cases these same polarities are linked, not to distress, but to creativity. She continues by explaining that within a family or other close group, conflicts and differences are conducted within the same unconscious polarities, and consequently the same narrative: meaning has been co-constructed and so holds the group together. I am interested here in exploring what polarities might dominate the discourses of TA and of education.

'Construction of meaning' is a central idea in TA. We call it script. Everyone creates, between the ages of three and seven years, a meaning-making story about themselves and their place in the world. This story, the 'psychological life plan' (Cornell 1988), changes as we grow up. We gain information, respond to significant events or refresh earlier beliefs. Sometimes, not always, the story includes decisions which can seriously damage well-being; even so, it will also include strategies and beliefs that promote survival and keep the little person safe. We are all storytellers, creating our own personal, family and social narratives to find our way in life. Every story – our own and others' – can teach us something, and learning is an intrinsic part of being human. Learning is also how we can change – change our own stories and open up the possibility of change for others.

Like Ugazio today, when Eric Berne originated the 'life-script' in the 1960s he used stories, from classical myths to fairytales, to reveal the power of his inspiration (Berne 1972). His aim, as always, was to make his ideas accessible and available to everyone, medical professionals, therapy patients and also the general public. His called his first book, in its second edition, *A Layman's Guide to Psychiatry and Psychoanalysis*, and he writes at the start that it is for those who are 'more interested in understanding nature than in using big words' (1957: xv). The question to ask, he goes on, is 'what can we change with our present knowledge and what can we not?' (1957: xxi).

What lies behind

Everything Berne went on to develop is based on the philosophy that people matter and are valuable in themselves, that everyone can gain insight into their own situation and can decide if, and what, they want to change. This beautiful (and to some, dangerous) idea is the founding myth of transactional analysis, from which other myths grow – myths of identity and hope (Moreau 2010: 37).

Myths are symbolic and significant stories that we recognize through our somatic response when we hear a story, see a play, film or a television programme, or hear a piece of music or song. 'Human beings are narrative creatures', the anthropologist Robert Bellah proposes in *Religion in Human Evolution* (2011: 34). He suggests *empathy* is the key emergent capacity that defines the beginning of humanity. Empathy enables us to develop the ability to understand others and to accept and share feelings. We learn to bond with others, to cooperate and to play, which means sharing attention and intention. Through bonding and play we begin to create meaning expressed in rituals – in Bellah's stimulating book, portrayed as the origins of early religion, but I believe his ideas can be applied to any cultural system. Meaning is shared through our joint social and cultural narratives, and from these myths or stories we derive concepts and ideas about who we are and how we relate. The social systems that we generate as a result can become normalized and accepted as inevitable – features of our everyday lives that Bellah calls 'online'. Or we may challenge this normality by staying aware of the 'offline' possibilities of empathy, bonding, playfulness, art, story, and so continually co-create new meanings in the present.

How can we relate this schema to the story of TA? I think that empathy or connectedness is the key – TA is not simply a system, it is grounded in a secure philosophy, and all the structures and concepts that have been built on this ground

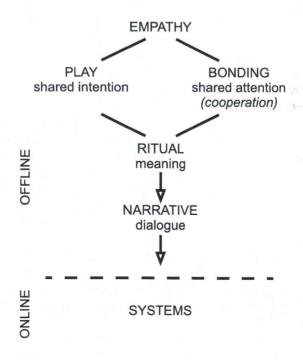

EMERGENT CAPACITIES

EMPATHY

PLAY
shared intention

BONDING
shared attention
(cooperation)

RITUAL
meaning

NARRATIVE
dialogue

OFFLINE

ONLINE

SYSTEMS

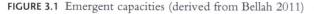

FIGURE 3.1 Emergent capacities (derived from Bellah 2011)

remain congruent with it. The 'play' of developing tools and models and the 'bonding' of a community that is based on mutual and self-respect, creates a narrative of hope, possibility, potential and change; although the resulting system has sometimes become more focused on pathology and deficit than on the back-story of health and value.

Like any other story, the story of TA is historically and culturally determined. Originating in the deterministic world of the 1960s, it can sometimes seem too structured and, in spite of its positive philosophy and accessibility, somewhat pathologizing. When we polarize pathology/health, and deficit/resource, the 'offline' of TA can sometimes get forgotten in the 'online'. A new story, however, has emerged; part of a 'relational turn' (Fowlie and Sills 2011: xxv) that moves away from the cognitive-behavioural towards mutuality and lived experience as a source of knowledge. At the same time, in co-creative TA, Summers and Tudor (2000; 2014) propose that, as well as being transactional analysts, we become 'transactional designers' – inviting people to use language and words to describe what they want to create more of, their desired future reality. Like Bellah, Tudor stresses the centrality of empathy, in this case as the prime method of co-creative TA practice (Tudor 2011).

While Ugazio helps us to see how we construct meaning and narrative, and Bellah shows how our narratives originate and are placed in cultural development, it is George Lakoff in his writing on metaphor who tells us how the language we use determines how we see ourselves and our world (Lakoff and Johnson 1980). As an example, when we have taken in a notion such as 'higher/lower', we assume that 'higher' (up) is better – we talk about 'high and low spirits', for instance. It may be true that high exam marks are better than low, but it doesn't have to read over into everything. Economic growth is an example – we rarely question that growth is good, even if it damages the environment and preferences competition over cooperation.

TA is a language and, like other languages, dependent on metaphors and polarities: 'winner/loser', 'higher/lower' (for example in the script matrix presentation and in diagramming 'OK–Not OK'), 'Parent/Child', 'adapted/free' (Loria 1990; Newton 2007). Sometimes the metaphors take over and become the system, instead of reflecting the narrative that gave rise to them. Similarly, Napper (2009), writing on Positive Psychology and TA, highlights the contradictions within transactional analysis theory between scientific 'objectivity' and recent constructivist thinking on 'subjectivity'.

More recently, Lakoff (2014) has noted how the language of political debate has changed, so that all sides use the same frame to understand or discuss 'reality', without realizing that we have created that reality and have the choice – and chance – to change it. So, we engage within a post-ideological, market-based model, and fail to address the more imperative narrative questions of, 'what matters to us – what sort of society do we want to live in?' Terms such as integrity, dignity, empathy, equality, are often excluded from debate. In contrast, from the more holistic perspective of social pedagogy or community education, we might consider:

people's well-being and happiness; how we bring up children to relate to themselves and others; what we can do about the social welfare of all, especially those at the margins of society (Cameron and Moss 2011). But we need to get these ideas to centre-stage rather than them being – like the people they are concerned with – marginalized.

All these writers – Ugazio, Bellah and Lakoff – are dealing with the stories we tell, and how those stories can bind us so that we think there is no other story; as if the story casts a spell and holds us within it (Sondheim 1987). How can we get back to the 'big story', the story of resource and thriving? Because a story is satisfying when it connects to other stories, and has a resonance with human functioning and deeply known metaphors and images.

What does this mean for the educational field?

Education differs from other fields of application in that it is always in the public space – there are social and political aspects to the contract, and there are witnesses to the 'doing'; the contract is always multi-party and is 'seen to be done'. Education is the pre-eminent way that a society or culture passes on its beliefs, priorities, philosophy, hopes and expectations to each generation. It is a community project. Different stories are often in competition here: is education about filling a need for qualified workers . . . for enabling and supporting its members' growth . . . for maintaining a society's myths . . . or for inviting political and social engagement? The stories we tell about education often seem to reflect the first and third, rather than the second and fourth purpose. Alongside this, and over a wide range of contexts, there has been a significant shift towards experiential and relational views of learning, a dialogue going on at the same time as some politicians aim to return to 'traditional' views.

Part of the relational turn being generated by TA educators is the 'turning' of concepts from descriptions of pathology or deficit, well intentioned as this might be, towards a resource focus. By investigating healthy normal development and the factors that promote it, by asking how can we talk about 'well-being', rather than 'remedy', we talk up divergence, individuality, interdependence and human capacity.

> Transactional analysis may, therefore, help promote the healthy integration of autonomous individuals within their cultural and political groups, developing healthy individuality with the capacity for belonging, intimacy and social responsibility. Specifically, a model of belonging combined with personal responsibility offers a healthy contrast to the contemporary development of what appear to be increasingly smaller and tighter social and political groupings – which seem to be the basis of the increasingly paranoid social structures that are replacing the narcissistic societies of recent decades.
> (Moiso 1998: 7)

We are telling a new story, and here are four examples of its 'chapters':

Re-imaging the Parent

One of the tales we tell is the metaphor of ego-states. Giles Barrow (2007) quotes Berne writing that he put 'Parent' at the top of his three circle diagram intuitively, because that way of thinking, he believed, has come naturally in all times and nations. But what might happen, Barrow asks, if we put 'Child' at the top?

How does this change the way we understand human experience and interpersonal dynamics (Barrow 2007: 206)? If we suppose that people are actually OK, for the most part resilient, and successful, and then observe that this is so for most people for most of the time, what does this imply for our theory and our practice? Barrow makes a connection between TA and Positive Psychology, with its emphasis on building a psychology of well-being and researching what enables us not just to survive, but to thrive (Seligman 2002). This, I believe is where we go back to the story behind the system; with parenting as the source of bonding, the supporter of play, and the provider and transmitter of good feeling in the narrative. In its apparent simplicity and visual impact, the CAP model contains the essence of re-imaging the Parent.

Two other models are also significant and influential. For many, new thinking about the Parent really began with Jean Illsley Clarke's work in re-focusing the cycles and stages of development model (Levin 1982) as a guide to healthy parenting (Clarke and Dawson 1989; 1998). Levin's work denotes stages of development from birth to adulthood, with developmental tasks to be completed, and needs to be fulfilled, for each stage. A great strength of her idea lies in its cyclic nature. As we become adults, individuals do not stop developing but continue to

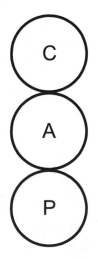

FIGURE 3.2 The CAP ego-state model (Barrow 2007: 206)

re-cycle the stages throughout life, first as youngsters, then as mature adults, then as older people moving towards death. Originally a therapy system for enabling clients to finish or re-do any uncompleted stages in infancy, Clarke turned it into a parenting model where the focus becomes 'what do babies, toddlers, children and adolescents need to create their own healthy script, and what do grown-ups need to discover or restore for themselves?'. This optimistic and enlivening approach, with its developmental and educational affirmations for each stage, has been further built on as a tool for teachers (Barrow, Bradshaw and Newton 2001; Barrow and Newton 2004; Russell 2009) and for tutors and managers in adult education (Napper and Newton 2000).

Another model that has had an enormous impact is Susannah Temple's *functional fluency*, described by Jan Grant in Chapter 17. Here I will simply comment on the great value of Temple's work in positively naming aspects of behavioural modes linked to the Parent ego-state: for teachers, and for parents, caregivers, social workers, all educators and trainers, the formulation of the Structuring Parent as an inspiring, supporting behaviour is not only a liberation from the 'guilty' label of 'Controlling Parent', but a permission to reinstate the Parent as essential. Similarly, naming the positive aspect of the Adapted Child as 'Cooperative' – the basis of healthy teamwork and all forms of socialization – removes another stigmatization from TA language. This lays the ground for 'being' in the teacher role as a fluently functioning person with all parts of one's personality available.

Updating the script

When we explore the positive threads from earlier writing about script, we find that English (1977) proposed that it is not all bad, in fact, script is essential. Everyone needs to create a personal story, and even seemingly negative stories contain something that gives comfort or security or helps to explain. Making meaning is part of the little person's learning, which, as Alison Gopnik and her colleagues have demonstrated, derives from evaluating what we experience, and involves experimenting with different behaviours, even when we are tiny (Gopnik *et al.* 1999). 'Learning' is our prime activity, the 'major adaptive process' of human beings (Kolb 1984: 32), and the way we construct meaning to craft our individual frameworks for future use and reference (Kelly 1955). Script formation is part of this learning (Newton 2006; and see Grant Chapter 17). As with the cycle of development, as we write our 'blueprint' story, we can go back and intervene for ourselves in that meaning-making, both individually and through communal activity. An example is the 'autonomy matrix' (Hay 1997), shown in Figure 3.3 at the base of the diagram – an upward-turned script matrix that indicates, as does the inverted CAP model, that caregivers, teachers and others support growth and physis.

Another example of an educational 'turning around' of the concept of script is Agnès Le Guernic's Social Roles Triangle, which takes fairy stories and folk tales as a guide. Psychological games and the Drama Triangle are both iconic TA concepts, and perhaps the most useful for conflict resolution, family dynamics and anti-bullying programmes in schools and organizations. Several versions of the winners' triangle are also well known (Choy 1990; Napper and Newton 2000) and serve a useful purpose in bringing about positive outcomes. However, the Social Roles Triangle (Le Guernic 2004) deepens an understanding of these dynamics. Starting with the idea of children being the heroes of their own stories, and benefiting from help and guidance from others, Le Guernic's model names the healthy, normal developmental roles of initiator, giver/helper and hero/beneficiary, which may become distorted into Persecutor, Rescuer and Victim if the right supportive input is missing. Stories enable children to choose positive relationship models and move towards personal growth and autonomy. A child can be the hero of his or her own story, benefiting from the help and direction given by others and learning to offer help and direction to others. Le Guernic presents a reading of fairy stories that contributes to the 'healthy, functional aspects of our personal reality' (2004: 216). This dialogue, between normal role-development and the limitations of the Drama Triangle roles, recalls Seligman's 'learned helplessness' and 'learned optimism'; both, he says, options for children growing up that are not random: children can be taught how to think, play, argue and express what they feel (Seligman 1996).

Healthy development and the health system

TA provides an excellent 'map' of child development, with key concepts expressive of each stage. Hewson (1990) brought these together in a 'systems' model. What happens though, if we gather instead the 'turned-around' concepts already described, in addition to others? The diagram below incorporates many of them.

This process began in a training group where I presented the Hewson diagram, and a trainee said, 'suppose we add the positive models to the diagram?' The eventual result (Newton 2005; 2007) has been updated here (Figure 3.3) to include the OK Box (Pratt and Mbaligontsi 2014), Social Roles Triangle, and CAP. The health system is constantly evolving as I respond to participants whenever it is presented, part of the ongoing discourse between a 'culture of remedy' and a 'culture of well-being' (Fregola and Iozzelli 2013). The outer line, the *resilience cycle* shows the assembled concepts, while the inner line is the original 'systems model'. The *preventive cycle* denotes that part where caregivers' support can enable healthy script development, the *restorative cycle* those ideas that can be used in aiding re-learning, new meaning-making, and recovery.

The philosophy of contracts

TA is a contractual system as a consequence of its philosophy and principles, and a contract – especially educational – always has a context. What we believe about what we do and how we learn, is the basis for what we contract to do as educators and how we do it. Biesta (2013) points out that to ask 'what is education for?' is not to give a definition, but to open up the debate. As referenced above, social

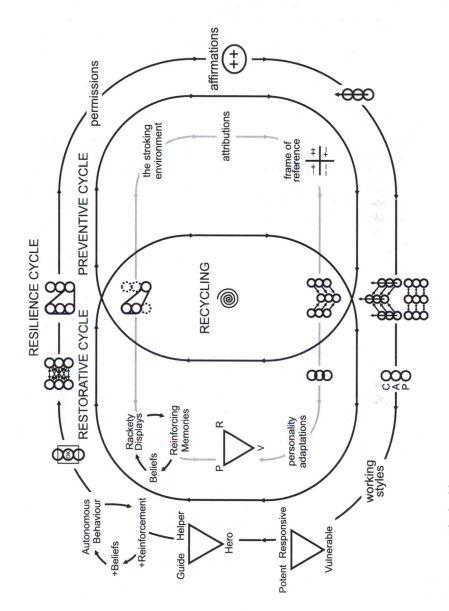

FIGURE 3.3 The health system

pedagogy draws attention to its purpose and the need to continually return to it, and not to assume that the question has been answered.

In exploring educational philosophies (Elias and Merriam 1995), I developed learning imagos to illustrate 'what is going on' in different kinds of learning groups, based on the 'group's group imago' (Clarke 1996), the collective picture we create in learning situations. TA can augment these ideas through the grounded-ness of concepts such as contracts, strokes/discounts, transactions showing transference and counter-transference or symbiosis (Newton 2003; 2014). This idea is more fully explored in the introduction to Part 4, along with its implications for adult learning. I include it here as a model through which we can look beyond the everyday experience of teaching or training to ask ourselves 'why': why do I do what I do and how can I show my beliefs about learning and education in my practice? What is my story, and how can I share what I have learned, be a transactional designer, and work with learners so that they believe in themselves?

When we take charge of what we do, consciously design our learning programs and interventions, and invite fresh encounters, we return to the radical origins of TA. We recover its potential for transformation.

PART 2
The identity of the teacher

INTRODUCING PART 2

Trudi Newton, UK

All those manifestations of teacherly will
Who join dozens of voices in dozens of schools
That make grownups of children and wise men of fools.

(Sophie Hannah 2003: 16)

What is a good teacher; one who can and does 'make grownups of children and wise men of fools'? Not simply someone who knows their subject and passionately wants to share it – although that may be very important – but one who both understands themselves and has an understanding of what learners, of whatever age, need. And cares about them: again and again, when people are asked to recall a teacher who was important for them, they will say, 'They saw me as a person'.

But what about the 'person' of the teacher?

A widely accepted facet of education now is the recognition of mutuality in the learning process: the teacher is someone who is themselves prepared to learn – from pupils and from circumstances, acquiring experience, comprehension and skills as they go. School, though, is not just about learning – for pupils or teachers – but is also a key way in which we absorb cultural and social norms; enculturation is a fundamental function of the school system, 'a crucial means by which individuals learn the norms necessary to exist outside of their immediate families' (Barrow 2009: 298). Teachers, as representatives of this system, take responsibility for defining reality for the students. So it is important to consider how the impact of this socialization process, as well as the sharing of knowledge, affects our beliefs about, and our understanding of, what it really means to be both a teacher and a learner.

Learning what we need to know and learning how to learn may be what we first think of when we think about education – but learning how to be part of our social environment is equally important. Yet even this understanding does not fully express a further domain of education, that of personhood, self-development, and freedom, which Biesta (2013) calls 'subjectification'. At first, I found this word rather ungainly for expressing such a vital idea, but then I found it helpful in its opposite-ness to 'objectification' – reducing someone, in all their multifaceted complexity, to the status of a simple object to be 'fitted in'. Rather, subjectification (or subject-ness) has to do with emancipation and its consequent responsibilities (Biesta 2013: 4); education becomes a process that contributes to the creation of human subjectivity (2013: 5). Like Freire, Biesta sees education as the practice of freedom, and teachers as demonstrating more than mere competence in playing their part.

Teachers need a combination of empathy and rigour – the understanding and compassion to be alongside learners in their self-discovery and growth, and also the strength to hold the boundaries and maintain the discernment and structure that provide the scaffolding to support healthy development in all its stages and manifestations; to balance risk and stability. This is what Biesta (2013: 130) calls 'educational judgement'.

Being competent to do things as a teacher is, of course, essential – but teachers also need to be wise, and to have the capacity for judgement: judging the right balance between potential gains and losses (2013: 129). This, says Biesta, lies at the heart of what goes on in the classroom between teachers and students – and goes on again and again and again. True education is a 'social art' (2013: 133) concerned with the interaction between human beings, not the interaction between human beings and the material world.

To bring us back to TA: this means above all having flexibility and awareness – and a strong, available OK Parent to reclaim 'the role of teacher in a way that does not diminish the learner. How does the educator maintain a sense of themselves, moment to moment in a way that relates powerfully with the learner, while honouring the contract in which the education takes place?' (Barrow 2015).

A *concentric* contract as illustrated in Figure 1 (Newton and Cochrane 2011) shows the overall educational contract – gaining knowledge, self-development and socialization – as the outer circle. Within this is the relationship – the middle circle in the diagram where real change and growth become possible. The moment-by-moment learning task is represented by the inner circle and *how* this is achieved will be affected by the two outer circles.

In exploring an unusual learning relationship, Giles Barrow employs the beautiful metaphor of an educator as 'cultivator' (Barrow 2011). He quotes Carl Rogers' wise words that educators, like therapists, do not make things happen – they provide the soil and nurture of cultivation to make the happening possible. The educator, like the farmer, needs to learn how to do this – which is also a process of cultivation, as Giles describes in his story of how he himself learned to become a farmer. He relates how his mentor, a retired farmworker, guided and enabled him, but also knew how to stand back and when to let go. Although the farmworker would not think of himself as a teacher, he showed Giles how to allow things to take

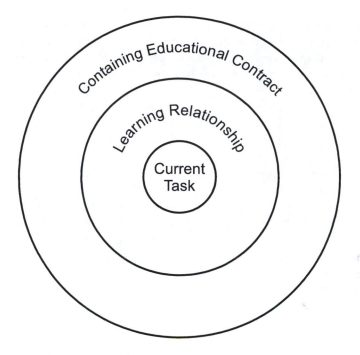

Containing Educational Contract

Learning Relationship

Current
Task

FIGURE 1 The concentric contract (adapted from Newton and Cochrane 2011: 23)

their own time, to be aware of the soil, and to act swiftly when something went wrong. The capacity to both learn and teach is in us all, an inevitable feature of what it is to be human (2011: 310).

Educators as cultivators are successful precisely because they own their experience and knowledge. Giles suggests that the 'cultivating' method of education intersects radical, humanistic and liberal models (Newton 2003; discussed here in the introduction to Part 4).

In this metaphor of cultivation, we see the role of the positive Parent supporting others' development, summarized in the CAP model (discussed in Chapter 3). In order to function in that positive, structuring, sustaining way, we need to pay attention to *how* we do that – and consider some recent thinking about the Adult.

One of the 'learnings' from the cultivator model is that of presence – what Giles calls grounded-ness – which includes containing the uncertainty in the process. Another similar idea is 'mindfulness': Žvelc proposes mindfulness as a key feature of integrating Adult (Žvelc, Černetič and Košak 2011). The term 'integrating Adult' has been used in various ways (Erskine 1988; Temple 1999; Tudor 2003) which all link closely to what the writers in this part propose: the importance of the person of the teacher, and how teachers can 'serve as models in the learning relationship which means that learners observe and notice intuitively the extent to which their teachers are authentic' (Dörte Landmann in Chapter 7).

Berne first defined the integrating role of the Adult (1961) as one of processing stimuli from the environment in association with the content of Parent and Child. He went on to propose the aim or desired outcome for the conscious person as being integrat*ed* – incorporating the warmth and spontaneity of the Child and the mature judgement of the Parent into the awareness and responsiveness of the Adult.

Integrat*ing* Adult is a little different – the ongoing, moment-by-moment activity of assessment and evaluation of context and available response and the activation of this with the flexibility to change (Berne 1961: 195). The way this idea is usually used now comes from the writings of two transactional analysts, Keith Tudor and Susannah Temple. Tudor returns to Berne's concept of the *neo-psyche* (meaning 'current mind') and deconstructs the traditional view of the Adult ego-state in favour of the integrating Adult as a present-centred, processing state of the ego (Tudor 2003: 220). This develops from the moment of conception; it can – and will – be expanded (rather than 'decontaminated') through experiencing authentic relationships. He describes 'a pulsating personality, processing and integrating feelings, attitudes, thoughts and behaviours appropriate to the here-and-now [. . .] at all ages, from conception to death' (2003: 201). Assume Adult, he writes, until proved otherwise (2003: 223).

Temple (1999; 2004) extends this idea, putting the integrating role of the Adult at the core of teachers' *functional fluency* – an ability to employ the full range of positive behavioural modes as appropriate in the moment. The desired outcome, in summary, is that in

> the co-created empathic relationship both teacher and learner stay present in their Adult, which in turn impacts their archaic Child ego states and introjected Parent ego states, both on a conscious and unconscious level, allowing them to extract new knowledge and make new meaning based on the shared emotional resonance between them. Such new knowledge and meaning is then integrated into their respective Adult ego states and this promotes the growth of an increasing acceptance of self and others for both teacher and learner.
>
> (Newton and Pratt 2015)

How can teachers use these ideas in developing their teacher identity?

Susannah Temple, placing the emphasis in her chapter on the teacher as a person, explores the way in which TA philosophy, principles and practice can support the journey of becoming a teacher – offering a coherent *framework for understanding* 'what goes on'. Her practical school-based understanding and clear descriptions of key concepts including strokes, hungers, the influence of the psychological level on transactions, and the importance of life-positions, show the true nature of educational TA as a practical psychology of learning. In doing so, she embodies some of its history from its beginnings as 'TA in education': the application of classic transactional analysis concepts in the teaching/learning context. But she does this from a much deeper, more soundly grounded perspective, that of a transactional analyst to her core, showing the learning and dedication that led to her developing the functional fluency model cited in many chapters of this book and now central to many educators' understanding of *how* we can make real familiar TA concepts. She cites neurological evidence that emphasizes the importance of both safety and appreciation in enhancing learning, and goes on to define what learners need: teachers who are confident in their own identity and their ability to relate positively to others; who can create trust and are sincere and congruent; who communicate well, with creativity and flexibility.

As she describes the concepts that support teachers in developing these abilities, Temple gives everyday examples of communication in the classroom, with a clear focus on problem-solving and positivity. Her conclusion is clear – if we leave out the personal development aspect of teacher education then teachers are not enabled to take on their leadership role effectively or, as above, develop educational judgement. TA can be both a support and an inspiration for building positive relationships in schools and enhancing the social art of education.

How does the teacher make a difference? In the following chapter, Henk Tigchelaar relates his classroom experience to exploring the polarity of pride and shame for learners – and shows how *reflection supports the integration of theory into practice*. An interesting aspect of this chapter is the research findings on teachers' communication, which confirm the classroom evidence. What is it that makes the difference in a pupil's encounter with a teacher? Similarly to Temple, he believes – and demonstrates – that TA concepts 'are very suitable to give shape to the process of getting a more conscious way of teaching'. When teachers give attention to, and reflect on, their behavioural modes with an awareness of the importance of these in influencing healthy script development for their pupils, they promote their pupils' freedom and augment their developing personhood.

Henk's concern is with the relational needs of pupils. In the next chapter, and in more detail, Nevenka Miljkovic writes about the application of the relational needs model (Erskine 2002) to education. While this is of interest from the point of view of learners' needs for identification, impact and affection, her concern is also with the needs of teachers and trainers. Those who have the *awareness to recognize their own script needs* will be more effective in responding appropriately to those of learners. Erskine's model has been widely influential in the therapy field, drawing attention to the 'missed' needs in relating to others that can bring people into therapy. To apply these same relational needs to the field of education and training and to explore, as Miljkovic does so eloquently, the potential effects for both teacher and learner, brings to light another aspect of learning, part of what Biesta calls 'subjectification' – the centrality of the learner as subject, not object. This is the kind of learning that has a potential to heal.

'Relational' is a relatively recent expansion of the range of TA theory and thinking. Another is 'mindfulness'. This idea has begun to be examined as an aspect of the integrating Adult (Žvelc *et al.* 2011). In suggesting that the Adult is not only a process but a practice, Verney describes it as:

> The ability to sustain presence in the neo-psychic, ever-changing Adult is crucial to our future, because it is in the ability to witness the workings of our own mind that we see the choice we make in every moment: to live with restraint and awareness in intimate connection to ourselves and our environment.
>
> (Verney 2009: 254)

Dörte Landmann and Gernot Aich place meditation at the centre of their perception of meaningful teaching as they *integrate TA into their personal world-view*. Central to their understanding is the 'person' of the teacher and the development of a mindful approach, which overcomes 'busyness' and a preoccupation with task and everyday pressures. Like Fanita English (1977), they see script as beneficial and the teacher as a model in influencing children's script formation. Their aim is to improve the effectiveness of the teacher's self in their role and, again, to be a healing presence. Both TA and meditation, they believe, are focused on improving the human condition. Both have the potential to generate answers to contemporary dilemmas in society about personal purpose. TA, they claim, has an important aim: exploring the question of how script can be changed in order to lead a more contented, successful and increasingly autonomous life. Their chapter resonates with that of Ferdinando Montuschi in the following part, an exploration of the importance of silence in the classroom, and as part of personhood.

This spiritual aspect of the person of the teacher is reflected in the idea of 'gift' (Hyde 2006), the gifting of goods, insights and expertise which has a long history in the development of communities. The gift must always be passed on, not remain with the recipient. 'Passing on' is the business of education – passing on culture, ideas, knowledge, beliefs and values. When we communicate our own experience and are changed by our contact with others, even though it may include anxiety, self-doubt and scare, we move towards the goals of 'making a difference' and a better world (Newton 2011). One aspect of giftedness is the gift of self.

Teachers – like Giles' farming mentor – often have the wisdom to serve and heal both individuals and communities. The self, and the willingness to be there for the other, becomes the gift.

4

BECOMING A TEACHER

An educational TA approach to personal and professional development

Susannah Temple, UK

Introduction

For those who work with people, personal and professional development are often regarded as synonymous. Teachers will say, 'I am the tool of my trade. Whatever I do, or don't do, my students will be learning from me; from the experiences I offer and the example I live'. In this chapter I will explore the ways TA philosophy, principles and practice can support teachers' development to enable them to inspire valuable, lifelong learning in their pupils and students.

Teachers are important people, in important professional roles. The journey of becoming a teacher is therefore an important matter and the main focus of this chapter. My context is the English system and, specifically, primary and secondary schools where most people spend a large part of their childhood. While the school experience is common to most of the population it is not, however, the same experience for everyone. The variables are many: matters of health, abilities, poverty/affluence, culture, neighbourhood – and political pressures. The effects are considerable and everyone in the community is involved one way or another. I think it is important to do everything possible to make the experience of school an enabling part of people's educational journey. We now have the knowledge and understanding to enhance the contribution that schools can make to children's lives. The issue is how to put that knowledge and understanding to use (Hénaff, Le Guernic and Salon 2012).

The most important variable for the purpose of this chapter is the relationship between children and their teachers. The focus throughout is on the teacher as a person. Teachers bring into school their efficiency and effectiveness, their competence and talent, their motivation and their ambition. Most important of all, they bring themselves, with their particular attitudes and ways of relating to others. Each child encounters many teachers during their school experience and

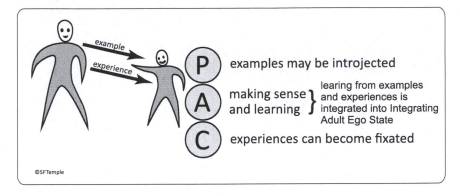

FIGURE 4.1 Teaching and learning

the relationships will vary. Each relationship provides a possibility for valuable learning, and practitioners need to ask themselves the question, 'When I am being a teacher, what are the children learning from me that will help them develop into effective lifelong learners?' (Deakin-Crick, Broadfoot and Claxton 2002). Teachers have a significant influence over us. They are authority figures during our years of immaturity when our beliefs and attitudes are forming. In TA terms, they are important Parental figures; 'powerful people in our past', in addition to mothers, fathers and primary carers. Teachers are inevitably role models and their influence, whether beneficial or harmful, can have enduring effects on our self-esteem, our self-confidence and our ability to learn.

This picture (Figure 4.1) is a reminder of the great influence of the teacher as a role model in school. It illustrates the psychological developmental process of ego-state formation. It shows how important teachers' congruence is for helping their students to make useful sense of the examples and experiences offered. Teachers must be aware that their influence will help shape the beliefs students build about themselves, others, life in general and learning in particular. What assumptions will they develop? How optimistic and persistent will they be in their future efforts as learners, based on what they have learned from their teachers?

What do pupils and students need from their teachers?

First and foremost is the need for pupils and students to feel safe, not just physically safe but psychologically safe. It is important to remember how fundamentally important this is, as laid out by Abraham Maslow (1970) in his hierarchy of human needs. Now, half a century later, we have the means to measure the physiological effects of operating in psychologically threatening situations using a neuro-imaging technique called the SPECT Scan. The researchers (Nelson, Amen and Lamare Calaba 2006) found that when functioning in a social medium of appreciation there was a good blood flow to the brain, whereas engagement in criticism, derogatory thinking and negative feelings actually lessened blood flow to the brain. The same pattern showed up in connection with heart function. Focus on the positive through appreciative thinking stimulates heart rhythm and pattern levels, which in turn enhance bloodflow to the cortex (Kline 2009: 57–8).

Educationally this evidence emphasizes the importance of safety and appreciation in school contexts if we want to enhance learning. In everyday terms, it means that having to cope with criticism, threats and warnings makes it harder to think coherently; the capacity of our brains is reduced. Teachers and students are affected alike. Inevitably some people are more susceptible than others if they are already low in self-esteem and confidence, so these facts are even more important with pupils and students who already, for whatever reasons, struggle with their learning. Denigration and judgemental criticism are counter-productive in the teaching/learning process. People function better, with less stress, when they can rely on respect, kindness and a focus on what works well and appreciation for their efforts. This is what engenders a desire to achieve more.

Pupils and students need teachers to feel confident about their own identity and role and their ability to relate positively to others; they need teachers to know how to create trust and rapport and to be sincere and congruent in what they do and say. They need teachers to communicate well and to have a creative and flexible approach that enhances their professional skill in delivering effective lessons.

Notice as you read the following story what doesn't happen – how the drama is diffused and the nature of the violent energy is transformed. The elegance of intervention is deceptively simple and rests on the teacher's positive attitude and ability to remain calm and objective in provocative circumstances. Instead of escalating hostility with negative reactions, he invites responsiveness (Temple 2005).

A real-life school story

I once witnessed a teacher faced suddenly with a group of upset adolescents very angry about being wrongly accused of something and all ready to act impulsively and violently. 'Hang on', said Mr Stokes, firmly and with a kind look at them all, 'This seems to be something tricky. Here, sit down for a moment. We need to think what to do for the best.' They all subsided, very tense and defensive. Mr Stokes was clearly thinking hard; then he said calmly. 'Each of us think of one small thing that would help this situation. When we are all ready, we'll list the ideas and choose what to do first.' In a quiet and business-like way he pulled out a large sheet of paper and found a board writer. There were five youngsters and he glanced round to see when they were ready. Most looked nonplussed and still rather suspicious, as though expecting the shouting and accusations to start. 'Right', he said, holding up the paper, 'If I fix this to the side of the board here, can you all see it OK?' With a small shuffle of chairs, they could. 'So, take turns and off you go; I'll write up the ideas, No discussion. We just make the list first of all.' They all realized now that he simply meant what he said – no tricks or plan to catch them out. [It seemed to me that one or two swiftly adjusted what they had first thought of. I could have been wrong.] There was a quiet pause. Then Darren, one of the three boys said, 'Each person says what they think really happened'. Two others were ready to argue about this, but the teacher shook his head and made a 'no go' sign. 'Just make our list', he said. 'Listen to each other', from Nick, then, 'Find Jack', Kate said suddenly. 'Tell Mrs Brinley the facts', came from Simon. The other girl, Sara, said, 'My idea is already there, really, – tell the whole story. None of us knows it all.' Mr Stokes added his idea, 'Learn all your names, I'm not sure of one or two.'

He added, 'This list OK with you now?' Nods. 'Any more needed on it?' They shook their heads, calmer now. 'So which is to do first?' 'Learning our names', they replied, so he put a '1' by that item. 'And next?' This was harder and finally, with some discussion, they agreed it was to find Jack. 'He needs to be here', they said. The mood shifted. After Mr Stokes learned the names, they asked if they could go and find Jack, get their lunch and come back to finish off before afternoon lessons began.

This was a key moment. The youngsters had engaged with the process and now responded co-operatively and assertively with a proposal of their own – a very sensible one too. The teacher agreed readily and they checked their re-meeting time together. The youngsters were following Mr Stokes' example with taking this lead. They felt better already and were thinking straight, with their plan they had made together, easily and quickly.

This had all taken place swiftly of course, in a corner of the school hall at the end of the morning. (It takes longer to write it down!) I didn't manage to see 'stage 2', but had some time to talk with Mr Stokes later in the day. He felt elated and somewhat surprised at how 'easily' it had worked out. The whole incident had in fact dissolved by the end of the lunch hour. It had been a case of serious misunderstanding over a misheard comment made by Jack about cheating. This caused threats of violence in retaliation which were overheard by Mrs Brinley who had promptly given two of them a detention, which was deemed unfair. Much accusation and blaming went on; Jack ran off to hide and tempers were rising whereupon enter Mr Stokes who knew nothing about it, but heard the levels of distress, frustration and fury and responded accordingly. When, in a more reasonable frame of mind, they went off and found the nervous Jack, they must have quickly done all the items on their famous list, so that they all knew all of the story as in Sara's idea. So they made friends again and that left the matter of the detentions, which was what they brought back to Mr Stokes.

He and I chatted about the roles he had played, including the one in which he approached Mrs Brinley to tell her a couple of key points in the youngsters' story and how well they had responded to the structure he had given them for dealing with the misunderstandings. He explained to her that he'd told them they must go and see her to apologize for their behaviour, tell her that the problem was solved and ask her if she would let them off the detention. Mr Stokes told her they were nervous about doing this, feared she wouldn't understand and that he had agreed to 'have a quick word with her on their behalf'. The two teachers had a friendly chuckle together and Mrs Brinley promised to listen to their case and make a fair deal with them.

In fact the story ran and ran, because it turned out the learning was catching, and various pupils and staff members got to hear of the incident and were curious. Both Mr Stokes and group members found they had to tell people what they did and didn't do and why they thought it had worked. Amazing, really. So simple. Yet, clearly, a learning experience for all concerned. I have often been surprised at how quickly adolescents grasp and make use of their learning about themselves and how deeply they seem to understand its significance (Temple 1996). This is practical educational TA in action; what it looks like on the ground. It is often quiet, quick and seemingly easy, because it is natural in fact for people to enjoy getting on well together and young people want to learn how to do it. When they feel safe enough and calm enough and have enough structure, stimulation and positive strokes, this is what they are likely to do. They enjoy the sense of mastery that understanding how people tick gives them. Mr Stokes used the power of his authority authoritatively to enable collaborative thinking and problem-solving. He demonstrated being a functionally fluent leader keen to collaborate and help through empowerment (Temple 2005). As the young people put it later, 'Mr Stokes was definitely on our side – at least there suddenly didn't seem to be any sides any more. We all wanted to make things better. He didn't try to find out who had done something wrong, so he could blame or punish us; he was just trying to help; and he did. We finished it all by ourselves in the end.'

This story is based on actual observations, though obviously all the names have been changed. I chose it for its ordinariness, because it shows that effective leadership at moments like this is not about magic or sophisticated techniques; it's about maturity and wisdom in action. At one level it is banal, no big deal. At another it demonstrates the amazing effectiveness of emotional literacy in action in everyday situations. It could all have been so different played out with blame, shouting, recriminations, punishment and resentment. The questions to ask with stories like these are, 'What learning is being shared?' 'Who will benefit and in what ways?', 'When this incident is over, will there be ongoing negative repercussions that will take time and effort to deal with, or will there simply be increased trust and positive social learning?' Preventive work is priceless and reaps benefits far into the future.

Reflect on this story and how Mr Stokes' behaviour benefited all concerned. Think about how he used his power. The list below gives some examples of what he actually did:

1   Relating to people, with Carl Rogers' unconditional positive regard, congruence and empathy (Rogers 1973).

2   Focusing on problem-solving rather than blaming.
3   Using authoritative behaviour (not authoritarian) to direct, soothe and restore order.
4   Giving time for consideration before acting by using the 'pause-button'.
5   Restoring the emotional balance of a group by meeting the psycho-social needs of the moment.
6   Inviting people to 'respond' rather than 'react,' so that they restart their own effective thinking.

What follows is a consideration of the educational TA approach and concepts that can help teachers develop the attitudes, assumptions and behaviours that underpin effective leadership such as that illustrated in the story. Teachers can use these concepts to widen their understanding of human psychology in a practical way for helping themselves as well as the people they work with – there is a mutual benefit effect from the building of positive relationships.

As you read further, you might like to use the list above to connect the story with the various TA concepts described below.

Educational TA as an approach for personal/professional development

A first and general consideration is that I view educational TA as a practical educational psychology; as a positively focused, optimistic approach with down to earth, practical ideas for helping people to function well. Its philosophy, principles and practice can be articulated in a coherent, consistent and congruent way (Temple 2008a).

Educational TA concepts encourage teachers to transform their growing self-awareness and understanding into practical relationship-building skills. They help teachers develop empathy, understanding and compassion along with the ability to be objective, fair, tough and courageous. Educational TA offers a framework for the development of the emotional literacy required for maintaining professional effectiveness, health, a sense of humour and the resilience to withstand the external pressure from a performance based culture.

The leadership role of teachers

Human beings feel better when they know who is in charge, and even better when they sense that those in charge know what they are doing and are competent. If they are not sure, they will 'test the water' to find out 'what happens if . . .'. They will want to know if the teacher says what he/she means and means what he/she says, and how far the teacher can be trusted. They want to know how safe they are; are they safe to be open to learning? Are they safe to make mistakes? It is, after all, impossible to be creative without making mistakes.

TABLE 4.1

Philosophy	Principles	Practice
Intrinsic value of all people – mutual respect – I'm OK – You're OK	Deep respect for self and others. (No power play, deception, manipulation or discounts)	Contractual method, openness and integrity in dealings with people
Each person is responsible for own thoughts, feelings and behaviour	Accept personal responsibility for one's own experience. (No blaming of self or others)	I-statements – congruence – emotionally literate interaction
A person's own experience is of prime validity	Recognition and respect for each person's personal experience. (Avoid interpreting or pathologizing)	Accounting for self, other and the situation – validation of inner experience – empathy
Each person constructs and decides own destiny, and can change those decisions. Problems are solvable	Focus on the positive, practical and optimistic	Search for solutions, using 'how' rather than 'why' questions

To be leaders for learning, teachers need to cultivate within themselves beliefs and attitudes that will help them inspire their students. They need to believe in their students' potential for success and in their own capacity to make a positive difference. Having the know-how and skill for engendering a classroom climate of hope and encouragement is vital, both for their own sakes as well as for their students. This way learning/teaching becomes a mutual activity and empowerment a two-way process (Deakin-Crick, Broadfoot and Claxton 2002). McCombs and Whistler (1997) identified that learners' motivation and achievement are enhanced by student-centred practice in various ways, and that the most important of these is the quality of the classroom relationships. Students' learning is more likely to flourish when the relationships are experienced as positive, understanding and enabling.

How educational TA can help teachers develop themselves as leaders

To be effective leaders in the classroom, teachers need to be authoritative and to exert authority in ways from which everyone benefits. For this they need to understand the difference between 'authoritative' and 'authoritarian' (Temple 2002), and to have developed enough self-awareness and understanding, along with know-how about human group dynamics. Veronica Lim, describing the essence of 'natural leaders', wrote, 'In nurturing a generosity of spirit with themselves, they extend the same generosity towards others. They fully realize their worth and they lead just by being the person they are, while always inspiring and allowing others to do the same' (Lim 2005: 25). Educational TA gives a practical framework of concepts to underpin the development of 'natural leadership'.

Integral to the philosophy, principles and practice of educational TA is the building of positive, enabling relationships. This focus is emphasized by educationalists from other disciplines. For instance, in *Becoming Partners: Marriage and its alternatives*, Carl Rogers wrote of the value people would gain if their schooling had enabled them to 'live as a person with other persons' (Rogers 1973: 219), having learned how to develop effective relationships. Much more recently, Nancy Kline demonstrated how to create a 'Thinking Environment' (Kline 1999) with ten components for 'igniting the human mind' and its potential for learning. All of these point towards the importance of listening, awareness, understanding and appreciation.

The TA theory of strokes is at the heart of human communication

Attention is a key word. Giving and receiving attention is what teachers are doing most of the time. TA maintains that human beings are relationship-seeking animals, that our psychological development proceeds through and within relationships and that we *need* to relate to people in order to become fully human, or as Carl Rogers put it, 'To become a person' (Rogers 1973).

The currency of human relationships is the attention that is exchanged within them. TA has a term for a unit of this attention or recognition. The word is 'stroke', in connection with the importance of affectionate touch for human beings – especially at the beginning of life. As people grow up the strokes can become more symbolic, though touch remains the most potent form of communication, for good or ill.

For psychological *survival*, human beings need strokes, they need to be recognized and noticed. The pain of being ignored taps in to primitive fears from very long ago, when I guess that if a child really wasn't noticed at all, if no one had an eye on it, then it might have actually got eaten up or left behind. I think it helps in education to realize that, deep down, getting enough attention is a survival issue. It is not a trivial matter. In order for humans to *thrive*, however, the diet of strokes needs to be positive and affirming, so that a healthy self-esteem can be built and a positive outlook on life developed. However, if there aren't enough positive strokes around that meet our needs, we are clever enough to make up the difference with negative ones. We learn to invite the negatives rather than go without. Important maxims are, 'any strokes are better than no strokes', and, 'the behaviour you stroke, is what you'll get more of'.

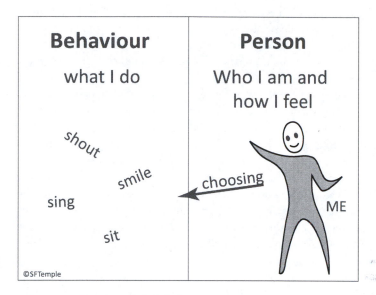

FIGURE 4.2A People and their behaviour

	Conditional	Unconditional
Positive	Approval +	Acceptance ++
Negative	Disapproval —	Rejection — —

©SF Temple

FIGURE 4.2B The Stroke Matrix

The above two diagrams go together, showing how important it is to think of the person as separate from his or her behaviour. They also show unconditional strokes are to do with the person and that conditionals are to do with the behaviour.

Using stroke theory in school

Every teacher has met children who will go to great lengths to get attention, steadfastly earning themselves negative strokes which you'd think they'd prefer not to have! Such children, stuck in negative patterns of attention seeking, are in danger of continuing to go without the positive strokes they need for psychological health and well-being.

A key task for teachers then, in TA terms, is to spot the child who craves attention and has learned to get it negatively, and to refuse to 'play the game'. Instead of accepting the child's invitation to dole out a negative stroke (a telling off or a punishment of some sort) the teacher finds a way to give that child the diet of positive strokes which will meet the child's individual need. This often means re-evaluating the whole way the child is dealt with in school. TA offers an extra dimension to the usual behaviour modification techniques. These can work well for children who are simply muddled about how they are meant to behave, and need some systematic training which will improve their social skills. However, children who are really stroke deprived and have settled for getting enough strokes in life by going for the negatives, need more than behaviour modification strategies, and in order to understand why, it's important to differentiate between the four different sorts of strokes that can be given.

Positive and negative strokes can both be in response to a behaviour (doing) or simply in response to the receiver's existence (being). In TA these are called respectively conditional or unconditional strokes. It is a vital difference. Unconditional positive strokes are the key to self-esteem. They are attuned in response to the person and how that person is feeling. They come for free and affirm a person's existence, worth and identity. They don't have to be earned. Often they are non-verbal – smiles, hugs, just a nod or a look of pleasure and welcome, someone spending time, listening, making room, preparing a place, or food or materials lovingly, these are all ways to give that positive unconditional regard so vital in person-centred ways of working.

Unconditional negative strokes are similarly in response to the person and are also unearned, such as name-calling and negative judgements of the person rather than the behaviour ('Stupid!', 'You wicked girl!'). Grimaces, gestures, ignoring, verbal and physical abuse are all attacks on the person, and are destructive and potent strokes.

So while unconditional strokes may be of acceptance or rejection of the person, conditional strokes are of approval or disapproval of behaviour. Whenever possible disapproval should be given in such a way that useful learning is invited, e.g., 'The next time, make sure that you . . .'. Limits and expectations should be clear and specific, e.g., 'No more jumping on the sofa, you can jump about outside'. Appreciation for desirable behaviour and for doing well should be offered frequently, in a way that is accurate, genuine and heartfelt.

The more that positive strokes are abundantly available, both for the being of the person and for desirable behaviour, together with non-blameful guidance with regard to unwanted behaviour, the better children will thrive and learn. It is hard for anyone to feel motivated and benevolent without enough positive strokes. Teachers themselves are often in deficit, and finding ways *as staff* to give and receive appreciation is a good first step in tackling behaviour problems!

The key stroke issue for children who disrupt

It is usually the case with children whose behaviour is disruptive and disturbing and who don't respond well to reasonable and consistent approval and disapproval, that they lack – and may always have lacked – enough positive unconditional strokes. They may well not actually mind much whether someone approves or disapproves of what they do. They carry on getting strokes in the ways they have learned, and hook the teachers into reinforcing the negative patterns, i.e. playing the games. What these children need more than anything else is an available and reliable accepting and loving relationship, so that by experiencing nurture of themselves as people, they come to care about others' approval or disapproval of how they behave, and learn to want praise and appreciation and how to earn it, while learning to give up earning condemnation and rejection as a way of living. What a risk! This is why a setting of psychological trust and safety is so essential (Maslow 1962; Steiner 1996). This is why the relationship with the child is the key to success.

Three psychological hungers: how to balance them

- Stimulation – we need to experience feeling alive.
- Recognition (strokes) – we need to feel that we belong, that we 'count'.
- Structure – we need enough predictability to have some idea of what will happen next.

These three basic human psychological needs, when in balance, help us maintain a healthy equilibrium for effective functioning, so this concept is useful for classroom management in addition to enhancing our own well-being. We can use the idea as a sort of three-way thermometer. When these needs are met well enough, we feel energized, comfortable and secure. We can get on with the job. When we have a deficit in any of the three, we feel unsettled, edgy and unable to concentrate easily. When we have an excess of any, we may feel wound up, the centre of the universe or boxed in or restricted. The greater the imbalance, the more we are inclined to escalate our behaviour, which gives clues as to the adjustments needed.

There are no 'right' levels for the three-way thermometer as people and situations differ. If we are in charge of a class and we observe evidence of deficit or excess of any of the hungers, we can take steps to adjust the levels and restore comfort ('Does this class need more activity now?', 'Would a set exercise be a good idea next?'). Teachers can also teach their students this concept as a life skill and an aid to self-discipline for study and as know-how for social situations. For more about applying this concept see Clarke and Dawson (1998). The original concept came from Eric Berne (1961).

Communication happens simultaneously on two levels: a social, more obvious level, and a psychological, more obscure level (Figure 4.3). In order for communication to be clear and helpful, the two levels need to be congruent. Congruence is

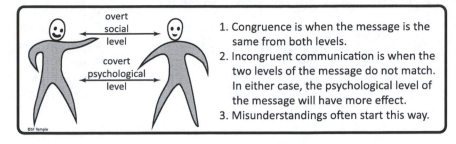

overt
social
level

covert
psychological
level

1. Congruence is when the message is the same from both levels.
2. Incongruent communication is when the two levels of the message do not match. In either case, the psychological level of the message will have more effect.
3. Misunderstandings often start this way.

©SF Temple

FIGURE 4.3 Congruence and levels of communication

when a message is the same from the open, social level as well as the hidden, psychological level so that the verbal and non-verbal aspects of the communication match up. Congruent communication is helpful, whether it is positive or negative, because the speaker is saying what they mean (and means what they say) and both parties know where they stand; mutual respect is easier. Incongruent communication is when the two levels of the message, social and psychological, do not match and the person is not clearly expressing what they actually mean. This is often experienced as insincere or manipulative in some way, though the speaker may not consciously intend this.

The most important factor to be aware of is that the power of any communication is fuelled from the hidden, psychological level, rather than the open social level. This doesn't show up in congruent communication of course. When communication is incongruent, however, the psychological level of the message, having greater potency, will have the greater effect. Imagine being greeted at the door with the words, 'Oh how lovely to see you!' said by someone in a dull voice, who just sighs and stands there with no smile at all. In spite of the actual words, it would be hard to feel welcomed and accepted. This is how incongruence often results in uncertainty and confusion and may cause misunderstanding or suspicion. It is also why so many arguments start out with the words, 'But I only said . . .!'

The daily dynamic of classroom relationships carries messages that can affirm and inspire or undermine and demean. It is important to note that humiliation and sarcasm, those enemies of classroom trust and confidence, usually employ incongruent communication. The dynamic works in both directions between students and teachers and is the main ingredient of classroom climate. The nature of this climate makes a huge difference to how people feel about themselves as learners, whether they feel understood or misunderstood, whether they think they are treated fairly or unfairly, whether they engage with the subject and whether they are motivated to succeed (Temple 2008a). The next concept builds on this one by pointing out how important it is to avoid wasting energy on blaming.

Life positions: To blame or not to blame?

This arrangement of life positions means looking at the OK Corral (Ernst 1971) in a new way that emphasizes a focus on the need to avoid blaming if we are to be free to get on with problem-solving in an I+U+ position (Temple 2000).

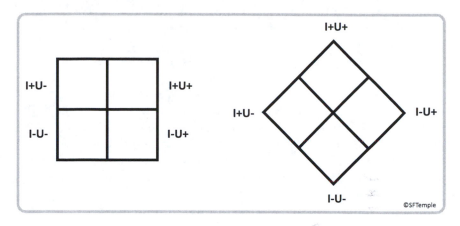

FIGURE 4.4A Franklin Ernst's 'OK Corral' rotated

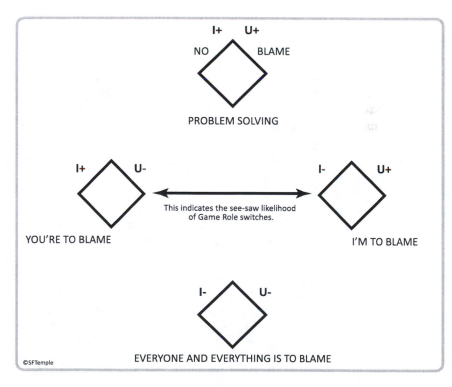

FIGURE 4.4B Life positions with a focus on blame-free interaction

The I+U+ position is the one for blame-free problem-solving, the Get-On-with-Life position.

The more that people can maintain an I+U+ position, the more their relationships are likely to be positive, satisfying and beneficial, and their behaviour effective.

In the I+U−, Get-Rid-Of, and I−U+, Get-Away-From, positions, energy is expended in blaming either the other people or oneself.

In the I−U− position of despair, the Get-Nowhere-with-Life position, blame is attributed both outwards on to others and inwards on to self, hence it is often called the 'futility position'.

People may have a familiar, or default position, which shapes their general attitudes towards self and others and the way they build relationships and deal with life. By avoiding the habit of blaming, they can learn to use the I+U+ Get-On-with-Life position more and put their energy into problem-solving.

Teachers can set the tone of the classroom communication dynamic by noticing and giving appreciation to what works well and making genuine requests for ideas that could help achieve successful solutions to difficulties; a more effective use of energy than blaming and punishing and much appreciated in turn by students − remember the story about Mr Stokes.

Conclusions

Becoming a teacher means taking on that authority role we were so familiar with from our student role position throughout our own school years. This shift needs to be done with awareness and understanding (Temple 1999). Teacher education must provide for enough reflection and discussion to support an effective taking on of teacher authority. These are some of the fundamental questions that trainee teachers need to answer: Who am I as a teacher? Do I want to have an enabling and inspiring influence on the students I teach? How do I develop this sort of influence? What examples and experiences do I want to offer my future pupils and students? How do I learn to manage my own behaviour so that I can help them manage theirs? What do I need to know and understand?

The danger of leaving out the personal development aspect of teacher education is that teachers are not then enabled to take on their leadership role effectively enough. This leads to the difficulties in classroom and behaviour management that makes delivering the curriculum well nigh impossible. First and foremost teachers are people. The positive relationships they engender in the classroom are the most important thing they do in setting the scene for learning to flourish. Confidence and know-how about positive relationship building are therefore vital goals for teachers' personal development. Educational TA can be both a support and an inspiration for this process.

5

THE TEACHER MAKES THE DIFFERENCE

Henk Tigchelaar, Netherlands

Pride and shame in the classroom

As a teacher and TA trainer I am very interested in the dynamics of the classroom, and especially in what promotes a safe and challenging learning environment. I developed an experimental workshop for TA professionals, called 'Pride and shame in the classroom', to investigate both what promotes such an environment and what the role of the teacher is in this situation.

As a former music teacher, I decided to start my workshop with an experiment by singing with all participants. Afterwards I ask how they experienced the singing and what experiences they had had with singing in the classroom. This is an important and vulnerable moment in the workshop, because there are always several people who report that they had bad experiences with singing. The teacher told them they were not in tune, their voice was not good enough, or made other negative comments on the quality of their singing. In other words, the teacher shamed the student. For many of them these remarks were even now determining their joy in singing – they still feel shamed while singing. Some of them reported that they decided never to sing any more with others. In all cases their teacher reacted from a strong negative Controlling Parent ego-state, and this wasn't helpful.

Others reported that they love singing and tell how they were 'stroked' by their teacher. Some for their beautiful voice or being in tune, others felt stroked by their joy in singing. They also reported that the teacher told them that everyone can sing and that if you like you can do exercises that will help you to improve your singing. In these cases the teacher reacted from Nurturing Parent and Adult ego-states. This, in turn, was definitely helpful in promoting pride and self-confidence.

In TA literature, I found some interesting theories about this issue. Fanita English wrote about shame and social control (English 1994). She explains that shame is a normal socializing process and the child has to find a balance between the Adapted and Natural Child. In the same article she also writes that shame and ridiculing are primary educational techniques to control and train children.

Landaiche writes about the social function of rejection. In blaming and shaming others you don't feel your own pain. He refers to scapegoating and passing on the 'hot potato'. He makes an interesting remark: 'What did your teacher feel when he shamed you? Maybe he was shamed himself. Is this what happened when the teacher shamed you for your singing?' In his conclusion he emphasizes the role of the Adult in stopping the cycle of pain (Landaiche 2009: 235).

Erskine has the following definition of shame: 'a self-protective process used to avoid the effects that result from humiliation and vulnerability to loss of contact in relationship with another person (Erskine 1994: 90).

With the underlying script belief, 'Something's wrong with me', there is a cognitive defence of needs in a relationship. Asking, 'If I become what you define me as, will you love me?' Erskine (2009) describes how the self will be split between a Social Self and a Vulnerable Self when we can't meet the expectations of the teacher; it's a strategy for trying to stay attached in relationship. This splitting can occur at any developmental stage when a teacher is neglecting the needs of the student, or when the teacher is too critical or has expectations that the student can't meet. An important underlying relational need is: the need to make an impact, to be seen as competent, and the need to be taken seriously.

From outside of TA, Erickson (1950) linked shame to the developmental stages two and four:

> Stage two (age 1.5–3): *Autonomy versus Dependency/Shame*. Anger is an important feeling because it helps in showing your own will; autonomy, anger and boundaries belong together. Ridiculing anger and the child's will decreases autonomy and pride, and increases shame.
>
> Stage four (age 6–12, i.e., primary school age): *Industry versus Inferiority*. In this stage the main task is the development of the self-image by learning competencies. What teachers can do is to give strokes, encourage students, have realistic expectations, give feedback in an I'm OK – You are OK way, and have an attitude that you can learn from your mistakes. This increases autonomy, pride and self-confidence.

All these theoretical findings indicate that the role of a teacher is very important in creating pride (Adult and Nurturing Parent) or shame (Negative Controlling Parent). Teachers who are aware of the effects of their communication towards students achieve good results. Teachers who use their positive ego-states consciously (Berne 1961) have a greater impact on the learning process of their students. This also contributes to the overall quality of their education. TA concepts in particular are very suitable to give shape to the process of getting a more conscious way of teaching (Napper and Newton 2000).

Education research shows that effective behaviour of teachers leads to successful learning processes and positive results (Marzano 2007). In what follows I will explore: how to apply TA concepts in teacher training; research about the effectiveness of TA; and the role of script formation in the learning process.

A stupid question?

Recently a student reported the following incident. She attended training where she had to analyse several real-life examples. During the preparation she didn't understand one of the aspects and asked a question about it. She was stunned when the teacher said. 'What a stupid question, you should have known'. Blood rose to her head and for a moment she didn't know how to respond. She felt very uncomfortable when the teacher criticized her in front of her fellow students. This created for her an unsafe learning environment. This resonates with a statement made by Ken Robinson: 'If you are not prepared to be wrong, you'll never come up with anything original' (Robinson 2006).

It looks like the teacher in this example handled her question from his negative Controlling Parent ego-state and had no idea what effect this had on the student. He sincerely believed this intervention was the best option for a positive learning result. Apparently he was so strongly focused on good results that a question was a direct threat to his goal. This seems like a reaction from his script. The lack of knowledge from the student, the question she asked, triggered the script of the teacher.

The teacher makes the difference!

The example above is not an exception. When people are asked about their experiences at school, they talk about the behaviour of teachers that had affected them, both in a positive and negative manner. The teacher makes the difference when it comes to creating a safe learning environment. The teacher has a significant impact on the script beliefs of the students.

It is very important that all teachers, whether working with children or adults, are aware of the effects they have when communicating. This means that they have explored the meaning of their Parent and Child ego-state, and know possible triggers for script behaviour, non-autonomy encouraging reactions and interventions. The difference between a script reaction from the Parent or Child ego-state and on the other hand an authentic response from the Integrating Adult ego-state (Tudor 2003) is reflection! When there is a moment of reflection between the impulse and the action, the communication will probably be effective. In the words of TA: everybody has options, you don't have to react in your script behaviour.

Being conscious of the ego-states

Temple (1999; 2004) elaborates on the importance of the process of autonomy. She argues that classrooms should be safe places where you can comfortably learn together, and that TA is very supportive in this. In order to let students acquire autonomy it is important that teachers expand on the topics of 'autonomy, consciousness, spontaneity and the capacity to accept intimacy' (Stewart and Joines 1987). Then entering symbiotic relations will decline. Besides that it is important that teachers are able to react flexibly, effectively use all ego-states and model various behaviours. Temple uses the term functional fluency to describe this skill. Through growing consciousness the teacher is able to make choices to avoid negative behaviour from the contaminated Adult (through Parent or Child). Decontaminating is an intriguing and dynamic process. Temple drew on the structural and functional model of ego-states in developing the concept of *functional fluency*. Even though one might argue the theoretical context, the power of the functional fluency model lies in the practical use. It gives a clear insight on the fact that ineffective behaviour (functional negative ego-states) comes from the contamination of the Adult ego-state within the structural model: behaviour that comes as a reflex from the Parent or Child and is from the script.

Temple designed a programme for undergraduate teachers, in which consciousness is central. It's a learning process in which ineffective patterns from the script are detected and the Child and Parent ego-states can be healed.

> People who enter this teacher training, particularly those in their late teens, will likely be doing so with many of these Parent and Child ego states as yet unintegrated and therefore available for transferential cathexis in moments of stress. In other words, until such teachers achieve the necessary Adult decontamination and integration, they will be liable in professional situations to be triggered out of Adult into replaying material from Parent or Child.
>
> (Temple 1999: 171)

Learning and script

In 'Teaching, Learning, Schooling and Script', Barrow (2009) suggests that the process of forming of the script is continuous and is not only the result of a certain period during childhood. Together with family, life events and other cultural activities school is a place where the forming of the script happens, not a place where the script is only 'performed'. As in each situation where you find script behaviour, the school can – by early symbiotic relations, transference and counter-transference – confirm someone's script. The difference between healthy autonomous behaviour and script-based behaviour of teachers is determined by the level of consciousness of this behaviour and the availability of options to do it differently.

In 'Script, Psychological Life Plan and Learning Cycle', Newton (2006) draws several conclusions in response to the formation of the script and the learning cycle (Kolb 1984).

> The child is a dynamic actor in the forming of the script; the script is formed through interaction and dialogue.

The script is for a child a way of solving problems and a way to create meaning from the available information.

The context in which the child forms the script is much broader than only in the immediate family; the script is formed within a community.

(Newton 2006: 189)

These statements underline the impact of teachers in the forming of the scripts of their students. The quality of the dialogue between teacher and student is determinative. Healthy, autonomy-enhancing communication from teachers will lead to healthy and autonomous behaviour from the student. Besides that, the extent to which the teacher is able to create a safe learning environment – with clear boundaries and a rich stroke climate – will have a positive or less positive influence on the forming of the script. The quality of the dialogue and a safe learning climate are conditions for good learning results.

TA training is proved to be effective

An article by two TA colleagues was published in the *Transactional Analysis Journal* (Çam and Akkoyun 2001), in which they discussed the effect of communication skills training, focused on ego-states and problem-solving behaviour. They demonstrate that, in line with the academic standards for research, training on communication skills for teachers with the use of TA is very effective. They based their research on findings from the 1980s, in which it was found that excellent learning results come from good communication between student and teacher. They also make use of research that proves that TA training is effective in influencing the behaviour of teachers (Rodriguez 1983). One of these findings shows a correlation between a high score on Adult and Nurturing Parent (with a low score on Controlling Parent) and high self-confidence in problem-solving behaviour (Çam 1995). The aim of this study was to test the effectiveness of a communication skills programme on the ego-states and problem-solving behaviours of student teachers.

With these facts as a basis, they started an academic research project with the aim of improving the communication skills of teachers. Ego-states (structural and functional), the analysis of transactions and options, were part of the training programme. The training programme also aimed to create an atmosphere of support, acceptance, confidence and intimacy among the participants.

Çam and Akkoyun worked with two groups. The experimental group participated in training, whereas the control group had no training. Both groups were tested before and after the intervention. The experimental group was followed up to test the durability of the effects of the training.

They used two measures. The first measure was the Adjective Check List, developed by Gough and Heilbrun (1988) to assess different aspects of personality. This test consists of several subscales, including the TA Ego-state Scale developed by Williams and Williams (1980). A Turkish adaptation of the TA Scale was carried out by Akkoyun and Bacanli (1990). The second measure was the Problem

Solving Inventory, developed by Heppner (1988) to assess the perception of problem-solving behaviours and attitudes. Both measures were applied to both the experimental and control group before and after treatment. Analysis of covariance test results showed that Controlling Parent, Nurturing Parent, Adult, and Adapted Child scores and problem-solving scores changed significantly within the experimental group. In addition, they tested the durability of change in the experimental group; this showed that results remained stable over 15 weeks.

In the training programme, participants learned to express themselves effectively and how to handle communication problems. In the evaluation of the training programme the egograms of the teachers that participated in TA training showed that the Adult and Nurturing Parent scored significantly high, especially when compared with the control group. These two ego-states are characteristic for people that are interested in development and in helping others to evolve, and are so called 'Guru Egograms' (Dusay 1977). People with guru egograms are often found in jobs such as coaches, counsellors, teachers and trainers. Their strong Adult guarantees that they are good instructors with a healthy and an autonomy-directed attitude. Their Nurturing Parent and Adult are equal or higher than their other ego-states.

This research shows the effectiveness of a training programme focused on ego-states and problem-solving attitudes for a specific group of prospective Turkish teachers. After the training programme, the participants reported they felt more confident in problem-solving behaviour with students. The outcome of the training programme also remained effective in the long term.

Meta-analysis of education research

In his book, *What Works in School: Research in action*, Marzano (2007) presents a meta-analysis of 35 years' education research, with the central question: 'What leads to more effective learning processes and good learning results?' In summary, the following conclusions were drawn.

> Effective teachers are very concerned with their students, give a lot of attention and are clear about their expectations of the students. They don't show much dominant behaviour. This is in line with the research of Çam and Akkoyun: a lot of Nurturing Parent and Adult behaviour is seen with effective teachers.
>
> A second success factor is the classroom climate: creating a safe group, being alert to events in the class and when necessary setting clear boundaries. This is in line with the statements of Newton (2006) and the study from Çam and Akkoyun (2001).
>
> The last success factor Marzano mentions is self-confidence. Teachers promote this by giving strokes for the successes of their students, by encouraging them to pick up new tasks and ask questions, and by giving them feedback in a 'I am OK, you are OK' attitude.

These are all interventions from a positive ego-state, to encourage autonomy and have a positive effect on the forming of the script.

Conclusion

Now you can see how determinative the interaction between teacher and student is; and how effective TA is to help teachers to make conscious use of their own autonomy to encourage autonomy in their students. When teachers explore their own script they come to know possible triggers for script behaviour, non-autonomy-encouraging reactions and interventions. Training to increase the use of their Nurturing Parent and Adult and decrease the Negative Controlling Parent is crucial in promoting healthy relationships and autonomy in the classroom.

Aware teachers will use the five P's (Crossman 1966; Clarke 1996) in order to promote pride in the classroom and a safe and challenging learning environment.

> *Power (Potency):* to set clear boundaries, to intervene when someone is ridiculing another, and to stop gallows laughter about so-called mistakes.
>
> *Protection:* to protect students from their own shame, to challenge with Adult examination, asking questions so that they can discover what is really going on.
>
> *Permission:* to give students permission to make mistakes, to know you don't have to suffer from them, to reframe it as real learning, to take them seriously, and tell them that there are no stupid questions.
>
> *Perception:* to look and see what's happening with the individual student, the group process, and intervene when it's necessary.
>
> *Practice:* to practise all these four P's and give students space to practise their pride and autonomy.

And all these five P's are in a circle of 'I'm OK, You're OK', the circle that says we are equal, worthwhile and that we deserve respect and love from our teachers. So that we can declare: 'The teacher makes the difference!'

6

RELATIONAL NEEDS IN EDUCATION

Nevenka Miljkovic, Serbia and Germany

What is a good relationship in the educational context? We learn in relationships. The brain is a 'social organ' – being shaped in relationships. So good relationships are essential for good education. But how can we recognize a good relationship in the educational process?

The concept of 'relational needs in educational context' enables us to observe and understand how all participants in the education process – students and educators – create and recreate their relationships in the way they need them in a specific moment. Like in a dance, they regulate closeness and distance, autonomy and the need for impact from the other, the need to feel accepted, or maybe the need to appreciate the other and to express it. So we can understand how we shape the relationships during our education.

'Relational Needs' (Erskine 2002) is a very useful model for the educational field; it can be used in:

- *Planning a course*, class, educational unit – on the basis of what needs will an educator probably have in this specific situation and what will be the needs of the students in the particular context.
- *Analysing and understanding the actual process* of training so the problems that occur can be seen in the light of the needs of students and educators – this understanding supports the educator to choose methods and content which make the learning process and personal development more successful.
- *Supervision of teachers and trainers* – most of the time problems in training or in the classroom show that specific relational needs are being discounted.

I want to show the potential of this model in the work of a trainer and supervisor. After discussing the model, its premises and implications, I describe my modification of it, taking a relational perspective on the educational context with examples of working with students' relational needs, and discuss the largely overlooked fact that teachers and trainers also have relational needs. I illustrate how these can be addressed in a beneficial way and also explore the ethical implications of this approach.

Relational needs in educational context

The relational net

The educational context is always complex: First there is the explicit formulated goal for learning; and then students are supposed to reach the goal; after the course, students should have attained defined competences, know defined facts, have developed their personality in a defined manner; and teachers are professionals whose task is to facilitate the fulfilment of these defined goals.

The quality of relationship is rarely an explicit goal of an educational process, but nevertheless it is the medium by which the goals can be accomplished or, alternatively, which makes the goals hard or impossible to reach.

Besides the learner and the teacher/trainer, several other significant parties interact and shape the process: those who pay for the education, those who organize the courses, those who evaluate the process, and in the background, parents, families, politics and so on. Even if we in pedagogy tend to consider the relationship between the trainer and the learners as the most important one, the effect of any other relationship can become dominant and influence the learning process strongly.

> *An example.* Some years ago I was offered the job of training one hundred policewomen in customer relations. During negotiation with members of the leadership team who were planning this training, I had a bad feeling because of the discounting way the leaders talked about the policewomen and their work. I tried to bring the contract onto the OK/OK/OK level.
>
> After that, the leadership started talking more respectfully about my future trainees and I agreed to do the programme. However, in the long run, the training was a disaster. It was understandable: if the policewomen had learned something important in the training and had acknowledged it, then their leaders would have been right to say that they had a lot to learn because their work was so poor. So the policewomen tried and managed to learn nothing in the training, which proved to the leadership that it was a mistake.
>
> Stating, and believing, that the training did not bring them anything new was a proof for the policewomen that they already had all the skills and their leaders were wrong and discounted them. In this case, my relationship with the trainees was OK but less significant than the discounting relationship between the leadership and the trainees.

In the process of teaching and learning, all parties develop relationships with each other and all experience relational needs and react to them and to the needs of

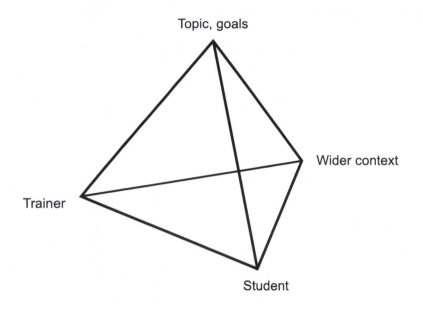

Topic, goals

Wider context

Trainer

Student

FIGURE 6.1 The three-dimensional contract

others. This is often an unconscious process, at the level that Berne called the psychological contract (or ulterior level communication). Usually, even if the process becomes conscious, it will not be discussed openly.

I use English's (1975) three-cornered contract to visualize this relational network. It becomes three-dimensional as I add the topic/goals over the top, because each party's view of these is of great importance (Figure 6.1).

The 'wider context' stands for any party outside the student–trainer relationship which becomes important in the relational network: training institute director, parents, market and so on. Systemic theory suggests that change in any corner changes the patterns and the relationships in the whole system and that the quality of the relationship of any two elements influences the whole. So, even where I as the trainer in a company where I am not responsible for the relationship between the students and their boss (the owner of the company), their relationship will have an impact on the training.

Here I want to mention the forming influence of 'the wider context'. Trainers sometimes offer the same course to similar target groups but in different institutes or organizations. They often find that courses with the same customer, or in the same institute, have important similarities. As a simple example: I have had a customer with whom every single training was kind of complicated, and another customer where trainings were always successful, emotionally moving and rewarding. So it can be useful to look at relationships and relational needs between the wider context and the trainer, or the wider context and the students.

Modification of the relational needs model for the educational context

Erskine and Trautmann explain:

> Relational needs are the needs unique to interpersonal contact; they are not the basic physiological needs of life, such as food, air or proper temperature. They are the essential psychological elements that enhance the quality of life and the development of a positive sense of self-in-relationship.
>
> (1996: 322)

> Relational needs are the component parts of a universal human desire for intimate relationship and secure attachment. They include, 1) the need for security, 2) validation, affirmation, and significance within a relationship, 3) acceptance by a stable, dependable and protective other person, 4) the confirmation of personal experience, 5) self-definition, 6) having an impact on the other person, 7) having the other initiate, and 8) expressing love.
>
> (1996: 322–4)

For practical work in adult education I have modified Erskine and Trautmann's model of relational needs and developed a schema to use as a diagnostic tool for consideration of the group process and specific personal relational issues of both the trainees and the trainers. My aim is to reduce the complexity of the descriptions and to find the key point of each need.

There are three specific axes, which refer to three different aspects in relationships:

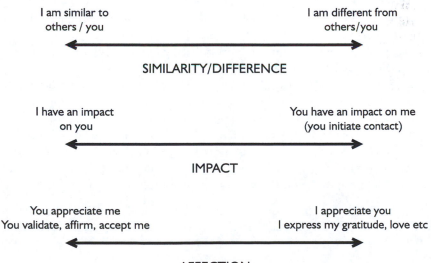

FIGURE 6.2 Axes of similarity, impact and affection

Besides these three specific aspects, each with two directions, there is one general need: to feel secure in the relationship. This need is connected with all other relational needs. We usually do not feel secure if any of the other important needs has not been satisfied.

Relational needs of trainers

Pedagogic literature and teacher education programme both have the same focus: the student. Usually, nothing is said about the teacher and about what they need in order to be able to work and live in their profession. On the contrary, in many papers it is simply demanded that:

> In a caring relationship, teachers must focus their efforts on valuing and appreciating students' needs and learning what their interests and desires are. Teachers should, as far as possible, suspend their own beliefs, feelings and values and listen attentively and generously to their students.
>
> (Thayer–Bacon 2004: 169)

But teachers (just like humans!) are relational beings, and they have relational needs too.

In Germany, we know that many schoolteachers fall sick during their professional life so severely that they have to be pensioned. There are many factors which contribute to this sad state of affairs, but I strongly believe that one is a systematic denial of the fact that teachers also have needs during their work in education, and the consequences which arise from it. I do not know of anybody in the educational field who does not want sincerely to have an impact on the students and the class. Otherwise, how and why would a teacher teach? In the long run, I cannot imagine anybody who does not care about getting affirmation and affection from their students. And where is the teacher who does not want to be remembered as different by their students? Each and every relational need emerges in the educational context, on the trainer's side as well as the student's.

Just as students can do many things to get their needs satisfied, the teacher/trainer is also doing the same. Whatever content they want to teach, they can use various methods to suit their specific needs. My experience is that new trainers tend to decide about teaching methods mostly according to the topic/content and do not consider themselves (with their relational needs) or the learners, as individuals or as a group. As they become more experienced, they vary their teaching methods according to the needs of all participants of the learning system: 'all participants' means themselves too.

For example:

I feel the need to be appreciated and validated	I can ask the group for feedback about their progress and what helped them to make it
I feel the need to be initiated and reached out to by others	I let the trainees discuss in small groups and present in plenum: what are the next steps to be taken?

Ethical implications

One question arises immediately. What are the ethical implications of trying to satisfy trainers' needs during the training? Trainers are not paid to get their needs met through the trainees. Are we allowed, as teachers, to take care that our needs are met, or should the pedagogical encounter just take students' needs seriously, and the teacher wait till the evening, or the holidays, or pension, or sickness?

In my opinion, we are actually obliged as professionals in the educational context to take our own needs very seriously and to welcome them.

There are many reasons:

- Students recognize trainers' relational needs within minutes, on a conscious or unconscious level. Often they react in a very friendly way, taking it as an invitation for symbiosis in which they protect the trainer, or as the beginning of a psychological game. In both cases they become more busy dealing with the trainer than learning the topic.
- Besides this, the trainer is an important model: if they are not aware of their needs or if they behave inauthentically, the mirror neurons of the students learn the lesson of 'How to discount one's own needs'. Model learning!
- And, how is the trainer going to support the students in their needs, if they discount their own?
- And, is the trainer not in danger of using their own script solutions if they discount their needs? Can they be responsive, validating, loving and respectful to their trainees if they are not to themselves?

In short, systematic sacrifice of trainers' needs to the needs of the trainees can be seriously harmful for both students and trainers.

Managing needs

This of course does not mean that all needs should be fulfilled in the educational context.

Students and teachers have very different roles. Schmid (1990) explains that a working professional acts in three different worlds: private, professional and organizational. The role of the person in these different worlds is a coherent system of attitudes, feelings, and behaviours. In each role a person has role-specific goals, values, visions, modus operandi, and ethics. We can assume that a person also has different needs in different roles.

In their work with students, the teacher acts in their professional role. In this role they are working on fulfilling their complex contract. The needs they experience in their role should help them to fulfil the contract. As long they act in their professional role, their relational needs will be age- and context-appropriate, and present-centred.

The teacher has to be able to differentiate 'here and now' relational needs from the script-bound ways of relating, in their students and in themselves.

Script-embedded ways of relating can be treated as any other personal issue which emerges in the educational process. If a student shows such behaviour, the trainer will decide how to meet it; if they observe themselves having 'embedded' relational needs, most probably the best option would be to look at it in supervision or in personal therapy.

It is an important task for the trainer to establish a learning environment in which the major relational needs of all participants in the learning system (both trainer and trainees) can be met as they appear.

• The trainer has to be aware of relational needs of the participants, and of their own, in all their diversity.

• The trainer has a special commitment to the goal and the contract and can value which and whose relational needs should be met first, second or not at all.

• The trainer can be an important model of how communication about one's own relational needs can be managed: open, clear and respecting of self and others.

Relational needs of students

In the learning process, students experience themselves as a part of many relationships: as a group member, with the trainer, with specific friends in the group, with the institute representatives and so on. Relational needs can and do arise in many directions, and often at the same time. We will discuss some of them.

The need for security

In the educational context the need for security is very important because the possibility of being shamed, and so getting hurt, is very present. To avoid the danger of being shamed students develop various defensive learning attitudes (Nagel 2009) which reinforce their script and make learning difficult.

Learning involves change, and this process is accompanied by feelings of insecurity. In addition, students (and sometimes trainers) often get assessed and compared; these processes are stressful, and again are accompanied by a sense of insecurity. This insecurity (the expectation of getting hurt) can be unpleasant and, further, harmful for the learning process. So, in the educational context the need for security arises often; it can be directed to any person in the system – a trainer, the group or the wider context.

The position of the student can be:

a) I (need to) feel secure in my relationship to the trainer. Am I confident that they are competent in their subject? Do I feel that they are offering the '3 Ps' towards individuals and the group? Do I experience that they are well settled in the wider environment, school, institute . . .?

b)   I (need to) feel secure in relation to the group: can I count on respectful behaviour from the group members?

c)   I (need to) feel secure in the wider context, in this school, university, institute . . .

Similarity/difference

To be different from others:

> Learning and teaching is based on being different. If we were the same, what could we learn from each other? Most people have the need that their being different is seen and appreciated.
>
> The student might think and feel: I have my individuality; I have my special strengths and weaknesses; I also have different needs to the others; I have also got different goals from the others; and this is good, and I can be open about this.

To be the same as the others:

> The student might think and feel, when this need is satisfied:
>
> It feels good to have the same views, values, use the same methods and have the same goals, same experiences as the others. I can feel relaxed, secure and calm. I feel connected by feeling the same.

Having an impact

The need to have an impact on the other arises in every relationship, and is important in every constellation of two or more persons. It shows that there are two in the relationship and that both are important. The educational context has a long history of students having less impact in the process. The student might feel and think: I want to express myself, my needs and wishes, my thoughts and feelings – and they should be seriously taken into account. In addition, we all have a need for the other to reach out to us, to have an impact on us, which can be enriching and invigorating.

Affection

Our motivation is connected to our wish to be affirmed, appreciated, accepted, loved. At the same time most of the people have the urge to love, appreciate and to express it. The students might feel and think: I am liked and accepted; I belong in the group and people seek out my friendship.

What do students do to get their relational needs met?

In order to get satisfaction for their needs, students/trainees undertake different activities during their training process: either they ask for what they need directly or symbolically, or they enact it in games. For example: a student has a need to have an impact on the trainer or on the group process. They can talk about it and explain it. Or they can propose some new activity, or they can demand something from the trainer or the group, or they can start a discussion about who is deciding what in the training. Or they can give some feedback that is supportive or aggressive. All these behaviours can be seen as attempts to change the relationship in the way the student needs it in this moment.

Trainer responses

Trainers tend to respond automatically to the needs of the students. This model offers guidance for doing it systematically and consciously. The first step is to use it as a diagnostic tool for reflection on the process in the group or between individuals. One very helpful question is: 'What needs are students trying to satisfy through this behaviour?' No matter how dysfunctional some behaviour is, it can be very useful to view it as an attempt to meet some important need. Though there may be different kind of needs which can emerge in the educational context, relational needs are so important that they should always be taken into consideration.

For example:

A new student has joined the group. They say almost nothing, even after some time. As a trainer, I start reflecting:

> *Security need*: They don't say anything – is it because they don't feel secure? Maybe they think that I am not good enough? Or the group is rather rude? Or the wider context is scary?

> *Or Similarity/difference axis*: I think they are not saying much because the group is quite homogeneous and they feel different and don't see their 'being different' accepted.

> *Or Impact axis*: Perhaps they are afraid of making an impact – or even, perhaps, they know that their silence will have a big impact eventually?

> *Or Affection axis*: I wonder if they hope that their silence will attract sympathy from me or the group?

This way I can reflect on all the possibilities and decide a possible diagnosis of the process.

The second step is to decide how to intervene:

In the educational context, we can use all kinds of interventions which are used in the counselling context – and in addition we can use different teaching and learning methods as powerful interventions. The choice of method is a genuine intervention in the educational context. Methods should optimize the learning process and have a strong relation-shaping impact. I consider this relation-shaping impact the most significant repercussion for the choice of method. Does the trainer do a piece of teaching themselves, or do they invite the student to do some teaching; do they organize the students to work in groups; do they work in stable groups or in changing groups; how big are the groups; and so on. All these decisions will create a different relational situation in the training and will highly influence the learning.

In the example above, the trainer can assume that the student needs:

1   More security in the group, so decide to create an activity for working in pairs or small groups.
2   More security in relation to the trainer: so a method will be chosen whereby the trainer can demonstrate some important competence.
3   Reassurance that students can be really different and this is OK; here the teacher may suggest a work experience where being different is necessary and helpful.

In this way the trainer can assess the relational need and choose teaching and learning methods that can be helpful for students to organize themselves in the way they need it at that moment.

Conclusion

An important question remains: Which needs of the students should the educator seek to meet, and when should they look for other ways of relating?

Society, the organizers of education, teachers and trainers, often see education as a space where, alongside learning and development, healing experiences should also take place. And indeed, even if teachers complain that they are not therapists – which is true – good education, with its relationships and constellations, offers a lot of opportunities for healing: 'to get what we didn't get on previous occasions or more of what we already have' (Barrow: 2006). Many students have had negative or shame-based experiences of schooling and, for them, simply to have a different experience of learning can be transformational. The educator can have a powerful role in facilitating such experiences of positive learning cycles, which help students to update their script through revising 'their theory in light of new evidence' (Newton 2006: 193). In this way, if we take Cornell's definition, 'life script is an ongoing process of self-defining and sometimes self-limiting psychological construction of reality' (Cornell 1988: 281), educators can and do influence this 'psychological construction'.

The educator dances on different floors. Sometimes they mainly facilitate the learning of the subject, and there they will usually meet present-oriented relational needs. Sometimes they mainly support the personal development of the trainees or try to offer a healing experience, where they will perhaps seek to meet the trainees' relational needs. Sometimes they challenge the student and offer something else – perhaps to explore the meaning of the ways the needs have been manifested. In addition to this, they have the same requirement to attend to their own needs – for contact, for impact, for satisfaction. The trainer who accepts and works with these not only provides a healthy model for their students but is usually a more integrated and congruent educator. In this dance, the model of Relational Needs supports the practitioner themselves within the educational process – and provides guidance in self-care and in the choice of interventions in the work with students.

7

MINDFULNESS AND LEARNING IN EDUCATIONAL TRANSACTIONAL ANALYSIS

Dörte Landmann and Gernot Aich, Germany;
with Giles Barrow, UK

Dörte Landmann (DL) and Gernot Aich (GA) are both German educational transactional analysts interested in introducing meditative practice into their work with adult trainees. Giles Barrow (GB) explores with Dörte and Gernot how this interest evolved, and its links with transactional analysis.

GB: Although I know that your current interest is in how mindfulness is useful in working with trainees, I am aware that your early experiences as educators were in the context of primary and secondary schooling.

DL: Yes, I started out as a teacher, and eventually was working across both primary and secondary schools in an advisory capacity. I had a particular interest in students with special educational needs. In fact, it was in working with disaffected students that I found TA most powerful. I recall introducing the process of contracting with one class that had suffered long-term neglect; they had been taught by interim staff, and the group dynamics had really deteriorated into game-playing. Although they were cautious at first, inviting them into contracting for learning resulted in them taking responsibility and re-gaining confidence in their capacity to learn. I was also involved in school development for a while, before becoming involved more fully in TA training.

GA: I also started as a teacher, and then I became a researcher in higher education. My focus, as a Junior Professor at the University of Education in Schwäbisch Gmünd, is research on the interaction between teacher, pupils and parents and the development of training for them. The goal of the training is the improvement of communication and conflict resolution in school education.

I have also had an interest in school organization and governance. Like Dörte, I am working as a TA trainer, though I continue to deliver training in schools and academies.

GB: So what has motivated you in the shift towards meditation in your work?

DL: It's come about because of our taking a more global perspective: in times of over-supply on one hand and extreme poverty on the other, it is not easy for the human spirit to concentrate on what is important. Many people find they don't have the time to reflect, due to being overworked, multitasked or stressed, and superficial entertainment only acts as a distraction. In this context, for some people, the question of the meaning of life and personal well-being is becoming more important. TA and meditation may ostensibly be two different methods, but both are focused on improving the human condition. Both have the potential to generate answers to contemporary dilemmas in society about personal purpose.

GA: In today's world we are faced with many challenges. Bauer suggests that the act of multitasking demands a permanent unspecified alertness. This poses situations of over-extension, which lead to loss of concentration or even illness (Bauer 2013: 46). Due to our minds having a natural tendency to distraction, our modern Western way of living can pose unsolvable problems. Our attention is stimulated by advertising, entertainment, sport or other activities, and can lose itself. There can be a tendency to think too much, and thoughts run between the events of the past and planning for the future. Teachers and trainers are subject to this process of agitation, both in themselves and also in relation to their students. Being able to achieve a separation from the high level of stimulation and establish a point of internal stillness has instructional benefits.

DL: We have found it increasingly important to incorporate meditation in our work to encourage practitioners to step up and above what might be a continual struggle for contentment.

GB: How do you see this connecting more specifically with learning?

DL/GA: A pre-requisite in our approach is that humans are learners and can consciously decide how they want to deepen their sense of purpose, and design experiences which support this. Individuals carry a responsibility for their own learning history and its resulting development. Learning in this sense means: to open oneself up to change; to take new directions. It means: to free oneself from a restrictive life plan; to develop new patterns of behaviour; to incorporate unloved traits of self; to be mindful of one's feelings. Learning, in this context, can also mean dis-associating and reflecting in order to find purpose in both personal and professional domains.

GB: It would be helpful to know a little more of your understanding of TA and the concepts which are especially important for you in your work.

DL/GA: We see TA as a humanist psychology. Berne's aim as a psychiatrist was to heal people; however, he did not appear especially interested in their spiritual development. For us, the work of Kiltz summarizes a more significant understanding: 'TA aims to lessen the pressure of suffering, minimizing the friction between people, resolving conflicts and problems, to learn to do things well and finally [. . .] to become more content and successful in having a higher quality of living' (Kiltz 2004: 1).

TA pedagogy has core themes, including observing, analysis and the intensification of conscious and constructive learning processes. This concerns the learning of new materials as well as understanding the group dynamic process. As teachers of school children, trainers and teachers in adult learning, educational transactional analysts have some expertise in these processes. We can serve as role models in the learning relationship, which means that learners observe and notice intuitively the extent to which their teachers are authentic. Incongruence is always picked up. We maintain that concentration and calmness are part of a learner's conscious learning process. A teacher who wants to instil these qualities as part of the learning partnership will need to have internalized these traits themselves. However, this modelling can present significant challenges for the educator.

As teachers of children as well as adults, we need to be aware of how powerful the educational relationship is for the personal development of the learner. It is a relationship that needs to be built on respect. If mutual respect and trust between teacher and learner is missing or even abused, the effect can have longstanding consequences which can influence how the individual thinks, feels and behaves in subsequent learning relationships.

GB: At this point, then, you are clearly moving into the arena of script and how learning influences its development.

DL/GA: Yes, perhaps the most important idea, for the purpose of this conversation, is the concept of life-script. This refers to the individual's life plan, which shapes thoughts, feelings and actions automatically and subconsciously. It also comprises the beliefs developed during childhood about self, other people, and life generally. We suggest that the individual's spirit is shaped and guided by script. The life plan provides structure and security; but it can also limit development, producing 'structure and stricture'. The personal life plan is developed by inner processes, experienced in childhood, which have also been subjected to external reactions within important relationships in infancy. Children interpret experiences, and how they interact in their relationships, in a child-like way; they have a tendency to generalize on the basis of specific experience. We see an important aim of TA as exploring the question of how script can be changed in order to lead a more contented, more successful, and more autonomous life.

A positive view of script was developed by Fanita English (1977). She argues that the script is a very complex compilation, 'in which some pages follow a logical sequence and some don't, with highs and lows, magic flipsides and assumptions, which can be positive as well as negative' (1977: 173). Instead of lamenting the development of the script determined by our childhood, we welcome the process. It is an expression of human creativity that children develop during one of the most imaginative stages of their lives, editing history for themselves.

Even if there are many irrational parts in a script – for example 'devouring beasts' and similar dangers and, often, a terrible end for a careless hero or heroine – there are also other fairytale elements: enthusiasm, adventure, love, and wonderful fantasy. Often the script contains all kinds of magic tricks and recipes for how a catastrophe can be avoided, and a mishap turned into luck. It is these aspects that offer clues of how we can find self-fulfilment through our script, rather than opposing it or fearing it. Even a script that has been developed through negative circumstances contains the intuitive knowledge of the childhood self. It demonstrates how individuals can seek inner aims in a creative way when certain malevolent faeries and adverse pitfalls obstruct the path. Without a script the child would function within a vacuum of time and space, without cohesion; through it, the past would remain unconnected with the future: we would be without roots, like a leaf in the wind.

GB: That last phrase catches my attention, and emphasizes the usefulness of script as having a kind of centring function for the individual – even though it is simultaneously at a cost.

DL/GA: That's right, and as educators we can learn to strengthen these intuitive and creative contents in the script. Meditation involves an inner process in which the individual pays attention to their conscience and promotes healing. The process develops openness, tolerance and empathy, in which the influence of script can be moderated.

At this point it's helpful to consider the structural ego-state model. Berne (1961) defines the ego-state as an 'interconnected system of thinking, feeling and behaviour'. If the individual changes the content of one of the ego-states, perhaps by addition or removal, the whole system changes. In the Parent ego-state, there is an archive comprised of potential role model material. It is clear that those earlier figures, such as primary carers and others in the original family in which the child grew up, all have an influence. A child is not able to consciously select from material generated by these figures; however, it is possible for an adult to make choices and identify new sources to fuel their personal progress.

As a grown-up I can integrate through the Adult ego-state, think about my conduct, and make a suitable emotional choice with regard to a particular situation. We have found the work of Susannah Temple extremely valuable in our work as educators. The idea of the Integrating Adult and its incorporation into her Functional Fluency model is in close alignment with what we see is achieved through meditation [for further explanation of Temple's model, see Jan Grant's chapter in this publication]. This model can be invaluable in a difficult conflict situation but also for a phase in our life, or for particular work tasks and roles. Even in adult life, an individual may lack sufficient resource to support this integration process, and it is here that meditation can be so useful.

GB: So you have explained your approach to TA; now say some more about how you understand learning.

DL/GA: Behavioural psychology talks about learning as a 'process based on experience, which results in a surviving change of the behaviour or the potential for this behaviour' (Zimbardo and Gerrig 2004: 243). Through the process of learning, we can access a new way of behaving, or changes in other less observable ways; for example: shifts in the individual's value system. In the field of meditation and TA, learning is more about the changing of inner attitudes – which are also not immediately measurable by our actions.

Cognitive psychology investigates higher mental processes such as perception, memory, problem solving and abstract thinking. In this context, 'cognition' refers to 'processes of knowledge including attentiveness, memory and deduction. In addition to this, the content of processes like concepts and memory content are being investigated' (Zimbardo and Gerrig 2004: 344). It is all about the building of cognitive structures, their content and their restructuring. Internal restructuring is important in meditation because in this process – similarly to TA – new insights and perspectives on previous experiences are anticipated.

In addition, from the viewpoint of humanist psychology, meditation and TA are intended to contribute to the development of human potential: 'Learning, concentrating, focusing on one area, not generalizing problems and developing a feeling of control are all part of this. In addition to this, a positive transfer of this ability to concentrate on other areas is expected' (Linden 1993: 209). In principle, both TA and meditation are about improving the effectiveness of the self. This construct developed by Bandura (1997) means 'that people possess self guiding abilities which put them into the position to gain control of their own thoughts, feelings, and actions'

(Mietzel 2007: 43). Schunk (2004) has identified some positive results in people's learning behaviour that link with high expectations of self-effectiveness. They included:

- Engaging in tasks with a high level of difficulty
- Endurance
- Increasing learning and performance behaviour.

Apart from these psychological benefits of learning, Schwerdtfeger has investigated the bio-psychological learning of teachers with high expectations of self-effectiveness, and found that high levels of self effectiveness are paralleled with:

- significantly lower heart problems
- lower levels of exhaustion
- lower levels of pressure to complain.

He concludes, self-effective teachers can deal better with stress, have a more optimistic attitude, a more positive mood and master critical situations in their job (Schwerdtfeger 2009).

Apart from the expectation of self-effectiveness, TA and meditation are meant to improve the concept of the self. In this context, one can define the concept of the self as a mental model of a person which includes their ability and their character. In this model, self-esteem plays an essential role as 'a generalized judgmental view of the self, which influences mood as well as actions and also influences a string of personal and social actions' (Zimbardo and Gerrig 2004: 634). TA and meditation can improve consciousness, the acceptance of reconciliation, the changing of one's own abilities, characteristics of personal self-esteem and the concept of the self in different circumstances.

Moral development is also increased; both meditation and TA aim to develop greater responsibility for self, others and the environment. Moral development and self-effectiveness can both be regarded as learning processes which are supported through TA and meditation, which stimulate cognitive and emotional restructuring – which have the potential to stabilize people in difficult situations.

We have experienced how TA and meditation complement and promote each other in a positive way, and how they can support a holistic learning process in people: we can learn to orientate our script in a healing direction, and so reach the targets we have set ourselves. That's why meditation in the context of further training in TA goes together with other methods. Almost without exception, trainees embrace meditation and regard it as a valuable support.

GB: In my experience, a heightened sense of awareness or integration is difficult to achieve. What's your view on this?

DL/GA: Yes, we agree, and Berne seems to have noticed this too:

> Awareness is the ability to view a coffeepot in our own unmistakable way, to hear the birds sing but not as we have been taught [. . . there are] only a few people left who can see and hear things in the old way. Most people on the other hand have lost this ability [. . .] the awareness forces us to live in the here and now and not somewhere in the past or future.
>
> (Berne 1970: 244–5)

What Berne doesn't show us, is how it is done. We believe it's possible to learn to develop these abilities – or awareness. To observe our own spirit in a mindful way and establish a habit of meditation, can be important in achieving this. Learning and training, to focus intently on the spirit in flux, is exciting.

GB: Sounds like you need to explain in more detail how you make sense of the concept of meditation.

DL/GA: One of the longstanding traditions in meditation is that its objective is to realize the power of the individual. The path to find this power is an internal process which leads to enlightenment and knowledge. The calming of thoughts and mindfulness leads to 'core self'. Meditation is the process of creating – or finding – a centre; it is an exercise in immersion.

Our perspective has a Buddhist influence which maintains that the soul has potential for being inherently clear and realizing, but is easily distracted to follow its own projections. We can learn to observe what is happening with our spirit, and which impulse it follows; if we choose, every moment can be full of meditation in which the wholeness of being can be experienced. As a result, individuals can remember significant moments in their lives – times when they have experienced something deeply, for example a great satisfaction, tranquillity, joy, love for their children, creativity and connection to nature. These experiences are ways of meditation.

GB: So, what does this idea look like in the context of adult training groups? How is it used in practice?

DL: When working with my groups or in counselling sessions, I regularly start with a meditative attunement which can vary in length and depends on the situation. I encourage people to be aware of their posture, to keep their feet in contact with the floor, straighten the spine, keep hands in the lap, eyes closed or focused on an object. I then raise people's awareness through the process of becoming conscious of their breathing and asking themselves how they feel, what they are sensing, what they need to bring to this session, and ending with affirmations to themselves. After this phase of calm self-reflection in the here and now, participants ca choose to share their experience. Sometimes it can be difficult if a mobile phone rings, somebody coughs or arrives late. I might comment on it in my instruction and after the meditation encourage people to reflect on the disruption: What did you observe when the phone rang? Were you able to stay with yourself? Trainees can be encouraged to learn to deal with external disturbances and to be aware of the present moment without judging – an opportunity to learn.

GB: OK, so I can begin to understand a link between Berne's idea of 'here and now experience' and what can be achieved through meditation.

DL/GA: Yes, exactly: meditation offers a wealth of experience drawn from ancient traditions, in order to experience inner happiness which is not dependent on external sensual experience or the acquisition of goods. Every meditation can lead to liberating insight and new realizations of a personal and existential kind. We can find peace and relaxation – and encounter difficult situations differently. We can bring something to the world.

We know that being in script can involve an engagement with archaic thoughts, belief systems and feelings that result in drives to maintain patterns that prevent us from being present-centred. When we concentrate on the stillness of our inner self, a more open and mindful way of existing becomes possible. According to Zimbardo and Gerrig, meditation puts 'the individual in the position of seeing known things in a new light; they free perception and thought from the constraints of automatic learned patterns' (2014: 230).

GB: I liked your comment about Berne not providing a 'how to do it' explanation! So how have you set about meditation practice for yourselves?

DL: First, we need to get clarity about our motivation to meditate and – practically – find a suitable space and a period of time. I need patience to go on this path of introspection, to develop my consciousness, to clarify my objective. Do I want to relax, practise concentration, or develop positive emotion? Or do I want to comprehend the nature of reality, to engage in an existential exploration, to increase my ability to observe and concentrate on the here and now and increase my capacity for openness, tolerance, empathy? This is beyond the relaxation process often experienced in the spa industry – accompanied by candles and soft music! To explore consciousness, it is very important to become calm and relaxed. We use techniques for achieving this, some of which are taken from the work of Thich Nhat Hanh and focus on the cycle of breathing:

> When I breathe in, I give my body calm. When I breathe out, I smile.
> I remain in the present moment, and now it is a wonderful moment.
>
> (Nhat Hanh 2007: 22)

Following an initial period of calming the individual experiences, there is a new level of internal awareness. Some of the more recent findings in the functioning of the brain appear to support the assertion that extended meditative practice can have positive effects on managing pain, specific disturbance and general stress. TA and meditation complement and promote each other in a positive way; they can support holistic learning processes in people. We have found that trainees embrace meditation and regard it as a valuable support in their learning.

The healing power of mindfulness is to accept what is. Its terrain is the present moment in its richness, in relation to the inner as well as the outer world.

Educational transactional analysis and schooling

INTRODUCING PART 3

Giles Barrow, UK

In this part we shift our focus to the context of schooling.

From its earliest days, teachers have used TA in their work in classrooms. *Games Students Play* (Ernst 1972) describes how psychological game-playing arises in teacher–student relationships, and is an example of how transactional analysts were making early inroads in schools. Today, educational transactional analysis has a stronger presence in schools, with a range of resources, initiatives and professional development to support educational practitioners.

The following eight chapters have been contributed by educators who draw on their experience of working with children and young people. Their perspectives cover a range of European contexts and include Early Years, primary and secondary education. What emerges is a useful educational psychology; it offers a framework for making sense of what goes on in the dynamic of the classroom and its impact on the quality of teacher–student relationships. A range of TA concepts are presented, both from classical TA and from developments of earlier models.

TA educators have a longstanding practice of adapting, translating and transforming concepts from a clinical frame of reference into a mainstream learning environment, and this is illustrated in the first of our practitioner accounts, with Evelyne Papaux's experience working with very young children and parents in the context of early years education. Papaux demonstrates the transformational theory exchange typical of educational transactional analysts. Using the innovative work of French psychotherapist Gysa Jaoui as a basis, Papaux presents a powerful rendering of the concept of permission through its integration with the qualities of autonomy. This deceptively simple shift generates a highly practical tool for working with parents, children and young people.

With access to an early draft of Papaux's educational permission wheel model, I have already witnessed its effectiveness; while working with a team of learning mentors in a school in the north of England, it became clear that they were struggling to make connection with individual students. I had not initially planned to introduce the model, though as soon as I did so it caught the interest of the team. This was due in part to its ease of use, but more importantly because of its clear orientation towards growth.

When I returned to the school after a couple of months, one of the mentors reported on a specific case: a 14-year-old female student had been uncommunicative, resistant to discussion, and demonstrated indications of autistic spectrum disorder. The mentor was surprised at how quickly this student began to complete the permission wheel. It opened up a new series of conversations, beginning with a deep sense of anger that the young woman had felt for many months. What was most interesting to me was that Papaux's initial adaptation of the earlier model had been orientated towards use by educators in support of children in the early years; yet her model had had an immediate impact when used directly by an adolescent. This highlights the inventive nature of TA educators and the generative nature of educational TA theory.

Not all educational TA involves a revision of classic TA models; Agnès Le Guernic demonstrates how her work as a primary teacher is informed by fairytales and script. This is a well-established connection, frequently occurring in the work of Berne and Karpman for instance, and has been the subject of more recent discussion (for example, Berardo 2014). Although there have been several ideas about script theory in TA literature, some of which are contra-positioned, there is a general consensus that one stage during which children appear especially interested in establishing a sense of identity is the period of 3–6 years. The potential richness of storytelling, script and childhood is introduced in Le Guernic's discussion of the tale of *Snow White*. Her concern is focused on the primary classroom and her work brings attention to how close teachers are to the process of script-formation among young children.

For those practitioners working in a mainstream arena, an awareness of script and the importance of story-making is of critical importance; however, it's not only younger children for whom stories can be a valuable resource. Elsewhere, in the context of her role as a school counsellor, Naughton has written about the tale of *Sleeping Beauty*, where the infant princess is cursed by a fairy. She describes how the newborn princess is cursed to die by a bad fairy at her naming ceremony: all seems lost and the court is dismayed; then the late-arriving twelfth fairy explains that, while she is unable to entirely eliminate the power of the wicked spell, she can offer the child a second chance: 'Take comfort, I have not the power to wholly undo what my elder has done but, instead of dying, the princess will fall into a deep and long sleep . . .' (Naughton, 'On Being the Twelfth Fairy', in Tudor 2008: 196). Naughton explores parallels between 'the role of the Twelfth Fairy and that of practitioners working with children and adolescents [. . . and] highlights the transforming influence that adults can have in the lives of young people with whom they come into contact'. I have explored elsewhere this potential for re-scripting in adolescence (Barrow 2014) which is underpinned by the idea of *re-cycling*, a basic feature of the cycle of development.

Not only does the concept of script connect educationally with the formative process of the student in general terms, there is also a more particular consideration: if script is understood as an ongoing, cyclic process – rather than a single, early childhood episode – then the relationship between student and educator will have further implications. The notion of recurrent script-formation has been proposed by Newton (2006), incorporating the stages in Kolb's experiential learning cycle. The implication of this is that the classroom provides an arena in which script is being formed, and not merely played out. Consequently, the sense of identity as a learner and all that entails – for example, competition with others for attention and approval, performing, shame at not knowing, permission to learn – is bound up in the ongoing experience of being in classrooms from the early years. This is a theme reflected in Shotton's chapter in this volume on 'power in education', and has been the focus of discussion elsewhere (Barrow 2009).

As well as a consideration of power, Le Guernic's account captures the vulnerability of the child in the period during which the script emerges. An early idea, which has possibly been overlooked since it first appeared, is the child's vulnerability quotient (Woollams and Brown 1978): the young child is compelled to create a plan for themselves as a consequence of their vulnerability in the world. Woollams and Brown identify five factors that accentuate the child's lack of power, and which are countered through the formation of the script. I have been increasingly interested in applying these ideas in the context of learning, in relation to both adult and children's education. I suggest that, when confronted with one or more vulnerability factors in the classroom, a learner's script is provoked and generates familiar patterns of experience and behaviour. In early childhood, the infant is quite literally vulnerable and engages in creating meaning that ensures survival and recognition. While this provides a template for coping with a lack of power during infancy, the same strategies may be deployed later in life, even when there are alternative options and the here-and-now vulnerability quotient is, in reality, much diminished.

The vulnerability that renders a young child dependent on a script-based strategy comprises the following factors:

Children do not have all the information that the grown-ups have. In the absence of this here-and-now knowledge, the child fills the gaps with all their ingenuity. In other words, they make it up from magical and fantastic possibilities – some of which can be found in the fairy stories Le Guernic features in her discussion.

A second vulnerability factor refers to the limitations around how the child manages their level of stress. Young children have less capacity to cope with anxiety, something which grown-ups can overlook and which further accentuates the child's lack of power. Combined with a lack of information or stress reduction strategies, young children do not have a capacity for extended thinking: unlike older children and adults, their cognitive abilities are emergent. *The Little Professor*, a source of intuitive and creative meaning-making, has its limitations and is likely to be 'over-generalized, global, exaggerated and appropriate only for the short run – not the long run', (Woollams and Brown 1978: 154). A final pair of factors – lack of options and lack of power – significantly impact on the child's ability to determine what happens to them: personal agency is limited while they are so physically small and weak.

When using the vulnerability quotient in education, I find the following mnemonic helpful: 'ISTOP': Information – Stress – Thinking – Options – Power. Educators working with young children might reflect on how their learning environment encourages a reduction in children's vulnerability through providing informative material, encouraging thinking, exercising personal power, considering options and accounting for children's frustration, anxiety and loss.

So we come to the contribution of Nicole Pierre, who brings the central TA concept of *contracting* into sharp focus when she discusses its application in the secondary school classroom. What is so striking about Pierre's account is the ability of contracting to empower students within a school environment. Through careful support and encouragement, Pierre claims the pupil can become the 'author of their success', which helps them 'progress towards autonomy'.

This remains for me a regular feature of using TA with students: educational contracting processes can be a sufficient first stage intervention; young people use the experience to test out the educator for authenticity, congruence and commitment. On the basis of this initial trust, students often take responsibility for claiming their part in the relationship. Three-cornered (or multi-party) contracting approaches, referenced in Pierre's account, can reveal a dynamic which students may have been aware of, but had minimal opportunity to explore. By using these approaches, educators can raise awareness of, and ask questions about, the power relationships that influence the teacher–pupil dialogue.

The topic of using TA directly with children and young people is more fully discussed in my own chapter, where I pay specific attention to children in specialist provision with additional or special educational needs. Here, the theme of *care and education* emerges as a feature of educational transactional analysis. In many respects educational transactional analysis can be framed as a social pedagogy in which the integration of care and education is essential to the character of a social pedagogic practice. Working holistically with the learner and integrating the environment within the learning process are additional features of this approach. In the stories about the TA Proficiency Award for Children and Young People (TAPACY), I show how groups of vulnerable children learn more, grow healthier and feel more resilient as a result of direct learning about TA models.

More generally, TA lends itself to a social pedagogic method. In this approach, not only is the emphasis on experiential process but the pedagogue enters the 'life world' of the learner as a collaborator. In presenting the perspective of a teacher who has been sharing TA with vulnerable students, an exceptional and powerful humility is revealed: 'We are now a little more confident in exposing ourselves, learning and working alongside our students', and this vividly illustrates the core of social pedagogy:

the underlying pedagogic response is not to deny the other person's capacity for social agency; people are responsible for their own actions, for their own creativity, for their own ideas. [. . .] Such understandings, informed by democratic and emancipatory intentions, allow the social pedagogue to accept the people with whom she works, open-heartedly, respecting and supporting their autonomy and avoiding stereotyping or stigmatizing them on whatever grounds.

(Kleipoedszus, in Cameron and Moss 2013: 82)

The direct classroom context continues to be explored in the work of Sylvie Schachner, a primary educator based in Vienna. Her chapter captures an especially contemporary theme in European schooling – the increasing challenge of migration and its multicultural impact on the classroom. Most teachers working across urban Europe are engaged with children from a diversity of cultural backgrounds; in many cases this brings a richness of experience, language, heritage and ambition. Schachner discusses how TA can support teachers in understanding and responding to the potential limitations that arise from cultural diversity. This is a sensitive area of modern-day teaching; it raises questions around power and authority also discussed by Shotton earlier in this volume. The problem of how teachers – who are often representative of the ruling hegemony – can carry themselves without contributing to underlying institutional discrimination is a very real issue for educators:

> Moreover, white cultural scripting fosters a lack of awareness through the messages transmitted to white children in their families of origin [. . .]. Through this process of discounting, the white individual is, in effect, groomed into a role of bland neutrality and passivity, whereby he or she benefits from his or her privileged place in society yet takes no responsibility for understanding how this status quo has come about.
>
> (Naughton and Tudor 2006: 160–1)

How educational transactional analysts account for the 'other' while in a position of power is linked to the development of what Schachner calls *intercultural competence*, supported by the use of TA concepts including OK-ness, accounting, and updating the Parent ego-state.

In reading the accounts of Papaux, Pierre and Schachner, I am reminded of Dennison's *Lives of Children* (1969), which details the establishment of a free school in New York's Lower East Side district; impoverished, multi-racial and enduring a time of educational crisis. Dennison provides forensic accounts of students' painstaking learning experience. Their progress is strewn with obstacles including brutal domestic violence, robberies and abuse. Arguably the most significant factor impeding their educational endeavours is the damage experienced in prior schooling experience. Expounding the objectives of a progressive approach Dennison exclaims:

Why is it then that so many children fail? Let me put it bluntly; it is because our system of public education is a horrendous, life-destroying mess [. . .] the powers of mind are nipped in the bud [. . .]. There is no such thing as learning except [. . .] in the continuum of experience. *But this continuum cannot survive in the classroom unless there is the reality of encounter between adults and the children.* The teachers must be themselves, and not play roles. They must teach the children, and not teach 'subjects'.

(Dennison 1969: 74, my italics)

Several of our contributors in this part share a similar focus on creating, understanding and maintaining the reality of a live encounter in the classroom. Jacqueline Goosens takes the experience of authentic relationship to a different level in her discussion of systemic constellations. Originally developed from psychotherapeutic and family systemic practice, the concept of family constellations remains a powerful and intriguing intervention, most often practised within the context of clinical work. However, Goosens explains how the principles of group dynamics and trans-generational scripting can be transferred across into educational work to alleviate distress in working with individual children and families. Drawing on the work of Hellinger and others, Goosens offers an explanation of the key principles, or 'laws' governing effective constellation practice, and how in doing so we create opportunities to reveal the archaic patterns which underpin current experience for children and young people. Hellinger suggests that the constellation has a similar effect on the relational system as sunrise:

When the sun comes up, you can use the light. You allow the light to work, helping you to see clearly. After a while, you see what you've got to do, you see things differently, or you see a new possibility. Then you do what needs to be done, but you don't need to talk much about the sun.

(Hellinger 1998: 258)

Goosen's contribution illustrates a particularly specialized area of educational transactional analysis, and the following chapter is similarly specific: Cesare Fregola is a mathematics teacher and researcher; we are able to reproduce a digest of a project he has been pursuing over a number of years using a TA framework, exploring students' reluctance and fear in learning maths. It is both informative and creative, and demonstrates the richness TA can bring to very particular aspects of everyday classroom practice. Just as importantly, Fregola's chapter offers a glimpse into the possibilities open to educators for developing a wider research base for educational transactional analysts.

This part on TA in the context of schooling comes to a close with an elegant consideration of silence in the classroom by Ferdinando Montuschi. 'Silence in class!' has to be one of those enduring Parent commands, familiar to so many who have spent long hours in classrooms. Montuschi begins his exploration in the classroom and considers how silence can be used to engage and liberate both teachers and students. His discussion progresses into a broader assessment of the power of silence allied with stillness and its potential for creating a mature, integrated state of mind.

This chapter resonates with Landmann and Aich's contribution in the previous part, in which the importance of stillness is connected with mindfulness and the TA objective of becoming script-free. As both authors develop their ideas the reader becomes acquainted with what Stern (2012) refers to as the *enstatic school*, in which loneliness is reduced and solitude is promoted. In this way, Stern suggests, the educator approaches the soul of the learner and makes more available the potential for living in the spirit of the school community.

8

ROUND AND ROUND THE PERMISSION WHEEL

An Early Years perspective

Evelyne Papaux, Switzerland

Introduction

This chapter focuses on the educational and social dimension of permission. Opening with a discussion of permission there will be a presentation of the permission wheel devised by Gysa Jaoui which was first published by Hawkes (2007). What follows are illustrations, based in the context of Early Years education and are taken from routine practice in my role as an educator with infants and young children. The discussion emphasizes the added value of educational transactional analysis as an effective and significant means of prevention in children's education, and as a powerful framework for supporting educational professionals. Transactional analysis theory and practice have the potential to enable professionals to become more effective in their roles with children and parents.

The concept of permission

In TA terms, permissions are 'messages, both verbal and nonverbal, that lead to the powerful decisions which make our lives rich and meaningful' (Alden 1988: 321). They are often positioned in opposition to injunctions, although interestingly some authors such as Alden consider that injunctions and permissions lie on a continuum, and avoid a more limiting on/off perspective on the concept. Furthermore, in TA discussion, permissions are associated with a liberation from script or an opening up from limiting decisions. In my work as an educational transactional analyst, permission provides an invitation to develop individual potential, the presentation of something as possible and achievable. Interestingly the word education comes from the latin *ex-ducere*, meaning *leading out*, and is close to the idea of opening up and unfolding towards a growthful direction. In childhood, an individual builds up a sense of self, that is to say the conception of self and how that combines with what is expected within a given environment, within relationships and social systems. When turning to the use of permission in the context of Early Years, consideration is given to the range of relationships of the child, including their social, cultural and historical environment. The aim is to assess if it is permissive or prohibitive. When Eric Berne and his successors wrote about permission, during the 60s, the idea had been developed on the basis of clinical observations and practice, whereas the context of this chapter is European Early Years education in 2013.

Jaoui's permission wheel

In the 1980s, Gysa Jaoui, a French trainer and psychotherapist, designed the permission wheel, a diagram illustrating the relative extent or limitation of an individual's sense of permission across various areas of relating and in experiencing the world. In 2007, Laurie Hawkes published Jaoui's contribution and explained its benefit as applied in psychotherapy. The objective here is to explore the concept from an educational perspective, focusing on its relevance for assessing children's development and specific needs and its usefulness in everyday life, for working with children aged from birth onwards. Furthermore the model is offered as a valuable aid for reflective educational practice.

> The permission wheel is a series of 10 concentric circles, the first of which represents 10 per cent permission, the second 20 per cent, and so on up to 100 per cent. The whole circular diagram is cut into four main segments, each of which divided into four or five subsegments. Each permission is seen as a slice of the pie chart, more or less extended depending on how free one is in that domain. So, if we imagine the person standing in the centre of the chart, he or she can turn and look about, seeing how far his or her freedom extends before being blocked by prohibition resulting from injunctions, counterinjunctions or decisions.
>
> (Hawkes 2007: 21)

Jaoui considered prohibitive messages not in black-and-white terms; 'you have it' or 'you don't have it'. Instead she preferred a relative view, in other words as 'being more or less' affected by it. Accordingly there is no such thing as an absolute prohibition. Jaoui also preferred to focus on the positive and on the resources of the person instead of concentrating on the lack and difficulties. Jaoui's perspective is particularly relevant for an educational application because of this positive assumption and in how it helps clarify the connection between permission and autonomy.

Permission and autonomy

Berne described autonomy as the release, or recovery, of three capacities: awareness, spontaneity and intimacy. He didn't develop this idea to the extent he did with other concepts and this leaves others with the opportunity of doing so. In 1984 Hagehülsmann, quoted in Tudor (1991), defined the TA philosophical basis, as 'the capacity of human beings for interpersonal relationships, openness and intimacy; their right to self-determination and self-responsibility' (1991: 12). I find it useful to incorporate interconnectedness to the idea of autonomy, by which I mean the experience of feeling connected to oneself, to others, and the world. Consequently, becoming autonomous involves being part of something larger than oneself, includes a sense of belonging and an urge to grow through co-operation. In other words, we don't experience ourselves as the centre of the world. As Clarke explains:

> True connection is a state of being in relationship. It may be close or distant, constant or infrequent, but it is held as a thread of real caring and it enhances the lives of everyone involved. It is a set of attitudes: mental, emotional and physical. It is congruence between commitment and action.
>
> (Clarke 1999: xv)

There is a social and dynamic dimension of autonomy: it is neither an outcome nor a final destination, but an ongoing process. It is a co-created phenomenon,

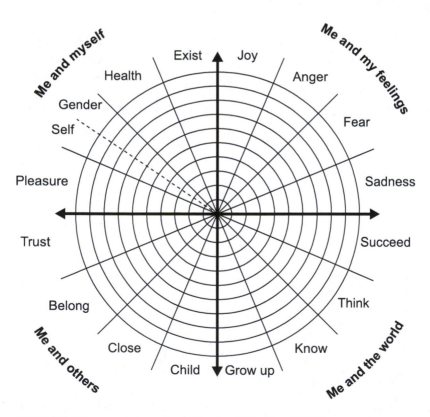

FIGURE 8.1 The permission wheel (Hawkes 2007; Jaoui 1988)

generated in the here-and-now circumstance through differing experiences and relationships. In clarifying the connection between permission and autonomy, Jaoui's model visually illustrates different aspects of relating through four clusters of permission: Me and Myself, Me and My Feelings, Me and Others, Me and the World.

I will take a closer look at two of the quadrants: 'Me and Myself' and 'Me and My Feelings'. They are both concerned with the connection to self, a sense of being, knowing what one likes and wants, and the expression of feelings. Permissions most relevant to these include: to exist, be healthy, be oneself, have pleasure, feel and express sadness, joy, anger, fear. This is arguably another way to describe what Berne referred to as spontaneity: 'the capacity to choose from a full range of options in feeling, thinking and behaving' (Berne, quoted in Stewart and Joines 1987: 266).

In the Me and Others quadrant, important permissions include: to trust, belong, be close, be a child. These involve how we connect to others in different contexts. Berne talked about intimacy as 'an open sharing of feelings and wants between you and another person' (1987: 267).

The permissions set in the Me and the World quadrant are: to succeed, think, know, grow up. Each of this cluster clearly links to awareness and our ability to connect to the world. This involves accounting for the environment's stimuli, being in touch with reality and being able to adapt to it. It is also implies having the conviction of one's ability to make an impact on the environment. Awareness was defined by Berne as, 'the capacity to see, hear, feel, taste and smell things as pure sensual impressions' (1987: 266). The permission wheel creates a visual representation of people's freedom while also providing a snapshot of the individual's interconnectedness, resources and of their specific way of investing energy to generate strokes.

Jaoui was flexible about the permissions themselves in terms of encouraging people to change the words, or add to the permissions as needed. There is no proposed hierarchy of permissions; Jaoui simply used the wheel as a way to find the most extended quarter and to use that resource as a contact door before then exploring a way to decide on which area to next focus. Some authors, however, have identified a hierarchy of permission in relation to child development. Erikson (1959), Levin (1980) and Clarke (2009) offer possible development stages with corresponding specific permissions or affirmations, as does Allen in relation to the well-being of individuals (Allen 1988).

My preference is to support Temple's regard for permissions: 'upbringing is a relational process unique for each individual, in which what we do or how we do it can either support a positive growthful dynamic or hinder it'. She continues by referring to Chess and Thomas, stating that the main question is; 'How good is the fit between the child's capacity and dynamic of growth and development and the carer's provision of challenge, stimulation and support?' (Temple 2008b: 217).

This brings us back to the idea of a co-created process and the importance of relationship. It also invites a reflective practice, building on both our knowledge and observation skills to account for the specific needs of the children with whom we are relating in our work.

The educational transactional analyst in Early Years education

The interventions of a transactional analyst are defined by the contract and the clients' needs. In the following case-study material, the global contract is to offer children an environment where they can develop skills according to their stage of development, and learn to live and thrive in a group in the absence of their primary caregivers. Apparently Berne liked to ask: 'What do I do when I am in a room with a client, if I am called a transactional analyst?' My question is: What do I do when I am in a room with a child, if I am called an *educational* transactional analyst? Or more precisely: How can I describe my way of being with a child?

My own immediate answer would be: relate in an OK–OK way; promote autonomy; give strokes and permissions. The following questions would be: How do I do it? And what evidence can I provide to demonstrate effectiveness?

What strikes me after all these years of experience with children and families is the fact that most interventions are regarded as invisible, remaining at an implicit level, and appear to most people to be natural and instinctive. I want to challenge these assumptions and account for the important learning that takes place in informal ways. It can be argued that any changes cannot be measured; the effects of our interventions will be revealed much later in time and in various contexts of the children's lives. What has become clearer for me after all this time is the need for educators to develop a high level of awareness of what is taking place and a capacity to name it so that it can be given due recognition. I have often noticed educators' consideration for physis and a commitment to the process itself, even if they do not claim it explicitly as part of their impact. However, staying humble does not mean discounting the significant impact of their interventions and validity of their work. I find it very helpful to read Allen (2008), who claims that children can find emotional support outside their families if and when they need it, and that such assistance is more than crucial. He adds that even small interventions can result in major changes in a child's life trajectory, which means: 'This is an area where the efforts of educators and organizational development personnel are especially important and potent' (Allen 2008: 209).

Working with children requires educators to be aware of the significance and impact of early relationships; they are direct witnesses to babies' neural development and construction of self, and they are actors in the creation of the child's life plan. Attachment literature has established that children develop internal working models of relationship based on their earliest experiences (Bowlby 1988). Stern's researches on that topic show that 'internalization involves sequences of relational experiences of being-with the other that produces being-with patterns' (Ligabue 2007: 298).

Furthermore:

> The caregiver's availability, the modes with which she or he relates, and
> particularly her or his ability to regulate her or his own emotional world is
> important in providing containment and support that are necessary for the
> infant's growth. . . . The caregiver is a psychobiological regulator of the infant's
> nervous system development and of its social and emotional experiences.
>
> (2007: 301)

In other words, it isn't possible to generate the attitude of self-care and awareness
of one's own feelings if someone else hasn't done it for you. The individual needs
to have an experience with another first, before being capable of reproducing it;
emotional intelligence is learned with others, and from others.

From birth, babies are active partners; contact and interpersonal exchange are
vital in their development. As they grow, they undergo a process of individuation
and progressively develop a sense of self and self-identity. There is also a strong
pressure within the environment to adapt to social rules and to become a socialized
human being. All through this process, children experience alternatively omni-
potence and lack of potency, and it can take time and support from others to discover
reality, while also building the ability to stay connected to and maximize their own
potential. Being potent involves being assertive and expressing needs and personal
ideas in an OK way. It means that they can also show commitment to their
community and environment. Furthermore that they have sufficient protection,
or know where to ask for help, and at the same time have enough permission, for
example, to exist, to belong, to think and feel. Combined with their rapid
acquisition of language skills, children will progressively be able to communicate
with others verbally, for example, by voicing their feelings and needs, and be assertive
about their wants and ideas. A further evidence of the impact of Early Years
education is offered by R. F. Massey:

> Through processes of mutual interaction between child and primary social-
> izers, a youngster solidifies and is reinforced for a script which establishes a
> life position, a stroke economy, preferred ways of transacting and structuring
> time and possibly racket behaviors. The cycle of experience and interactions
> in a child's social life, both inside and outside a family, shape a 'group imago'
> which influences the expectation – like a map or a blueprint – of how the
> system should operate.
>
> (Massey 1989: 186)

Imitation is a key element in a child's development and, consequently, in the
educational relationship: 'People learn by example and from experience, especially when young. In the classroom, it is inevitable that teachers, whatever they
do or don't do, are setting examples and influencing the experience of their
students' (Temple 2005: 10). Educators need to 'walk the talk' and be an inspiring
model. Children from birth to 4 years old are particularly sensitive to non-verbal

communication and emotional states. This specific need for congruency is often required, not only during a one-hour session, but for the eight hours of presence in the group of children.

In my role in pre-school provision, I have had the opportunity to explore the impact of permission in my interpersonal relationships through observing children's interactions and activities with their peers. This is an important period to provide the relationships within which 'the children and young people develop their respective identities and abilities to relate to others in a social group' (Temple 2008b: 217).

> What is needed is a good fit between the child's unique developmental needs, stage by stage, and what upbringers provide so that the two way dance of upbringing and growing up supplies the right balance of demand and support for the child . . . To start with, this is in the context of feeding, bathing, dressing and the playful exchanges and routines that are the stuff of infant-carer interaction, and later of relationship-building and the progressive mastery of the environment by the infant.
>
> (2008: 225)

Temple is addressing an essential point: the educator's interventions take place by the way of casual and down-to-earth actions, which means that it is easy for an outsider to discount their meaning and importance. It appears to be what any care-taker would do, and this may be the case – except that transactional analysts are aware of what is at stake, are able to name what they are doing, how they are doing it, and to what purpose.

The permission wheel in the Early Years context

Woollams (1980) describes 'permission level' as the amount of stress the individual is able to cope with before turning to script behavior. Allen (2008) invites us to look at the roles of permission and protection in terms of the promotion of resilience and positive emotions. In addition, I see permission as playing an important role in self-esteem development and life position formation. As transactional educators, how can we use the permission wheel to promote reflective practice within a preventive and developmental perspective?

> Ultimately each person needs to give themselves the permission they need. However therapists, counsellors and educators as well as parents can directly foster an atmosphere which will facilitate this. . . . Supportive individuals and groups are helpful for they imply, if not actually say, we back you.
>
> (Allen 2008: 206)

How can we offer a protective and, at the same time, permissive environment aiming at preventing unhealthy script formation and facilitating autonomy, expanding children's integrating Adult? What follows are examples of how I use the permission wheel with babies and children in an educational setting, with a developmental and preventive perspective focusing on normal development and growth.

I see the permission wheel as a frame of reference enhancing reflective practice and as a basis for raising the following questions.

What is the actual meaning of each permission in this specific context?

Let's begin with the 'OK to feel' permission, divided by Jaoui in four slices for each emotion – joy, anger, sadness and fear. This means that children need to receive the permission to feel what they feel, but also to know what they feel. Steiner (2005) stresses the fact that children need to learn words to describe their emotional state and differentiate them in order to go over the chaos level. It is also because they can explore all of them that they can connect to their authentic feeling and won't develop a racket feeling that is regarded by Parental figures as more appropriate or acceptable. 'The full range of emotions is molded in the relationship with the caregiver, which then determines the capacity to understand, feel, differentiate and describe one's own and the other's emotion' (Ligabue 2007: 301).

Due to this ability the individual can develop empathy and connect to others through understanding their emotions, without feeling overwhelmed or disconnected. If we consider the 'OK to be yourself' permission, we realize that Jaoui's choice of separating the permission into 'self' and 'gender' is relevant when observing children. The question of sexual identity is an important part of their development, but does not need to be separated. I also think that the permission to know, identified by Jaoui, is an important one; it incorporates the permission to ask questions, to get information, to make meaning of the world and one's relationship with others.

I have a specific observation on the permission to exist, which is a key element in people's lives: taking care of babies has been a learning experience for me, the connection taking place mostly through a tonic dialogue. The permission to exist will be 'told and heard' mostly by this channel and requires authenticity and interconnectedness. A tonic dialogue is the variation in the body tonus, which is used as a way to understand the other, so there are actually no words at all. I cannot forget how babies were staring at me, and the feeling that through that look they could actually connect with my true self and see behind the appearances. They are indeed active partners in the relationship, and the permission to 'exist and be yourself' is consequently bilateral.

In what ways am I offering and modelling these permissions?

I am responsible for a group of ten children, aged 3 to 5 years old, which is a standard arrangement in Switzerland. It is winter-time and everybody needs to dress warmly before going out for a walk. This moment can be the occasion to offer children various permissions: 'Where are your shoes?' (permission to think);

'Try and put them on' (permission to do, permission to succeed). I can also encourage the children to help each other (which suggests permission to be close). I can invite children to state clearly if they need some help (permission to acknowledge needs). This may initially appear straightforward, but sometimes it would be so much easier for me to fetch the shoes myself and put them on the child quickly. It would take so much less time, and we would be ready to go out. In these instances it is not so easy to refrain from repeating 'Hurry up!', 'Stop dreaming!', or 'Let me do it, because you can't do it yourself!'

So the process starts with my own permission level and stress management, and children will sense my patience or impatience, my agitation or enthusiasm, and they will check the congruence between what I say and what I do. In addition, this particular exchange may take place after a few hours of attendance in the group when my own needs might also be challenged.

Marco, 18 months, is playing with a wooden stick. He puts it on a radiator and the stick falls down and rolls. He bends, takes it again, and puts it on the radiator. Marco will continue this action at least ten times before trying to put the stick on a different surface. In terms of permission – if nobody interferes with his activity – Marco is experiencing the permission to do, to think, to succeed, to grow. He also gets the feeling of being important and experiences pleasure as he masters his actions.

Not far from Marco, Tessa, 3 years old, is playing with Killian. Tessa is wearing high-heeled shoes and they are pretending that they are going to the restaurant with their baby. Killian is talking in an angry tone to the doll as he sits at the little table: 'Now you have to behave! We are in a restaurant!'

During this role-play, Tessa and Killian explore various emotions and, through playing co-operatively, they develop permissions to be important, to be close, and to belong to a group. Play has long been recognized and valued in child development, considered as a crucial process for making meaning, taking account of their environment and experimenting with physical, cognitive, social and emotional abilities. I further suggest that play offers the opportunity for the child to connect with the body; to develop co-ordination, balance, body-image; and to connect with the world: collect facts and learn to think, to organize time and space and develop problem-solving skills.

> This opportunity to play in a safe way, without undue concern for external demands or pressing inner drives, allows the child self-expression and the chance to create something unique in the outside world. It forms the basis for autonomous, creative living . . . Imaginative play may be one of the great untapped resources in the amelioration of pathology or in developing socially constructive orientations in all children.
>
> (Singer, quoted in Shmukler and Friedman 1988: 81–2)

If this observation appears obvious, care must be taken not to discount: 'The origins of play and creativity in childhood are dependent on good enough environmental facilitation and care' (1988: 82). If children can develop their own creative way, the attitude of the caregivers continues to be essential in the process. The carer needs to offer a secure basis and a holding environment: 'While our ability as humans to play is innate, it is only developed through interaction and encouragement' (Day, in Tudor 2008: 174). The caregiver has an important role – and not an easy one – because it requires humility: they need to be present, both physically and emotionally, yet without direct intervention. The quality of the carer's presence is fundamental as it offers protection and permission and gives the child a stroked experience. The child experiences that adults show a respectful interest in their experiments, ensuring for example the necessary time to develop play in a space where they can feel safe. We might ask in observing carers: Do they keep a distance or do they give comments, advice or warnings? Are they expecting a performance, or a result?

Do I offer specific permissions for each child in order to provide a 'good fit' with individual specific needs?

It's story-time; Alex is asking me for the story of the little owls. I ask him if he would prefer a new one, the one that we just chose in the library. He shakes his head, sits and waits; the story he wants and asks for, over and over again, is the story of the little owls and how they can cope during their mother's absence. Children love stories; they offer a useful way to make meaning of their environment. They discover options about life issues, such as being jealous of one's sister, being scared of starting school, not wanting to wear glasses, and so on. Stories convey various messages and models of behaviours, and they present a wide range of permissions. It is important for educators to take time and consider the stories they are reading to children and to ask: what kind of permission does this story convey; what sort of stories could be interesting for a particular child; or what metaphors could they create especially for the child?

We shouldn't discount what it means for babies and children under 6 to live within a collective and deal with the consequences in terms of personal needs and rhythm. After the experience of the family, the playgroup or day-care centre is often the child's second experience of living in a group. In transactional analysis it is well understood that these primary experiences will be part of the individual's group imago, which will inform their experience of group processes in childhood and adult life. Young children are building up their sense of self, are discovering their identity and at the same time are expected to socialize and cooperate within the group. As an educator this has been one of the biggest challenges I have encountered: how can I take care of each child and give him or her a 'good fit' within the reality of the group?

Adapting Jaoui's model to the educational context

When Jaoui was presenting the permission wheel she invited others to adapt it to their own reality and observations. I appreciate this consideration, and suggest a

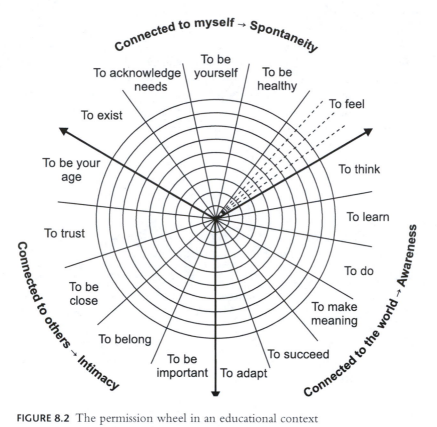

FIGURE 8.2 The permission wheel in an educational context

modification of the original model according to my understanding and observations of children's development.

The permission wheel is divided in three equal parts, each one representing one component of interconnectedness: connected to myself, to others, to the world. In the educational setting the permission 'to be a child' and the permission 'to grow' are similar, and I envisage them as set on a continuum. My preference is to use the permission 'to be your age'. It means it's OK to behave and think according to the developmental stage and the child's well-being in relation to the here and now, and not to pre-empt the future. It is combined with it being OK to grow at your own pace, to play, to dream, to ask for stories, to say no, and to learn structuring their time and space, to make choices.

Some additional permissions are offered on the educational version: the permission 'to do' comprises the permissions to take risks, to deal with mistakes and doubts, to experiment fear and learn to cope with it. The permission 'to be important' refers to showing capacities and to take a role in a group, to be a leader when needed and become part of the connection with others. I suggest naming the permission 'to make meaning', instead of Jaoui's permission 'to know', in order to give it a wider scope.

Ramond (1994) proposed a new cultural injunction 'don't change' as the basis for a script that supports the teenager in avoiding integration into the culture of a new country. In turn, I suggest the permission 'to adapt' as a positive answer to the injunction, as I consider the question of interculturality as an issue of growing importance in a European society. Finally, I propose the permission 'to learn', as it is central in children's development and growth.

Conclusion

TA offers a model of human psychology which emphasizes the influence of social and cultural process that promote change and growth. The main questions for the educator include: What kind of design do we have? What role do we want to play in this process? In what way do we want to be influential? And, if having a design is a necessary start, it is, however, not enough. Educators need to ask how they can relate this discussion to everyday professional practice: What kind of identity are we co-creating in our relationships?

> I will start saying that as children we have to learn how to get along and get ahead, upbringing is therefore providing the relationships within which the children and young people develop their respective identities and abilities to relate to others in the social group.
>
> (Temple 2008b: 217)

The quality of the relationship is essential to the process of permission development and Early Years are essential. This is the time and space where children connect with their potential, receive permission from inspiring role models and test their capacities in a protective and permissive environment. I invite educators to take a step back and look at the environment offered to children in terms of permission and protection, and check if it is well balanced. This question is relevant not only to the individual, but at social and cultural levels. How do we consider children in our society? What kind of messages are we giving them regarding their abilities? What kind of opportunities are we providing so that they might have an impact on their environment? And how might they become progressively our fellow citizens? 'We cannot refer to children separate from their relationships or their environment: rather they are subjects-in-relationship-with. That is, intersubjectivity is a primary process' (Ligabue 2007: 295).

A final observation is that I have been an educator for young children for more than twenty years, and I am quite struck by the current tendency in Switzerland to create a 'no risk' environment for young children: educators tend to avoid all activities where children might, for example, get dirty or be bruised; there is such a fear of coping with consequences, that children are prevented from important experiments. There is also an increasing tendency to value precocity – wanting children to learn early and fast – to encourage results and productivity instead of supporting the learning process and the individuality. Not much time for dreaming and playing, not many opportunities to make discoveries at one's own rhythm and according to one's own interest. This is an issue that I currently face in my work as an educator trainer and a consultant in education involved in meeting parents.

The permission wheel offers a useful model to support addressing the cultural challenges: It can enable educators to name their interventions in terms of permission; it can give value to and reinforce the educator's strategies, and help them explain the preventive dimension of their actions to parents, colleagues and society. My hope is that educators can use the permission wheel as a starting point to think about the society and the various groups in which we are living and raising children, and in what ways we can make a difference.

9

SNOW WHITE

The triumph of beauty

Agnès Le Guernic, France

Introduction

Fairy stories, read to little children, either at home or in the nursery school, belong to an oral tradition. They were passed down from generation to generation and, in Europe, they were written down during the seventeenth and nineteenth centuries. Perrault's and Grimm's versions (Grimm 1984; Perrault 2010) are the most well-known ones, but scholars all around the world have made collections of national tales, which can give us an entrée into cultural worlds different from our own.

The fairytales, which are often read to children by their parents at bedtime, are our first narratives. They tell us about what can happen to a child as they grow up, and they help to develop imagination and to anticipate futures. They offer lessons about life, managing emotions and encountering danger – and they have happy endings. They serve as a model from which life stories might be created and that can lead to rewriting the narrative of our lives over and over.

For the purpose of this chapter I have chosen the first version of the Snow White story, by the brothers Grimm (1984), in my view the strongest and most poetic account. In the text below, all quotations are taken and translated from this version in French (Grimm 1986).

Later versions, both in text and film, are often made more sugary; Disney's animation of Snow White is purged of the strongest details, for example, referring to just how young Snow White is, and defines it primarily as a love story – when Snow White is sweeping the dwarves' house, she sings, 'One day, my prince will come!' Adapting the story into a film, with all the inevitable distortions necessary in accommodating cultural expectations, further ensures that it becomes firmly rooted in the both children's and adults' memories.

Perspectives on fairytales

In the following discussion, I consider three approaches to using fairytales in working educationally with children in the primary classroom. The three perspectives considered are the psychoanalytical approach, the narrative approach of Vladimir Propp, an expert on Russian fairytales, and the life-script approach of transactional analysis.

In *The Psychoanalysis of Fairytales*, Bruno Bettelheim (1976), suggests that fairytales help children to understand themselves and to find solutions to problems that are worrying them. He goes on to caution that adults should resist explaining the meaning of the tales to children, or turn the reading of them into instruction. He proposes that the story of Snow White explores the difficulties a girl-child goes through during puberty, the position a child holds in a family, and mother–daughter rivalry. It speaks directly to children's unconscious minds.

Vladimir Propp (1968) analysed the structure of fairytales and identified recurring elements to be found in traditional stories. He highlights the elements which are often present in the narrative, and that teachers frequently use to encourage children to reflect and talk. Imagine it is story-time at nursery school and the teacher is reading a story to a group of children sitting in a circle all around. They are shown illustrations in the book and invited to talk about the characters and think about their dilemmas. This is a time for language. There is a move from one linguistic register to another, from the written code to the oral code; at which point the meanings of the terms used are absorbed and the meaning of common situations is understood, and it is also a time for articulating feelings. The children learn to put what they are feeling into words, and they hear other children express what they are feeling too. The process fuels consideration and absorbing of social norms and the development of values, for example perseverance, courage and a distrust of wrong-doers.

Transactional analysts since Berne have taken an interest in both Greek myths and in fairytales. The Greek myths provided models of life stories which relate to the passage of time and end tragically. Berne referred to mythic characters to capture process scripts (Berne 1972). 'Never' comes from the Tantalus myth, 'Always' from the punishment of Arachne – who was turned into a spider. 'As long as' is drawn from the trials of Hercules, 'Afterwards' from Damocles, and 'Almost' from Sisyphus – who almost managed to reach the top of the mountain. Meanwhile, traditional fairy stories like Little Red Riding Hood or Cinderella offer scripts for everyday life. They help a young child to answer the question: What happens to children when they grow up? The fairytale characters are on the side of ordinary men and women, while the Greek myths are on the side of the gods and show how they triumph over human beings.

It was analysing a client's favourite fairytale that led Stephen Karpman to the concept of the Drama Triangle (Karpman 1968). The dramatic roles of Persecutor, Rescuer and Victim emerged from analysing Little Red Riding Hood. The dramatic climaxes correspond to twists and turns in the story. In contrast, Fanita English (1977; 2007) regards the stories that we tell children as a resource; they satisfy our 'thirst for structure' and 'help us to develop from childhood to old age' (English 1977: 340). She emphasizes that 'stories which have influenced our scripts often give us models of courage, of perseverance and of helping each other as well as of hope in the future' (1977: 343).

As nursery school children, the stories that were read aloud to us by our parents or our teachers fuelled the ability to imagine possible future scenarios for our lives. The narratives of fairytales are about real life. The heroes are those who are in positions of weakness, who are ordained to face a future where perils and successes take turns with each other. The tales teach children how to overcome dangers with the prospect of surviving. They help them discover the world of feelings. They promise success through happy endings and are optimistic. The heroes are learning from life; they make mistakes and find resolution. Fairytales explore what it is to be part of a family – a place which is both safe and dangerous. They raise questions about the potential for the family they will make for themselves, and how they will achieve it. They evoke work, endeavour, social and emotional success. The lessons they teach are implicit. Individuals create their own understanding from these tales, so that adults too find both permissions and warnings in them.

In the following discussion of Snow White, I will explore the ways in which the tale can be used with children, identifying the themes at both explicit and implicit levels and how educators can relate it to a contemporary frame of reference. Snow White is primarily a story for girls, although has relevance for boys too. It is essentially about the rivalry between women and the role of beauty in competition for love and power. The theme of beauty runs through the story, closely linked to the theme of time. It is also a story about apprenticeship, and gives pointers to children about possible paths to follow from their birth family to the family they themselves will establish, and the transition from childhood to adulthood.

The story of a little girl who is incomparably beautiful

Beauty, the dream of perfection, the dream of happiness and the dream of power. How do we create the way that we see beauty – its role, its power over us and the power that it gives us over others? Snow White is the story that tells us most about this. It has all the elements we need to understand the dream of beauty, the feelings that it arouses, and our efforts to attain it, and sometimes to destroy it; because beauty can give rise to ambivalence.

What do we feel in the face of beauty? Fascination, admiration, a deep joy? We are full to the brim: happy, possibly. The spectacle of beauty can indeed make us happy. Beauty is an aspect of the divine: the beauty of goddesses in mythology, painted virgins in churches. Beauty is always exceptional. Nature is the primary source of beauty; and the primary source of beauty in nature is a spectacle. The tale of Snow White starts off with a queen dreaming of a snow-covered countryside, described as a picture with three colours; the white of the snow, the scarlet of the three drops of blood which fell on the snow when the Queen pricked her finger sewing, and the ebony of the window frame.

It was so beautiful, this red on the snow, that when she saw it, the Queen thought: 'Oh, if I could have a child as white as the snow, as scarlet as the blood and as ebony haired as the wood of this window frame!'

As is often the case in fairytales, the wish comes true; but in a way which has unexpectedly harmful consequences. The Queen had a baby girl a short time after, but she died as she brought the baby into the world. It was named 'Snow White'. Dreams can come true; misfortune can happen.

Women's beauty and the risk of rivalry

After a year, the king marries again – to a very beautiful woman. Beauty is an important criterion in the choice of a wife, particularly a king's wife. Being beautiful promotes a better chance of a prestigious marriage. This socially divisive rule is experienced by children in their own lives, in how preferences play out in the heart of their own family and at school, where the best-looking boy may become the teacher's pet and the loveliest girl a sweetie-pie.

The stepmother is not satisfied with being very beautiful. She wants to be the *most* beautiful: 'She was so proud and so arrogant about her beauty that she couldn't bear the idea of someone being more beautiful than her'. Here, the fairytale introduces rivalry between women for beauty.

A puzzle is presented: How can you be sure that compliments are sincere if you are a queen? The new Queen has a magic object, a mirror to which she asks questions and receives replies, and it does not lie. She is reassured when it tells her that she is most beautiful woman in the land. This passage describes the happiness which looking at her beauty in the mirror gives the Queen. It is a source of pride and a source of power. It is not the sight of beauty which fills her heart to bursting, but the thought that she is superior to others. Simultaneously, she is scared of the reply: she is gnawed by doubt: What if she stopped being the most beautiful? This is a poison induced by rivalry. She can only be happy at times when the mirror has confirmed that she is the most beautiful woman. The source of her confidence is not in herself, but in the mirror. How many times will it continue to give her the same reply? An honest mirror alerts someone who is open to seeing to the marks of time.

The threat of the younger woman

The fairytale is precise about the moment in time when Snow White becomes a rival for the Queen. Six years have passed; Snow White is still only a child. When she had her seventh birthday, she was as beautiful as the day, much more beautiful than the Queen herself, and this is revealed to the Queen when she questions the mirror. Perhaps we might find it strange that a little seven-year-old girl could be considered as a rival for an adult woman. But what do we know, after all? In any case, astonishment, jealousy, a heart which reels with the pressure of hatred – these are the sorts of feelings the Queen experiences. She is obsessed. 'Pride mixed with jealousy swelled in her heart, like a weed grows, leaving her not a moment of peace, neither day nor night [so that] she would no longer see her before her eyes.' She ordered the huntsman to take the girl away into the forest and to kill her.

It is significant that the Queen needs to hear the verdict of her mirror before she notices the beauty of the little girl, even though she was right in front of her eyes. Her self-confidence had made her blind. Hurt pride is compared to a noxious weed which overruns everything; jealousy which is at the same time a desire for what another person possesses and a fear of losing what one has. This in turn attracts hatred, and hatred arouses the wish to kill. Snow White is endangered by her beauty even though she is only a child. Taught by fairytales, children know very well that being conspicuous is not necessarily a good thing for them. When they are the focus of admiration, they easily become potential prey. Yet the Queen has all she needs to enhance her beauty and make it even greater in terms of dresses, finery and treatments. All the same, in the fairytale she is not the one who carries the day, but Snow White is. We will return to this later, with the fairytale's implicit messages.

Implications of power

The fairytale's proposition is that someone such as the Queen, who is eaten by rivalry and who also has power, can use this to physically eliminate rivals; and that jealousy can push her to murder. It is useful to consider what the Queen loses when she is surpassed in beauty. She was chosen because she was very beautiful, but the real power belongs to the king. A woman can have a share of the power when she becomes queen. According to the tale, her power allows her to eliminate people who trouble her, even if the victim is the king's daughter. When she commands, she is obeyed; which for a child is the true definition of power. What we don't know at the beginning of the story is that she also possesses other powers apart from being able to make her mirror talk: the power to create magic spells which arouse desire, and to make fatal poisons. This queen is also a dangerous witch. So the danger for the heroine is first of all in her own home, from which she must flee.

The next part of the fairytale describes a flight from danger and searching for a hiding place to escape death, from which to grow up and become a woman without the support of her birth family. The heroine's beauty then becomes her greatest asset, as it ultimately leads to her being loved by a prince.

The role of men

The King, Snow White's father, is an absent father. He only appears when he marries a very beautiful and proud woman, one year after being widowed. He does not appear after this point. The huntsman is given a task by the Queen, which is to lead Snow White far away into the forest, to kill her, and return with her liver and her lungs as evidence. The little girl softens his heart with her tears and promises him that she will run away and never appear again. 'She was so beautiful that the huntsman took pity on her and said: "Run away, my poor little girl".' He feels pity and, above all, relief that he hasn't had to kill her himself, because he is sure that 'the wild animals will soon have eaten her up'. So in effect he is a murderer who satisfies a good conscience by handing the task of eliminating the little girl over to the wild animals. He is moved to pity by her beauty, not by her predicament or her youth. Beauty has the power of softening hearts, but only to a certain point. He deceives the Queen by cooking her a young wild boar's liver and lungs, which she eats later with great satisfaction. A little later on in the story, Snow White meets the Seven Dwarves, mini-men, who will help her. Then finally the prince appears; but we will return to that later.

The flight into the forest

For children, the vast forest symbolizes the world outside their house and all the dangers of the unknown territories. They are afraid of being left there all alone, and of being abandoned in an unknown world. For Snow White, danger is inside her home – the Queen's palace – but danger also lies in the forest. She is frightened as 'she looks as it were behind every leaf and every tree'. She runs, gets scratched 'by the thorns and sharp stones'. The wild animals come to brush against her, although do not hurt her in any way. The animals are not hostile like human beings and the narrative softens: 'She ran straight on as far as her little feet would carry her.' The child knows that she is vulnerable, but she is brave.

Refuge in the Seven Dwarves' house

The dwarves' home is a miniature house, fitting for a child. Everything is small, clean, charming and tidy. The repetition of the word 'little' for each detail conjures up an impression of order and of safety, appealing to a child's mind: the little table with its white table cloth, the little plates, little tumblers, little knives and forks, and the little beds with their fresh, white sheets. Snow White is hungry and thirsty and, although she is tired, she adapts herself to this miniature world. She eats a little bit from each little plate, drinks a little drop of wine from each little tumbler, eats a little mouthful of each little bread roll, then tries out the beds and eventually falls asleep in one which is the just the right size for her. She has been well raised and acts in a way that will mean she is accepted. This is a lesson for children, who can find it hard to control their desires.

The Seven Dwarves track her passage through the house asking questions about the intruder, and then they discover Snow White asleep in their bed. What a beautiful child she is! They feel so full of joy that they leave her to sleep. The dwarf whose bed Snow White has taken sleeps for an hour in each of his companions' beds. Children enjoy this detail because of the sharing: no one has suffered because of Snow White's arrival, and all has been fair.

In the morning, Snow White and the dwarves get to know each other; she says who she is, tells them about her misfortunes, and they suggest that she keeps house for them. In exchange, they will look after her and she will not lack for anything. She agrees, and gains board, lodging and security in exchange for her labour. During the day the dwarves are away at work and, when they return in the evening, everything has been prepared. Snow White is alone all day long, which is why they put her on her guard against her stepmother and warn her not to let anyone enter. So, in relation to the little girl, the dwarves play the role not only of childminder but also of protector.

Being put to the test

Within a short time, Snow White is put to the test. The Queen is keen to learn from her mirror that her rival has really been put aside. Despite the dwarves' warnings to put the little girl on guard against the Queen, she does not heed their words. Such are the challenges of education! Snow White is innocent – and ignorant. She puts her trust in appearances. Parents are kings and queens to a young child. They have both a childminding and a protective role, but they are not to be believed. Parents talk of the challenges of education and the impossibility of preparing children who live in a closed environment for the dangers of the world outside. Taking risks is inevitable.

The Queen, who has found out that Snow White is still alive and discovered the place where she has taken refuge, decides to eliminate her directly because, 'jealousy was eating her up and wouldn't leave her any peace'. So she disguises herself as an old pedlar and on, two occasions, arrives at the dwarves' house and attempts to trick Snow White. Each time the dwarves save her. On the third occasion the witch is ready to take more risks, although they carry a possibility of her own death. She makes an apple, half of which is poisoned, and then dresses as a peasant. She manages to convince Snow White to taste the apple, after she has herself taken a bite out of the good part. This time Snow White is lost. The dwarves are not able to do anything for her.

The death which is not a death

They had to yield to the evidence; Snow White is dead: 'She was dead, their dear little one, and dead she stayed.' They grieved for her for three days, and then they decided to bury her; 'but she was still as fresh looking as if she was still alive and she still had her colour and her beautiful red cheeks.' They could not bring themselves to bury her in the black earth, and had a glass coffin made so that she could be seen from all sides. They had her name and title as a princess engraved on the coffin, laid her in it, and 'carried it to the top of the mountain, where they took it in turns to keep watch over her'. The animals came too: an owl, a crow, then a dove – and they all grieved for Snow White. Time passed.

Waking, meeting and marrying, and punishment

A prince appears, who has lost his way in the forest while hunting. He spends a night in the dwarves' house and sees Snow White in her glass coffin. He is filled with admiration for her, and gains the dwarves' permission to take her away. His argument is interesting: 'I cannot live without gazing on Snow White, and I will look after her and worship her as my beloved, as the thing which is dearest to me in the world!' He arranges for the coffin to be carried away, and his servants stumble on a root as they carry her, which dislodges a piece of apple which had been stuck in Snow White's throat and sets her free. Restored to life again, she lifts the lid, asking questions. The Prince's replies, explains what has happened, and invites her to marry him. She falls in love and leaves with him.

The Prince's reply is charming. Apart from her stay in the dwarves' house, Snow White has only known a solitary life. Yet here is someone who is young, good looking, and is there for her. It is a promise of intimacy, security and joy. The wedding is an occasion of great celebration from which the wicked Queen could not stay away. At this point the Queen has a terrible punishment. She is condemned to put on some red-hot boots which have been heated in the fire – and to dance until she dies.

The potential power of the fairytale for children

Perhaps most importantly, the story explores the life which lies ahead of children, a combination of *aspiration and security*. A child's home – their parents' house – is by its very nature a place of security. The outside world is experienced as dangerous, and it is symbolized by the forest and its wild animals. The physical dangers are multitudinous for children. They can get lost, be knocked down by cars, injured, killed, kidnapped. How can we reconcile the things we say to warn them with what we say to instil confidence in the future? This is the challenge the dwarves come up against – children struggle to distinguish between a pleasant expression and real kindness. They can believe appearances and what others say to them. When she sees the disguised witch, Snow White sees a harmless old woman. Children fail to see evil and, furthermore, they do not know how to defend themselves against it, because they are weak compared with adults.

Throughout childhood, children have to learn to think, to check out the truth of what is said to them whenever possible, and to ask for help from a position of vulnerability. The situation is worst when the danger is inside the home: the risk of being beaten or killed, the risk of incest. It is here that children who have been blessed with great beauty can be most in danger. They are objects of desire and become preyed upon, undefended by other members of the family who may be jealous of them. Passions are exaggerated, and they are the first victims.

The tale tells children that beauty, which everyone highly values, is a powerful factor in succeeding on the social ladder. In a traditional society, this can lead to envy and feeds rivalry, leading to a difficult life and loneliness. It is other qualities that generate affection, such as work, love, helping each other. When she arrives at the dwarves' house, Snow White takes care to eat a little bit from each plate and to drink only one mouthful from each tumbler. She is worried about not upsetting anyone. She agrees to work for the dwarves and to keep house for them.

The dwarves help Snow White, but not without compensation. A sort of contract binds them: food and security in exchange for housework. They work hard in the mines in the mountain to extract precious minerals. They help each other. When the prince arrives, he asks the dwarves if he can take Snow White away with him. He has to convince them with sound arguments. There is no question, either for him or for them, of buying the glass coffin, but he promises to look after her and worship her as his beloved, as he cannot live without gazing on her.

The story also initiates children into the realm of *emotions and feelings*, which prepares them for their future life. As they go through the story, the reader observes, in turn, a range of experiences:

- the way the good Queen is filled with wonder at the world's beauty
- the joy of her wish coming true
- the sadness of her disappearance, which makes Snow White an orphan
- dread aroused by the bad stepmother's jealousy
- fear of being killed and even terror when she is in the forest
- joy at being sheltered by the dwarves
- pleasure and ultimately, love.

Children can also identify with feelings that are unknown or forbidden in the family. They understand the physical or psychological expression of these feelings: jealousy which makes people turn yellow then green; pride which harasses and does not lead to peace; hatred which drives to pushing others aside or having them killed; the anger and fury which follow failure; the despair which leads to considering dangerous action. Other feelings are pity and guilt; the cowardly relief of the huntsman who avoids having to kill Snow White with his own hands. There are other possible connections which the young reader might make: The dwarves' surprise and admiration; their joy and grief when they lose Snow White; they demonstrate compassion for the prince and, later, admiration and worship. This is different in nature, as it gives birth to love which is at first one-directional, and then reciprocated. Children can put words to these experiences.

The visceral signs of emotion are described. The Queen is happy as her mirror tells her the truth; but pride is like a noxious weed which leaves her without any peace. She cannot see the little girl who is right in front of her eyes. The huntsman takes pity; he is relieved of a great weight as he avoids having to kill her with his own hands, and only then does he feel the guilt. Snow White is desperately lonely, so very afraid, but she moves ahead with courage as far as her little feet can carry her.

The power of beauty comes from the emotions that it arouses in others. It elevates a beautiful person as it arouses extreme emotions in others; for example, the admiration of the dwarves who are awestruck with wonder and adoration. The stepmother's envy, jealousy and hatred are also prompted by beauty. The prince's need and his desire to take her away, which defeats the dwarves' desire to keep Snow White, is also fuelled by beauty. Beauty gets what it wants without even having to ask, and without having to insist.

The central concern of women's lives: love, power and children

The story of Snow White is told within the frame of reference of a traditional society, where the central concern of women is love and marriage. Finding love and a good husband, while simultaneously avoiding a destructive and unhappy marriage, is a complex challenge. Fairytales present a range of versions of this theme: Sleeping Beauty finds herself with an ogress as a stepmother. These paths will lead them from their birth home to one where they will live with their husband's family and their children. The model is clearly exogamic. The prince gets lost in the forest and finds his princess while on a journey or as he loses his way. The lesson of needing to move outside the original tribe in order to survive or find love is integral to the story at an implicit level.

In fairytales, the woman is most often passive in the quest for a loving partner. In the case of Snow White, this can be explained by her age: she is only seven years old! The time she spends in the glass coffin, which keeps her on the mountain top as if she was hibernating, allows her to mature physically so that the prince discovers a beautiful young woman, aged at least sixteen, where the dwarves had left a pre-pubescent girl. Again, nothing is made explicit – fairytales teach us indirectly.

In the Snow White tale, the heroine's key asset is her exceptional beauty, which inspires love. However, the tale suggests that great beauty has disadvantages too: having others held in thrall does not provide a good preparation for the realities of life and its tests; women who are too beautiful often get the message, 'Be beautiful, and shut up!' It may seem pointless to them to think about things. People see the individual's outward appearance, and remain unconcerned with their personal qualities. What permissions has Snow White? Permission to live, to be a child while she is with the dwarves, but not permission to grow up: the adults are dwarves; there are neither children nor adult women around her. She has permission to please others, as demonstrated in the care she takes with her appearance, but little permission to think for herself.

The role of the child in the tale is special: we do not find a single reference to her birth parents. The first queen dreams of a child with whom she may already be pregnant, and for whom she is sewing. The child has no gender; it is described only as perfect. We see here the power of an archetype, which is an important element in Grimm's fairytales. It is a mechanism in which a dream provides a way in which people are trying to make a reality in the present – our very own child, and a perfect child!

When the tale tackles desire, it is initially in the form of desire for a child, expressed as a wish. Wishes often come true in fairytales, even when they are harmful or ridiculous. Dreams which have come true do not necessarily bring happiness. This is a recurrent theme, and the implicit lesson is that individuals should not dream too much, and that it is better to take action.

Finally, the theme of time in the story is important. Time connected to the family, the family of the past, of childhood, and the family that we will create in the future. It is found too in the idea of physical maturity; it takes time to develop a man's or a woman's body. Feminine rivalry, which starts for Snow White at the age of seven, puts her in danger. On the other hand, youth is an advantage which is inseparable from beauty. Wanting to stay beautiful leads to battling against time, a battle which is lost anyway, even more so if 'being the most beautiful queen' is the dream.

Snow White today

Two hundred years after it first appeared, the tale still speaks to us, both children and adults. Its power over our imagination is intact, and the different ways in which society has evolved resist altering the dreams to which it leads, or the dangers of which it warns.

Children remain as vulnerable and dependent on adults, whether they have given birth to them and brought them into the world or whether they have been put in charge of looking after them in a school. Women dying in childbirth has become a rarity, but hazards of family life have become more complex: a single-parented family, by default, circumstance or choice; abandonment by the father before a child arrives in a couple's life; divorce and re-forming of new couples, with or without siblings; organization of children's lives to accommodate the different homes of parents and step-parents. These different ways of living scatter snares across children's paths.

The road and its predators replace the forest. The trinkets offered by the witch disguised as a pedlar are the same – we find them on shop shelves; the poisoned apple is replaced by substance misuse. Love emerges as the source of hope. The theme of beauty, and of the mirror which encourages children to become pre-occupied with how they are perceived by others, is current today. The posters on street hoardings, the photos of models in the pages of magazines, offer ideals to fuel aspirational dreams of achievement. The ideal physical identity whose secret lies in a particular skin care product or type of make-up, or the possibility to resist time due to anti-ageing creams or cosmetic surgery – this impacts from a very young age. Beauty competitions for children and Botox for teenagers are witness to this madness. People endeavour to destroy rivals so they can be the most beautiful and, in doing so, destroy themselves. Little girls aim to look like Barbie from their sixth birthday – and some manage it.

Men who, in times gone by, also used to give great importance to their appearance but ceded this preoccupation to women, now begin to take part in the same cultural game: 'Mirror, my beautiful mirror!' What power does beauty give us when it is no longer a rarity? How can we stay alive, forever watched by others, and avoid being thrown into the dungeon of anonymity? Perhaps one theme has been changed, that of women's power. In the fairytale, power comes from marriage to the king. Arguably, the way that society has evolved has made it possible to access power through merit and political action, rather than by birth and beauty alone. And one dream remains: that of finding, one day, a person who in response to our question, 'Where am I?' will answer, 'You are with me!'

10

CONTRACTING FOR LEARNING

Nicole Pierre, France

What is a contract?

Contracting is a powerful tool which features in my professional practice as a teacher. Contracting is a process in which one or more people commit themselves to do something. Steiner defined four conditions for the creation of a healthy contract: mutual consent, reciprocal obligation (consideration), competence (of both parties), and legal objective (Steiner 1974). Claudie Ramond writes in *Grandir: Éducation et analyse transactionelle*,

> to break the symbiosis which characterises education, rescuing, psychological games, and games of power should be avoided; it is therefore necessary that the two parties engage their three ego states in relationship and gain their autonomy.
>
> (Ramond 1989: 304)

This also implies that the parties have at their disposal all the necessary information from which to make decisions that lead them towards agreed objectives.

Different contracts

At the start of each academic year, I use the three-cornered contract with my classes so that the two parties – the class group and myself – have all the necessary information. I draw a triangular model on the board and explain what constitutes a contract.

There is also a second contract – that between the college and the pupils. Students are minors, under parental responsibility, obliged to attend school until the age of sixteen. Parents are obliged to the institution by a social contract in the sense of Rousseau; a convention that exists between the governing and the

NATIONAL EDUCATION
COLLEGE

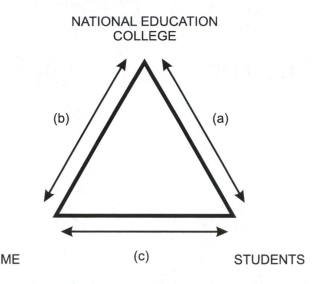

(b)   (a)

ME   (c)   STUDENTS

FIGURE 10.1 The three-cornered contract (adapted from English 1975)

governed, or between the members of a society. Children adapt to the rules of
the establishment and receive in return knowledge and know-how, which enable
them to progress to the next level of class. The process culminates in obtaining
diplomas. As the class and I start to make the contract, we read together the internal
rules of the school. I explain that this part comprises the non-negotiable rules of
working together.

A third contract, the one between myself and the college, is discussed. I teach
German in the 6th grade class according to a defined programme. At the end of
the school year the students are expected to have acquired certain capabilities. In
the course of the year I must evaluate and give grades. Additionally, I am the class
tutor and, in order to attain the objectives defined in the curriculum, the head of
the department is informed as to the techniques which I might use to manage the
process, including transactional analysis. I receive a salary for all these activities.

We then explore the contract between the students and myself. I ask them to
remind me of the non-negotiable rules, e.g. college hours and use of time. Then
the negotiations begin. A pupil might ask: 'If a teacher is absent, can you change
the time of the lesson?' – with my possible reply: 'Yes, according to my availability
and with the agreement that you take responsibility for asking the head of
year.' Thomas Gordon (1974) identified the qualities that help establish a good
teacher–pupil relationship:

- frankness, honesty and truthfulness, which enables each person to express
  themselves openly
- care towards others, which enables each person to feel valued and appreciated

- interdependence, which replaces dependency and submission
- individuality, which allows each person's creativity to blossom
- respecting others' needs, which removes all personal privilege and potential frustration.

Using a table drawn on the board (Table 10.1), I lead the discussion into acceptable and unacceptable behaviours for students and myself.

TABLE 10.1 Acceptable and unacceptable behaviours in class

1	Unacceptable for all of you
2	Zone of acceptance for all of you and for me
3	Unacceptable for me

This is where student values emerge, for example:

> Justice – 'When the teacher nods her head towards someone it shows she has her favourites'

> Respect of the other – 'There are some who tease, or who call us all sorts of names, and tell us we're worthless'

Then I share my values, including honesty and openness. In the area of acceptance ('2' in Table 10.1), I introduce the three Ps: Protection, Permission, Potency (Steiner 1974). I really like Ramond's contracting diagram which shows that 'each one has

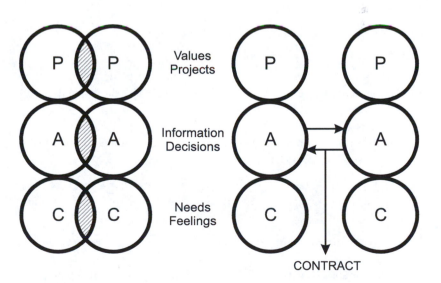

FIGURE 10.2 Ego-states and contract (Ramond 1989)

to renounce in some way his own demands: those which are unacceptable for the other', and 'there is a sharing of projects, negotiation of methods and means of evaluation, permission to express one's needs and feelings' (Ramond 1989: 307–9).

These important points are noted by the pupils who sign the contract, get the parents to sign (for information), and myself. Our contract is established for the school year, with opportunities for review during the term.

The contract for individual sessions

At the beginning of each lesson, I establish a contract for the session. Lewin states that 'the desire or intention to complete a task successfully establishes a system of tension which both feeds and drives the activity so that the task is not fulfilled' (Gellert and Wilson 2002: 200).

I pay attention to the pupils' demands: Post-it notes might be left on my desk, questions written on the board, which might be questions about organization, exercises for relaxation or stimulation. For example: 'Madame, we've just had a maths test, we need a relaxation exercise', or 'We're tired this afternoon, we need some energy.' I then make these requests a part of the work that I have planned, and we establish the programme together, with objectives to achieve by the end of the session.

Initially surprised by this method of working, the pupils soon enjoy taking their part, moving out of passivity, connecting with their Adult and Free Child. I offer strokes – I congratulate them for their ideas, their creativity and their humour. I take into account the interventions of those in opposition, those who are in a phase of counter-dependence. As we work on our project, the energy circulates among us and promotes a move towards autonomy and OK-ness.

Contracting for individual success or improvement of behaviour

It is this type of contract which I regularly use in the 6th grade as a method of support. The student chooses a subject or a behaviour which they would like to improve, and in doing so I observe how they use their three ego-states. An example:

> 'My project is to improve my grade in maths, it will be useful for me: I want to move up to the next class' (Parent)

> 'I know how to do it and I've decided to do it: to review the lesson the same evening and re-do the exercises (recall); and then ask for explanations' (Adult)

> 'I really want to progress in maths; I will be happy if I succeed' (Child)

I refer back to the ideas of neuro-linguistic programming (NLP) and apply them to a chart which the pupil completes after a shared activity.

TABLE 10.2 Changing behaviours

Current state	Future state (the objective)
Precise description of the issue (Just one problem; a single problem or single incident)	– Stated in the positive – Realistic, no more than 2 points of a improvement per contract – Observable (for example: better attention in class) – Time-bounded (e.g. within 15 days, a month maximum)

The means	Obstacles and sabotages
To decide a way to reach the objective: – Clearly defined – Realistic	– Specific examples

The most difficult phase, and also the funniest – the ingenuity of the Little Professor triggers laughter in the others – is the emergence of sabotage: for example, 'I've got shopping to do this evening . . . well, perhaps I will ask my mother to help . . .' or, 'On getting home from school, I settled down in front of the TV to relax, and then I forget the time . . . '. At the point of feedback, the pupil considers if the methods they have put in place are working or not and adjusts them accordingly. In the process of these stages, my role is to accompany or mentor, to answer their questions. This form of contract renders the pupil the author of their success, which helps progress towards autonomy.

The contract with an individual pupil and his parents

The work with parents and pupils is developed as needed during a meeting with all parties. Each meeting ends, in the case of a problem, with a contract to check during the following session. The concepts that I use are:

- active listening, for conflict resolution (Gordon 1974)
- transactions, for the analysis
- negotiation, as proposed by Ramond (1989: 307–9).

The three-cornered contract (English 1975) may be a 'multi-contract' because it takes into account that 'the relational network, like a system, interacts at different levels: the people present, the implicit agreements, the contracts concluded with different parties' (Sichem 1991: 147).

For example:

> Yvan has very bad results. During the meeting with his parents, his eldest sister, Valerie, proposes to help him, and the aim is the creation of a multi-contract:

- with Yvan: sharing the intention, the content of the work, mini-contract
- with the parents: support to help them in their activity of educational support
- with the sister: definition of the role, time, duration and form of help.

My class-teacher contract with all parents of my year 6 students

At the beginning of each year, I meet the parents to co-create the contract which will contain the various aspects of our collaboration. The aim is to share or learn:

- Detailed information on the programme, the planning and the meetings in the year.
- Taking into account their expectations; for example 'how can we help our children at home?'
- What I bring to them: I take advantage of the time for them to discover my techniques by way of small exercises, methods which they could learn and use in times of difficulty.

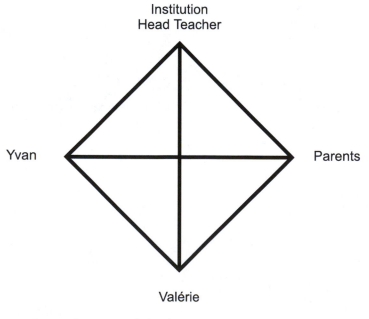

FIGURE 10.3 Contract with family

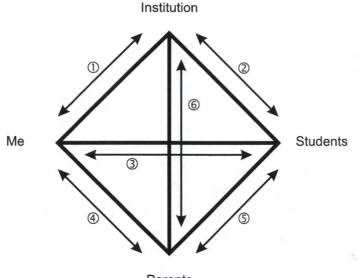

Institution

Me

Students

Parents

FIGURE 10.4 Contract with parents

In fact, it is a double three-way contract which links me to the institution, to the pupils, and to the parents. I present it as follows:

1 My contract with the institution, the college
2 The contract between the college and the pupils
3 The contract between the pupils and myself
4 The contract between the parents and myself.

And what doesn't concern me directly:

5 The contract between the parents and the pupils, that is to say, their children
6 The contract between the college and the parents.

Here is an example of a pastoral care contract with a pupil from the 6th year:
    Contract for Isabelle:

- If you are sick, I commit to taking your homework and explaining the lesson to you.
- Isabelle, I commit to help you and to explain regularly if you have not understood me.
- Made the 14th October 1991
- My telephone number is: 38 xx xx xx xx

Example of a more detailed contract with the 4th year class:

Contract with the 4th year:

- Humour, letting go.
- Respect the rules of non-violence, non-verbal and verbal.
- In case of absence or failure, I commit to help catch up.
- No homework, no writing in the exercise books after being submitted.
- I am responsible for myself.
- Maximum of three things forgotten each term, then, warning at the beginning of a lesson when work has not been done and committing to catch up.
- In case of minor lateness or excuse and apology – I use my discretion.
- Evaluation or test of knowledge on Monday, to ask the previous Thursday at the latest to delay homework.
- Each piece of work done at home can be marked.
- I commit to say the exact number of points that I've had – including negative points.
- I accept confrontation/challenge from the other pupils.
- Possibility for the first 10 minutes of every lesson, taking turns, of either speaking, laughing with what one has in one's heart, in German (or in French if it's a problem in German).
- Accepting of oneself and of others.
- Signed the 10.09.93.

Introducing *gestion mentale*

Once the contracts are in place and there is understanding between the pupils and me, I ask what will enhance the learning? I combine TA with *gestion mentale*, to describe the self-management that students can learn to reinforce their own learning. This is a French term which is taken from the work of Antoine de la Garanderie, who explained:

> The human being must be recognized in his capacity to lead his life by himself and so prove his autonomy . . . the role of the educator, of education, being . . . to reveal the means . . . to lead his life, to become more autonomous.
>
> (de la Garanderie 1991: 57)

I use these self-management techniques combined with other approaches including yoga, relaxation therapy, visualization, to 're-centre' the child in readiness for the learning process; active listening and NLP to conduct dialogue which leads to help and support.

Here is the exercise through which I ground *gestion mentale*, or self-regulation, in my class. The objective for the pupils is to create an awareness of different mental processes, different forms of mental recall which allow students to pay attention, to memorize, understand, reflect, imagine and consequently develop confidence in themselves.

I invite the pupils to close their eyes and to go back to their last year class with their teacher. They relive a pleasurable session where each of their five senses is re-activated. Then, if they want to – the exercise is voluntary – they talk about it. One child, for example:

- Sees his class, his teacher, he describes them (visual third person).
- Sees himself in the class (visual first person or auto-visual).
- Hears his teacher talking, his friends talking (auditory third person).
- Hears himself speak (auditory, first person or auto-auditory).
- Feels his pen in his hand, feels his fingers on his pen (kinaesthetic).

I make them notice that it is quite normal to have difficulty in remembering the type of pen, the smell of the class, since there was no plan. So we make a plan of re-establishing other mental images:

- Perception.
- Pause to allow them time to 'go back inside' (introspective recall).
- New perceptions to check.
- Pause (second recall).
- Return to the present.

Active listening, precise questioning and help with explanations, allow the pupils to be conscious of their lead preference (for example: third person visual). In addition, by articulating the process through the shared conversation, it allows the 'pairs', when it's their turn, to see their own cognitive process more clearly.

Asking them to 'go inside' themselves or 'return into their heads' requires them to introspectively create an image: a phrase; a subtle noise, such as chalk on the board; a taste, for example a fruit. It is often a discovery for some pupils, and they will say among themselves, 'That works!' It helps them to open up. I offer them strokes enthusiastically for participating.

From this moment onwards, the pupils are training themselves on each occasion to recall in order to know how to use their potential. It is in this way that, on re-hearing inside their heads the original word or phrase from the tape or the teacher, they can correct the German pronunciation themselves.

The practice of TA and gestion mentale

From this exercise, protection is established through methods put in place so that the new experience succeeds. Permissions – for example seeing without hearing, hearing without seeing, taking your time and having your own rhythm, pause, practising recalls – allow potency to emerge within the child, demonstrated by their capacity to engage Free Child. In this approach to learning, the pupil passes from dependence to autonomy, as Jacques Dekoninck proposed:

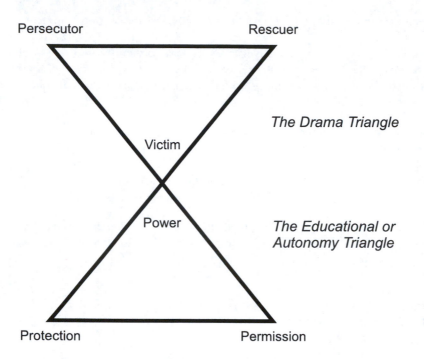

Persecutor   Rescuer

The Drama Triangle

Victim

Power   *The Educational or*
Autonomy Triangle

Protection   Permission

FIGURE 10.5 The Drama Triangle (Karpman 1968) and the Educational Triangle
(Dekoninck 1994)

The teacher . . . teaches the methods of learning and thus acquires another
relational dimension. He no longer says what you have to do: 'Be attentive!'
(P)→(C); but how one becomes attentive: (A)→(A).

(de la Garanderie 1988: 165)

To be attentive is having a plan to give oneself mental images of what one
is perceiving.

(de la Garanderie 1984: 109)

This approach implies an invitation from the teacher to the child to leave the position
I–U+ and move to the I+U+ position through the I+U+ invitation.

The child can say that they don't understand or that they can't manage to
learn a lesson; they are no longer frightened of being annoying or being
judged, because the teacher can help them diagnose the causes and determine
what will lead them to success.

(de la Garanderie 1984: 109)

With a pupil who says that they have not understood, I ask them to start again
with the explanation from the beginning, to know what they have understood

(for which they deserve strokes) just up to the 'sticking-point' – the moment where the explanation is no longer clear.

As for the child who says, 'my head is empty', who is in a state of confusion because they cannot find the text of the lesson, I guide them so that they can 're-see' the image of the manual – from which they can 're-see' a fragment of text, or 're-hear' the instructions. In other words, I give the child a way of reconnecting with his Adult. The pupil who puts together a plan of paying attention, of memorizing for example, is active and therefore avoids passive behaviours (Schiff, 1975):

> *Abstention/Withdrawal*: focused introspective recall is a mental activity and avoids the possibility of being psychologically elsewhere.

> *Over-adaptation*: the child chooses, by way of very clear instructions, to do the mental management exercises according to their own preferences. For example: with the mental exercise of reflection, they have a plan to apply either the rules, to 'say again', or the examples, to 'see again', in relation to the presenting problem.

> *Agitation*: 'the impatient emotion' and 'the paralysing emotion' are produced by a shortcoming or gap in the practice of the mental methodology. This leads the student to recalling differently, and allows them to manage their feelings.
>
> (de la Garanderie, 1987: 106)

Motivation

In the practice of self-management the child aligns their three ego-states accordingly (Ramond 1989: 194–5):

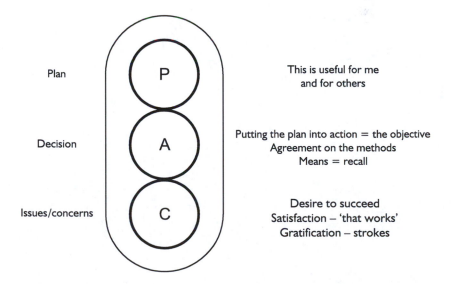

Plan	P	This is useful for me and for others
Decision	A	Putting the plan into action = the objective Agreement on the methods Means = recall
Issues/concerns	C	Desire to succeed Satisfaction – 'that works' Gratification – strokes

FIGURE 10.6 Aligning ego-states (adapted from Ramond 1989: 177)

In conclusion: TA and *gestion mentale*, a happy combination

De la Garanderie (1989) centres his approach on introspection. The introspective recall of the intra-psychic preference enriches the Adult:

TABLE 10.3 Combining TA and *gestion mentale*

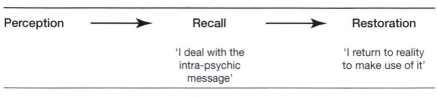

Perception	⟶	Recall	⟶	Restoration
		'I deal with the intra-psychic message'		'I return to reality to make use of it'

The Adult deals with the information that they already have, along with the new information provided via perception which renders them more powerful. De la Garanderie offers an understanding of mental images and provides a technique. However, he neglects the relational aspect which TA brings. I find that TA and *gestion mentale* complement each other and, combined together, are a powerful tool in the field of education.

This chapter is a translation of Deuxième partie, '2: Les différents contrats' from Nicole Pierre's book *Pratique de l'Analyse Transactionelle dans la Classe*, published by ESF éditeur (2002), pages 60–9, with additional material from pages 70–6.

11

USING EDUCATIONAL TRANSACTIONAL ANALYSIS WITH CHILDREN AND YOUNG PEOPLE IN SPECIALIST PROVISION

Giles Barrow, UK

Introduction

When I am teaching transactional analysis to educators, especially schoolteachers, I am often asked if it's possible to introduce TA directly to students. In response to the question I am aware of how teachers have been teaching children TA for several decades in many different contexts; it is a well-worn path. This chapter attempts to contribute to the limited published material describing teaching TA directly to children.

When asked the question, I invite the teacher to check their motivation for sharing TA with students. I have found that often the teacher's enthusiasm for their fresh learning about TA builds a momentum and an impatient desire to go straight back to their class and make the children understand just how important TA can be! When the teacher begins to describe a rationale for working with students a number of issues emerge. Sometimes the teacher begins to talk about behavioural and relational struggles in the class, or instead, it is the emotional needs of one or two students that become a focus. Occasionally a pressing reason is the teacher's frustration at not managing the group as well as they would like. Sometimes the central factor for using TA is to broker a better partnership with other adults, for example parents and colleagues, including in-class support staff. As the discussion unfolds the teacher is drawn into a pre-contracting process that invites them to consider the professional and psychological levels of a possible contract with the children within their school context.

Children on the edge

In my own experience of teaching TA to children I have found those students regarded as at the edge of the mainstream the hungriest in taking up the ideas. By 'the edge' I mean that the school has identified pupils who have poor attendance, or are academically under-performing. It may also refer to children who have additional educational needs, or mental health issues. For some it will be because they are at risk of exclusion, either formally by the school, or socially from their peers. The general sense is that the child experiences some level of struggle in belonging in the classroom, school or to the learning process itself. I have found teaching these children TA a qualitatively different process than when I have been sharing ideas with mainstream classes. At risk of over-simplifying the distinction, mainstream groups of relatively able and stable children demonstrate an enthusiasm for TA and a pleasure in using it to make sense of their relationships with teachers, parents and peers. The higher need group brings a similar enthusiasm, in addition to a keener sense of connection with the models. It is as if transactional analysis gives voice to an unarticulated, yet felt desire to be understood, both internally and in relationship with others.

This distinction becomes clearer still when I have been working in specialist provision – as opposed to mainstream schools. In the UK specialist provision has taken the form of pupil referral units (PRUs) which have been designed for students excluded from schools, or who are long-term non-attenders. It also includes special schools which serve children identified as having a need that is beyond the scope of a mainstream school. Occasionally specialist provision can be found within a mainstream school in the form of an on-site base/unit, or a specially identified group programme. In these instances students are identified as being at risk of exclusion, poor attendance or poor achievement and the on-site arrangements are aimed at preventing further deterioration. For the purposes of this chapter, my attention is focused on using TA directly within specialist contexts. I want to share several stories about this kind of work and in doing so highlight what can be achieved, some of the inherent challenges in the process and consideration of professional and ethical aspects of engaging children with TA.

Giving voice

The earliest experience I have of using TA with young people was with Trudi Newton in a PRU in south London. The provision was specifically targeted at 14–16-year-old students excluded from school and/or at risk of custody. I was a member of staff at the unit and Trudi had been commissioned to deliver an introduction to TA. Unusually, the group was comprised of both staff and students and from the outset it was clear that it would be an exceptional learning experience. Even before the contracting process was fully underway the students began to show signs of powerful involvement. They were surprisingly spirited in their engagement with the notion of three-cornered contracting and declared both a commitment to the group process while also making their needs clear. The language of TA, its use of visual metaphors and diagrams and the ease at which it immediately applied to what is happening, all combined to capture the interest of the young people. The remainder of the day generated a dialogue between students and staff that had not been previously experienced. The constructive and creative potency of the young people took staff by surprise, as did their passion and determination for change. Simultaneously, the young people became increasingly aware of the context in which staff were working. The contract process enabled some students to understand what were limitations within the educational system and to de-personalize their frustration with staff.

This intense response has been typical of similar situations where TA models resonate with the felt yet unarticulated experience of the students. This connection is also made with mainstream groups of students, although for those in specialist provision my sense is that the need for the students to be understood and to become attached, is both greater and less familiar. I find it most helpful to link this keen connection with the concept of physis (Berne, 1957); learning about TA gives voice to the physis energy in the student. It's as if the young person realizes; 'At last, here's a way of describing what happens to me, both to myself, as well as to other important people in my world'.

Ego-states in the moment

I had been working with staff in a secondary school in east London. The school had recently established an on-site base where students at risk of exclusion could be re-engaged with learning, experience better relationships with staff and return to mainstream lessons. The provision was staffed by a small group of learning mentors. One of my visits was due soon after opening the provision. My plan was to meet with the mentors and consider how TA might best be used directly with referred students.

I arrived in mid-morning, during the school day and met the four mentors in the empty classroom at the base. We had arranged a cup of coffee and were just scoping out the purpose of the session when the door of the room burst open and a student stormed into the room declaring, 'Miss, I am NOT going back to that lesson! That guy should never have been allowed to teach – he can't teach us anything and he's gone and kicked me out!' So began a tirade of anger from the young man, who I will call Tom. The mentors and I were initially taken by surprise as we were not expecting interruptions. Clearly the student was upset and not ready to return to the classroom, nor be sent anywhere else at that moment. It was also evident that despite having been operational for a short time, the provision was already being regarded as potentially safe by students.

The mentors soon became apologetic to me for the disruption to our meeting and we were unsure of quite what to do. The student briefly paused having exhausted his profane and comprehensive criticism of the teacher's incompetence. Here was a moment, I thought. I asked if it was OK to join the discussion and reached for a white cotton sheet I was using in my work. I spread it out on the floor and on it revealed in large print two ego-state diagrams alongside each other on the sheet. Between Tom, the mentors and myself we began to explore first the idea of ego-states and then, second, the dynamic of transactions. Throughout the exercise we stepped into and across the large ego-state diagrams on the floor sheet.

After several relapses into Adapted Child rebellion, Tom gradually began to restore an Adult awareness. He began to integrate his justified anger with a need to regulate in order to stay in relationship. At first his focus was in achieving this balance with the mentors and myself before considering how he might transfer this new-found groundedness with his teacher. Crucially, the mentors began to use the sheet to explore how they would support both Tom and his teacher in this process. What struck me most about the episode with Tom was the immediacy of his learning about TA. It spoke to his condition with vital urgency. He now had the language, the framework and the options which he had previously lacked.

TA and care in education

Empowering educators using TA to provide care to vulnerable students is a theme that has interested me in teaching TA directly to students in specialist provision. Several schools have used TA in providing students with a route back into the heart of school life and the joy of learning. The following case studies illustrate how schools can extend their impact beyond the limitations of exclusive academic agendas.

In the early 2000s an experiment was carried out in west London. A middle school headteacher decided to use TA as the over-arching model for how the school went about establishing, understanding, promoting and repairing relationships and her experience was subsequently published (Rosewell 2003). There were several outcomes, in terms of individual pupils, whole school performance and staff development. There was also a resource created for teaching TA to children, a TA Scheme of Work. This material formed the basis of similar initiatives from which emerged the TA Proficiency Award for Children and Young People (TAPACY).

TAPACY was, and continues to be, operated by the Institute of Developmental Transactional Analysis (IDTA) in the UK. It is a programme aimed at introducing children to TA and encourages them in understanding and applying basic concepts to their lives at school. The IDTA arranges a moderation and award ceremony at which students receive a certificate and badge in recognition of their involvement in the scheme. Initially trialled in east London, the scheme has now been introduced across the UK, several European countries, Taiwan and South Africa.

The case studies I want to focus on are from the earlier groups involved in TAPACY. A small number of PRUs provide for a minority of children who have significant mental health difficulties. These children may have high levels of anxiety, eating disorders, phobias and other internalized disturbance. For most they will neither be able to attend mainstream school, nor meet the criteria for long-term specialist provision because they are too vulnerable. It was one of these small units that formed part of a group of schools involved in TAPACY. All of the young people involved at the unit were in their last years of statutory schooling and the aim of teaching them TA was to support them in preparing for transition back to school for final examinations, or to post-school options. The tutor at the unit was in regular TA supervision and often expressed a combination of apprehension on behalf of this especially vulnerable group, while being hopeful that staff could make a difference. All students came from poor backgrounds, with several coming from families where mental ill-health was inter-generational.

Engaging some of the students in learning about TA was a challenge in itself, let alone inviting them to join children from other schools to moderate and celebrate their work. On this occasion the event involved over seventy children from primary and secondary schools. Despite this potentially intimidating environment, the power of the learning and sense of achievement was so great that all but one of the students at the unit came along.

During the moderation session children and adults were given time and encouragement to circulate and give strokes to each other, based on the work and experience of the TAPACY programme. Again, despite this exposure, the students from the unit took part and proudly accepted their certificates and badges. The group's tutor wrote sometime later:

> I wanted to update you about the use of TAPACY in our unit. This is the third year of our following the course and every year we are adapting and learning something new. We are now a little more confident in exposing ourselves, learning and working alongside our students . . . We enjoy the challenge as do our students.
>
> The students seem to enjoy the course and have made great progress. Do you remember Dennis – a tall young man who was very damaged and traumatized by a variety of social and emotional factors, not least of which was having parents with chronic mental health issues? He entered into the TAPACY course, initially very reluctantly, with our clear focus being 'moving on', hopeful at that at some stage returning to school would be possible. He was incredibly nervous at the accreditation ceremony but was absolutely thrilled to receive the certificate and badge. Dennis chose the affirmation: 'Moving on is a normal part of growing up' and used to carry this in his school coat pocket. Dennis returned to school part-time and has been there for over a year. He is due to take ten GCSEs this summer and then A-levels, then university. Then the World!
>
> He benefitted from the TAPACY course and still carries the affirmation and has his certificate proudly displayed in his bedroom . . .

The story of Dennis demonstrates how TA provided both him and his tutor with a language and framework that enabled care in learning. While care might be regarded as an obvious feature of all learning relationships, for students on the edge of school life a more systematic and concerted approach is often needed. Many teachers will not have a way of thinking about how to create such an approach, which is why TA can be so beneficial.

A second example, drawn from the TAPACY programme, is that of a primary school in an inner city area. In this case the school identified a small number of children who were experiencing significant disruption in their lives outside school and who were presenting challenges in the classroom. The children were all in the penultimate year of primary school and it was felt that teaching them TA during the summer term might help get the best from them in their following, last year in junior school.

The children learned about ego-states, 'windows on the world' (Hay 1995), strokes and affirmations. They were supported in using these concepts in the playground and classroom, and staff became increasingly impressed with how the behaviour and attitude of the children changed in such a positive way. Eventually the group was presented with a special task. They would be the TA ambassadors for the rest of the school during their last year. Having achieved the TAPACY award they were positioned as the in-house experts in TA, which began to be shared across the whole school. Younger pupils learned TA from these older students who took on the role of peer mentors. From being out on the margins of the school life, this group became central to its work on improving relationships.

Both of these accounts, drawn from work with disadvantaged students, show the dividends for both the individual pupils specifically, and the school generally. Staff experienced change and development as a result of getting alongside students and teaching TA. Most schools have not needed to adopt the TAPACY programme to be successful in using TA, although it provides an organized approach to doing so. In either case, sharing the language of TA becomes a powerful tool for all involved where it is most needed.

Professional and ethical issues

There are several considerations regarding professional practice and ethical aspects of teaching TA to children. In all of the case studies previously discussed the contracting process was critical in ensuring success. To return to the opening of this chapter, reflecting on teacher motivation for sharing TA with children is absolutely crucial. This might be self-evident; however, it is surprising how quickly educators can discuss TA with children without pre-empting important questions about why the work is taking place.

Linked to clarifying the underlying rationale, accounting for the wider context in the contracting process is important in terms of ensuring ethical practice. There have been some reports of where children have been introduced to TA concepts by enthusiastic visiting teachers, only to find that students rapidly become more literate in classroom dynamics than their class teacher. Similarly, a school may see the need to teach children ego-states and overlook the importance of discussing the project with parents. This again can lead to problems where children have a language-specific model to deconstruct what goes on at home which carries the potential for confusion. Being clear across all parties about purpose, language and application can forestall problems.

In the UK most teachers are trained in a curriculum model of teaching. This is often in the absence of training in learning through process. Working directly with children using TA requires confidence and competence in understanding and working with process. Many teachers I have worked with have been anxious about teaching TA because they mistakenly believe that 'knowing' everything about TA is a pre-requisite for teaching it. It is extremely important that this frame of reference is challenged if children are to really learn about TA. Students do best where the educator is prepared to get alongside them and be open to 'not knowing it all', and this is especially the case when they are learning TA. Students need to have a sense that there is room for their experience, their creative response, and the freedom to co-create with the teacher. An important consequence of this alternative frame of reference is that teachers using TA with children will best safeguard their practice through taking supervision. This is particularly pertinent regarding a final consideration.

Teaching TA to children is different from engaging children in TA psychotherapy. Again, this might be self-evident, but deserves attention. For the most part, children attend school primarily to learn. The social contract is educational, and this needs to be accounted for when embarking on an intervention. Obviously, TA has its potential as a psychotherapeutic method of work, but for the most part it is an inappropriate application in the context of the classroom. Consequently educators need to be doubly sure that the contract and its delivery are clearly educational in terms of substance and direction. This is not to rule out the possibility of therapeutic impact. In each of the narratives featured in this chapter there has arguably been a shift in the individual's frame of reference that might be explained in terms of therapeutic process, but the contracts throughout are essentially to support learning.

One practical strategy for dealing with this when working with children is to set up activities that expressly invite reflection on the student's experience of school or learning. In other words, the arena set out for intervention is boundaried within the limits of school life. This is helpful in creating safety for both educator and learner; that the personal and home arenas will not be subject to investigation. The child might choose to refer to non-school matters and relate ideas outside of the learning, but the educator does not provoke these incursions into the private world of the young person. Second, it is worthwhile in raising a discussion among staff about the difference between psychotherapy and educational work. This keeps the boundary issue alive and at the forefront of the practitioner's mind during the programme.

Summary

Teaching children TA can be a powerful intervention if the educator establishes a clear multi-dimensional contract with all parties. Furthermore, children experiencing difficulties in schooling and learning are especially receptive to transactional analysis. For educators thinking about using TA in their practice there are important considerations, primarily regarding motivation and purpose. Where these considerations are built into the planning and delivery, educators can reach further into reducing barriers to success for students most challenged by the schooling process.

12

INTERCULTURAL LEARNING AND TEACHING IN MULTICULTURAL CLASSES

Sylvia Schachner, Austria

Introduction: The meaning of intercultural learning for schools

Picture the scene of a contemporary classroom in a central European primary school. You would see about twenty-five pupils, running around, sitting in groups, writing, drawing, playing and talking away with one another. There would be books and other learning materials with lots of pictures and letters and numbers. You would also see one, two or more adults interacting with the children – either as a whole group or with individuals. You wonder what's going on. The children come from five or more different countries, speaking four or more different languages – but often not the teaching language – and coming from different national, social and educational cultures. This is the multicultural classroom, typical of so many in Europe. Learning and teaching in multicultural classes is a very current pedagogic issue. It is also a social and cultural subject which greatly influences everyday life. Intercultural learning concerns all Europeans, regardless of age, gender or profession; this subject has importance to us all.

Changes in our social systems are happening. The most pertinent current questions are, how are they to be managed and understood, and how can we best use the resources they present? 'Foreign workers' become 'staying guests', sometimes living in one country for two or three generations but still seen as 'the other'; and there continue to be people needing to leave their home countries because of war, necessity, hardship or other crises. Consequently, a lot of children from very different backgrounds are living and learning together: in some schools we find more than 70 per cent of students with a migrant background. As these developments continue, those children with knowledge of only one language and one culture will become a minority; and it is these children who will most need special support in a multicultural society.

Already today, it is usual to find places and situations in which people from different cultural backgrounds meet, live, work and spend their free time together. We find different cultures, rules and values within families, organizations and schools; These are sometimes conflicting and significantly divergent. There are explicit and implicit boundaries; instead of being integrated, people live side by side, separate, in different classes, different schools and different language patterns. Strangeness and difference grow rather than becoming less so, or developing into something new. Experience from the past shows us the danger of living side by side without any understanding of, or interest in, the other; consequences may include racism, fundamentalism and terrorism. We need to account for these things in our role as educators.

Intercultural learning and TA

To handle such intercultural complexities demands differentiated approaches, attentiveness, awareness of processes and flexible strategies for interaction.

The relevance of intercultural learning is linked to the basic assumption of transactional analysis. Models of TA offer many possibilities to address these challenges, in terms of planning, reflecting on learning situations, and in-the-moment decision-making. We can create the basis of a vision for living together in a good way, growing out of human rights and the TA ethical framework, in which everybody is equal, everyone can think, and individuals can make decisions irrespective of their nationality, gender, religion or age.

The key questions that are explored in this chapter include:

- How does the personal frame of reference have to change, and how does this impact on the social frame of reference?
- How does our thinking, feeling and behaviour have to change, what changes in the ego-states are necessary?
- What decontaminations are necessary in order to realize the basic assumptions?
- What new decisions are necessary to solve problematic aspects of script behaviour and become increasingly autonomous, interacting with people with different manners, values and rules?
- How do we manage the challenge to interact from an authentic OK+-OK+ position?
- What strategies and methods of contracting can be used to solve problems and conflicts in a constructive way?

None of these questions can be answered generally. Individuals develop their own answers, based on individual experience, individual script and frames of reference. The next step is a critical evaluation of the values, the norms and assumptions of the individual. Using Adult assessment, it extends to cover the organization – the school – and the wider political and social system. The goal is *intercultural competence*, which is composed of three elements:

- *emotional* competence: *awareness* of one's own culture and its values and rules, awareness of personal feelings and emotions
- *cognitive* competence: *knowledge* about other cultures, experience from travelling, speaking foreign languages
- *aptitude* competence: *capability*, behaviour, strategies.

Intercultural competence includes knowledge of the resources and limitation of one's own culture, to have a measure for differences and similarities and to describe and value cultural information. Feeling safe, understanding situations and finding meaning are fundamental.

When these capacities are absent, individuals tend to generalize, building stereotypes and acting in rigid ways and misinterpreting situations. This cultural knowledge is passed from generation to generation, including strategies for communication, behaviour and attitudes. This knowledge forms part of a national mindset and is strongest in more traditional communities. Globalization diminishes this at a superficial level, but it continues in a deep and unconscious dimension; for assessing and interpreting situations, it is necessary to validate both the individual and their cultural background.

Implications for educational transactional pedagogy?

At present the following situation is typical of classrooms throughout Europe:

- About 25 or more children between 5 and 7 years start the first year of school together.
- Most of them have spent several years in kindergarten, some of them an additional year in pre-school.
- In these pre-school institutions they have had different experiences with learning, expectations about behaviour and strategies for success, combined with their family experiences. These can be diverse, and they are deeply anchored.
- Children have begun to build a first assumption about themselves, their role in a group, and their learning abilities.
- Some children have become over-adapted, while others struggle to obey rules.
- Many pupils will neither speak nor understand the teaching language.
- Some of them have had traumatic experiences leaving their homelands, or because of problems within their family.

Children and teenagers spend a total of about 10,000 hours in schools. If these hours are to be beneficial, the first contact with educational establishments is very important.

Commonly, parents have strong feelings, expectations and, occasionally, anxiety how their child will manage their first steps outside the family. As the child begins school, the opportunity arises to integrate with cultures different from that of the parental home and their own cultural background. An attitude of OK-ness, openness and curiosity towards different ideas and an objective sense of observation are basics for success. Kindergarten teachers create space for learning (potency), safe rooms (protection), and an invitation to discover, to learn, to pose questions, to think and to grow up (permission). There is space for development – and for learning the teaching language. Projects that include the parents are especially successful.

Specialities of multicultural classes

a) For teachers

Berne described the different stages of group development as 'imagos', the mental pictures we carry. For teachers, it is important to know their individual inner beliefs about being a 'good teacher', the attributes of a 'good' class and of 'good teaching' – beliefs often constructed on the basis of personal school experiences and previous experience of teaching.

The following questions are helpful to find personal answers and to update existing imagos:

- What pictures do I have as a result of my professional role as a teacher?
- Which parts of my beliefs come from my own school experience?
- Are these beliefs significant for today's teaching, for the present conditions?
- What are the expectations of the institution where I am working?
- What are my preferred pedagogic models, and are they connected to the beliefs of the institution in which I currently work?

At the same time as teachers have pictures and beliefs about school life, and associated strategies for being successful (or not), pupils and parents bring their own experiences and beliefs. Where these pictures were similar in the past, they may not be so today. Philosophy, goals of teaching, and expected behaviour in schools, can differ sharply, either at national or international levels.

b) For pupils

New situations evoke stress and activate script behaviour. Some children over-adapt, others show bravado behaviour. This particularly develops if children don't understand – or don't quite understand – the teaching language. In multicultural classes, between 70 and 90 per cent of children speak two or three languages – but not the teaching language. These children are multilingual, and yet have a reduced capacity for speaking. Sometimes they speak their known languages incorrectly, so their intuitive knowledge of the teaching language is subsequently reduced. They have a lot of experience of travel across different cultures and a great flexibility to accommodate to different situations; however, they lack a deeper knowledge of the cultural frames of reference of countries in which they have lived. As a result, there can be imbalanced development with a wide range of difference. Based on family circumstances and their first experiences in kindergarten or preschool, they may have developed differing rules and strategies to generate strokes.

The first weeks in school can be turbulent and stressful. It takes a lot of time and effort to build up a working group. Communication with children with no knowledge of the teaching language demands creative new strategies. It is important to be very clear in speech and gesticulation, and to use visual support. Children may use the body language and behaviour of younger children to get contact with others. It is necessary to discriminate between aggressive behaviour and contact behaviour. The learning steps have to be very clear, supported by visual and non-verbal signals, and orientated to the individual's potential. Step by step language competence is built up in connection with reading and writing competence.

The diversity of experience and the different strategies to get attention can be used as models for flexibility and tolerance. In everyday life, children have contact with others' alternative frames of reference. Together with guidance from the teacher, they construct common rules and values in their classes. These values can be integrated in the homeland values, but children can also learn to 'stand alongside them', and figure how to switch between different cultural attitudes. This needs a lot of time and effort and, in effect, models the establishing of a constructive Parent ego-state.

Different levels of development and language capacity stimulate new teaching methods, flexibility and creativity. From the beginning, children need additional individual learning programmes, working in small groups with various tasks, supporting one another in an atmosphere where there is permission to think, to experiment and to make mistakes. Tasks differentiated according to the capacity of each child increase self-confidence and offer permission to think and learn. Positive strokes are helpful to promote a positive motivation for learning and working.

TA models helpful for teaching – how it works

I have 25 years' experience teaching in primary school, 15 of them using TA models in the classroom. Here, I present the situation of a typical class in a primary school in Vienna, and describe ways to handle this complex situation using TA approaches.

Twenty-five 6-year-old children start in the first class. We find a group of Asian children, over-adapted and used to saying 'Yes' to everything, avoiding speaking without being asked and very polite. Another group of boys from eastern Europe are used to being first, use strong body language, move a lot and take a lot of space. A group of children with an Islamic background follow their religious and cultural rules, bringing a lot of gender-orientated conventions and behaviour with them.

Seven of the children do not speak or understand German, ten have little knowledge of the language, while the others have sufficient to get by. The vocabulary differs from expressing understandable phrases to elaborate description.

Some of the children were previously at a Montessori kindergarten. They are very organized, used to expressing their needs and choosing their activities in a self-orientated way. At the same time, they are not used to following common rules or doing things they do not want to do at a particular moment. Others have rarely taken any decisions for themselves, and have few strategies to organize their affairs. Some of the children are experiencing family problems, such as the divorce of parents, loss of a family member, birth of brothers and sisters, changing their home, city or country. Each of the children has their personal history, their personal resources or frailties and their own strategies to get attention. All of them are excited, perhaps anxious or nervous about the new situation.

Applying TA models

1   *OK–OK approach*: Using OK-ness is more than a gesture; it demands an attitude of openness and an acceptance of the whole person with all the individual's resources and limitations, and the opening of a space for development. Non-verbal communication, gesticulation and tone of voice are paramount. Short, clear transactions give orientation. Confrontation is in three steps: first, stopping unwanted behaviour, second giving a clear description of the preferred behaviour and, finally, a positive stroke when a modification of behaviour is made. In doing so, it is clear that the classroom is a protected and safe space for everyone.

> *Example:* The first day in school is a special and very important moment. Every child finds a name label and a little present at their place. The teacher speaks to every child personally in a friendly way, using short and simple phrases. The teacher first gives opportunities to demonstrate the knowledge and resources that have been brought into school, with questions like: What do you expect to learn at school? Do you know some letters or numbers? Do you want to show us? Children are offered permission to think and to experiment, and the furnishing of the room and its atmosphere show that every child is welcome.

2   *Contracting for the classroom*: The aim is to create a culture for the group which is helpful for living and working together. From the beginning, there are two important non-negotiable rules;

- no violence
- nobody will be shamed or derided.

Following on from this are some behaviour rules and strategies, such as asking for support, working together, solving conflicts, apologizing. These will be built up through role-play games, in exercises, in presenting sentence structures and in contracting for activities.

Example: The first weeks of school are over. In the classroom, the two important rules are established. One boy has a way of running into other children and colliding with their schoolbags or bodies, then running away, shouting and laughing. Here is a good opportunity for the teacher to give an example of a resource-orientated confrontation. The teacher describes the behaviour; instead of seeing the behaviour as interference, they propose other assumptions: Do you want to be in contact with the other child? Are you angry about something? Do you want to play? When, together, they find an answer, the teacher can stop the undesirable behaviour and establish a new, more effective one.

3   *Observation or meta-perspective*: Knowing about different cultures and their behaviour, finding out about the distinct ways of constructing meaning and strategies, prevents labelling behaviour and using stereotypes for interpretation. Questioning observed behaviour, describing it and sharing the child's own thinking, enlarges the frame of reference and avoids misunderstanding. It is important to use the Adult ego-state! Pupils see a model for handling complex situations and diversity in a good way.

Example: The teacher observes that a Japanese girl is sitting in her place without speaking, without eye contact. When the teacher speaks directly to her, she doesn't look at him. She seems to be sad, anxious or bored. When she is playing with other pupils in the break, she is happy and has good contact to the others. Because of experience with school culture in Asia, the teacher knows that this pupil is attentive and focused, and showing the behaviour of a 'good' Asian pupil. To help her adapt her behaviour, the teacher tells her directly, but in a very polite and careful way, what she has to do. She is also used to saying 'Yes', and in the way she does so the teacher can recognize whether she really means yes, or is over-adapting – in which case the teacher shares their observation and encourages her to say 'No'. All the children have an opportunity to speak and decide, not just the powerful ones.

4   *Clear and heedful transactions*: Communication is a meeting point between different cultures, through language, personal style and professional technical terms. Using the same words doesn't always carry the same meaning. Every speaker is orientated by his own reality and often assumes that the other shares this reality. In important teaching situations, as well as in talks with parents, there is an intensive dialogue. Repeating questions and using active listening are helpful, so that dialogue slows down and became rigorous and clear. The frame of reference of the dialogue is opened and a deeper understanding grows up.

In every profession there is a certain vocabulary, including shortened messages and phrases to organize situations. There are also lots of unspoken rules and expected behaviours.

In multicultural class contexts it is especially important to speak more about rules and expectations, including explanations about our thinking, our observation and presumptions. On the other hand, it is also important to ask questions about the experiences that the children and parents have had before with school systems.

5 *Learning contracts and individual learning goals; the promotion of autonomy.* The often diverse situations of children require on the one hand a clear structure and clear rules, and on the other, opportunities for individualized learning. Multi-professional teams work with different learning levels to support language acquisition, and children are invited from the start to support each other to design learning processes and to achieve learning strategies.

> *Example:* The first year is almost over. The children have become a group, learning, working and playing together. They have a confident attachment with the teachers and some experience with different methods of learning. 'Becoming a good reader' is one of the important goals of the first year. Significant differences have emerged by this point. Two reading lessons per week are 'free' lessons. The teacher has contracts with the children for the learning needs during this week, such as becoming familiar with two or three new letters, working at reading texts containing familiar words, or reading new texts and solving tasks in order to understand content.

6 *Discount levels:* it is possible pick up the pupils precisely where they are positioned in the learning state or in problem behaviour. By recognizing and bringing into awareness (and challenging the discounts around) the existence of these issues, it becomes possible to develop tailor-made solutions.

> *Example:* In the second year the understanding of situations, and of children's feelings and expressions, comes into focus. During the break, two boys begin to fight. They are shouting, swearing and very angry. The teacher stops the fighting immediately and separates the two boys. For conflict-solving he uses several stages. Both of the boys consider the following stages of the episode, while the teacher avoids taking sides.

a. Expression of the problem situation, expression of the feelings in an emotional way. Here the children are allowed to shout or to show their anger, but without hurting or touching the other person.
b. Exploring what the intentions were of the children involved in this situation. My experience indicates that it is useful to ask, 'What did you want to achieve?' instead of, 'Why did you do this?'
c. Finding better ways to achieve a solution.
d. Contracting for new behaviour and reviewing later if it works.
e. These steps of conflict-solving can be done orally in the present, or later on, when the agreed steps can be written down.

7   *Passive behaviour* is a widely diffused phenomenon, particularly in the context of traditional schooling. The pupils listen to the teacher explaining and finding solutions. The pupils do not understand, and the helpful teacher shows the right answers. Here it is important to remember the famous slogan of Maria Montessori: 'Help me to do it for myself' (Montessori 1991).

> *Example:* A maths lesson, in the second year. The pupils have to solve different tasks, all of which are familiar to the children who have also been well prepared. A boy and girl are sitting and not working for several minutes. The boy is playing with his pencils, the girl looking around helplessly. Behind them, three other children begin to speak and tease each other. Suddenly one of them screams, 'I hate maths, I hate school!' All of them are demonstrating passive behaviours to avoid working.

The teacher does not stroke any of this behaviour. Instead she forms a group with these five children, sitting with them, and says, 'We will work together for ten minutes to solve these problems'. She poses different questions in a resource-orientated way, without thinking for the children or explaining too much. She strokes every right answer and encourages the work. After ten minutes, the teacher asks the children, who are now working, how they want to continue, and strokes their efforts.

8   *Dealing with feelings*: Common to all people is the perception of four basic emotions: fear, sadness, anger and joy; however, there are differences in the way in which, and the depth to which, feelings are permitted to be expressed across different cultural contexts. Some children and young people with a migrant background may have been exposed to traumatic experiences. The move to another country may have come about without warning or preparation, and in difficult circumstances. Experiences in the home country remain unprocessed, the children and their parents are traumatized. There are also psychological and linguistic barriers to speaking about and processing their experiences. With this group of children, transactional analysis for working with emotions may be useful to identify excessive, inadequate, or lack of, expression of feelings. Employing emotional competence and support to express the teacher's own feeling and thinking, is an important area of personal work incorporating the permission to think and feel. This developmental experience can became part of personal and social competency, and can be integrated across cultural frames of reference.

> *Example:* The expression of feelings is a good introduction to social competence behaviour. In different stages, the children learn to name their feelings and to show them to the others. A set of cards, designed in the art lesson, helps to make their own feelings visible and to find simple phrases about them. With the help of pictures, but also through drama, children learn to express and to handle different emotional situations, they learn in a playful way to take care of others, be sensitive and to handle emotional situations.

9 *Frame of reference*: In the school curriculum, there are many topics that can be used on a large or small scale to support the positive co-existence of different nationalities. Imagining one's own country, learning a basic vocabulary in another language, reading children's books and hearing the speech, celebrations in the typical style of a country, are just a few examples. In a playful, robust way, not only is knowledge extended, but also tolerance and curiosity about the unknown are encouraged.

Summary

My experience of teaching multicultural classes has been both challenging and enriching. The language barriers and differing experience of children and young people can be especially complicating in the first weeks of teaching. More time needs to be devoted to establishing rules and structures; the group phases are stormy and often unpredictable. Due to the limited vocabulary, there are often conflicts that are played out non-verbally, and it can require creativity and ingenuity to handle them. Learning content must be developed more intensively and be differentiated, and teaching plans must be well prepared. Use of gestures and visual teaching material must be reinforced, and the learning content must be offered in smaller learning steps. The learning groups are heterogeneous and individual learning receives more attention from the start; this also requires increased preparatory work on the part of the teacher. Teamwork with colleagues is of great importance, as is first-language instruction – additional instruction in the teaching language and supportive incentives have to be coordinated well to be efficient.

It is also important to see the opportunities this form of teaching offers. From the beginning, children learn to handle different frames of reference and different ways to construct reality. Imperceptibly, practice in everyday situations trains tolerance and expands children's knowledge about the world. Dealing with others with childlike ingeniousness reduces fear, and teaches them the many similarities of people despite their different modes of expression. Children play, especially in the first years of life, similar games and experience similar stages of development. People have similar desires and longings as they think, decide and develop.

The complex conditions in school and classes today are practice areas and images of our complex world. They prepare children adequately to be successful in a globalized world. In those teachers who exemplify tolerance, diversity and appreciation, they have good models to overcome racism and intolerance. Multicultural classes and schools can be the basis for a new society in which the coexistence of different people is self-evident.

In transactional analysis pedagogy there are many elements that are essential for ensuring that learning and living together in the school succeed. Students practise learning strategies and different ways of working. Passive behaviour is confronted. By knowing the discount levels, the learner can be challenged at an appropriate level to support accounting. Students experience and learn confrontation culture, and gain insight into interviewing and conflict training. They have an opportunity to share their culture of origin and their characteristics in the classroom, and experience appreciation. Children's frame of reference is extended. From the beginning, children learn strategies and behaviour to act in an autonomous way in the here-and-now context of the classroom. Such a colourful and vibrant education system can make a significant contribution to the integration, and the wealth and resources, of a multicultural society.

13

FAMILY CONSTELLATIONS IN EDUCATION

Jacqueline Goosens, Belgium; with Trudi Newton, UK

TN: Jacqueline, I know that, as well as being an educational TSTA, you also work with family constellations. How to you relate constellations to TA?

JG: The family systems approach is systemic, that is to say it is oriented towards the individual, and at the same time always towards the various systems to which they belong: family system, ancestral, tribal, ethnic or national. This immediately connects to script, cultural script and cultural Parent (Drego 1983). Bert Hellinger, the founder of constellation work, was inspired by psychodrama and role-playing, and also by TA – Hellinger worked with Fanita English for a time (Hellinger and Horel 2001). Other influences are ethno-psychiatry and symbolization, as well as psycho-magical healing work known by traditional communities.

Family constellations emphasize the power of the system on the individual. The process regards the morphic field as composed of the awareness of spaces, structures and of the relationships existing between living and deceased individuals as well as current, past and future events. A morphic field of resonance is a process whereby organisms inherit a memory from previous, similar systems, such as families – or classrooms.

The familial system is a force field within which we live and grow. It determines our personal way of thinking, acting and feeling. Each family system is determined by the whole past of our family: parents, grandparents, ancestors, their respective thinking-schemes, beliefs, religion, nationality, and ethnic group. This force field is structured by significant events of these individuals' lives. These may include: illnesses, abortions, miscarriages, death of children, suicides, accidents, wars, adoptions, incest, an ancestor guilty of or victim of a crime, psychiatric placement and detention in jail.

TN: So you link this to family scripts and imagos?

JG: Yes. Positive and generous actions give a balance to the force field and reinforce its strength. The health of a system will be indicated by the presence of life, freedom, and creativity as well as solidarity, human warmth, interdependence. No one is guilty in a system, although some are responsible. We are not guilty of our thoughts, actions, beliefs generated by previous generations' experiences; however, we are responsible for transmitting them in a conscious way.

These statements are valid in any system, institution or association, and they appear in Berne's organizational theory (Berne 1963); there is a similarity between constellations and imagos.

TN: I see that, and it seems to me that constellation work is a lively way of using imago theory. What sort of circumstances do you encounter?

JG: Trauma is an event that often happens without any warning – people experience a shock: sudden bereavement for instance. Behaviours appear as a protection in answer to the shock and are passed into the whole system in an unconscious way. There are four biological responses to a trauma: fight, flight, freeze and fragmentation.

An example of flight is Christelle's family, where the mother developed an inappropriate fear of any medical symptom. She interpreted them as a death threat and kept going to the doctor, hoping for a dramatic diagnosis that would allow her to justify her permanent stress.

Going back in the history, it was possible to identify the origin of this behaviour, going back to a trauma. In this case, two generations ago, a mother died giving birth and the unconscious memory of that event continues to fuel Christelle's mother's behaviour.

In some families, there is a freezing or despair which may show as an indifference towards a child; there is a blank look in their eyes. It is not uncommon that a succession of early deaths has taken place: a parent dying before their children are grown up, a child deceased as a baby or a series of dead children. Again, in that case a restitution of the familial history can relieve the isolation, remove the guilt and the shame from the child.

TN: So how do you detect these traumas?

JG: There are three 'roots of being' we can identify to help us detect trauma and design healing interventions.

First, the root of *clan, land and ancestors*, which naturally connects to the cultural script (Drego 1983). The knowledge of the familial history which meets and intersects with global history, nationality and cultures, the origins of beliefs, but also sufferings – above all in adolescence when existential questions are raised about how to become a man or a woman.

What constellations have demonstrated to me is the recognition of the seriousness of traumatic death: an abortion, a miscarriage as a result of an illness or an accident, the serious impact of a hospitalization, a birth, challenges that ended well – but during which fears of death that were not expressed. Here at last the word is mentioned: fears of death cause the system to vibrate and disturb the spirit, the soul and the body of descendants. It is as if life is not totally available for the descendants, a 'piece' of humankind is missing, caught in the earlier dramas.

Fortunately, resources often lie behind these traumas. Back in school, history and geography lessons can be so important in reconnecting these dramas to the full life that stands beneath them, for example by re-playing a piece of history – as in this story:

> Monique, a teacher in primary school invites the 8–10-year-old children to work on the origin of their village, based on the steel industry. It involved emigration experiences for the forty or more workers coming from Italy, Portugal and, later, Morocco. The children put on a show; they prepared a video telling the history of the village and revisited their familial stories. This experience gave them a strong feeling of belonging and also recognition of an earlier life's reality, its dramas and joys. They ended up more aware of their humanity and of the strength of historical events lived by those that have existed in the past and, most importantly, by their own ancestors.

Second, there is the *familial root* consisting of four generations: father and mother, brothers and sisters, grandparents, and great-grandparents.

TN: This is where we talk about family script and epi-script, as Fanita English described?

JG: You can see it in this way. Before the age of three, before the establishment of script and the consequent discounting and the formation of beliefs about themselves, others and the world, a child should have an emotional access to their history. The child needs information, and will express their curiosity and emotions. When they feel supported in expressing themselves, they will return to their natural position. This involves becoming aware of the deaths, accidents, difficult births, times when child and mother were in danger, as well as love stories with their happy – or unhappy – endings.

In their early years, before the age of five or six, family traumas are felt by children and if they can't put words and emotions to them, they won't know what 'belongs' to them or to somebody else. Constellations are helpful to identify what the feeling is about, what children may carry without knowing it, and without their parents noticing it.

> Nadine is an adopted child; she was abandoned by her mother when she was born. In the USA, at that time, when a mother decided to give up her child she couldn't go back on her decision and the baby was taken away immediately. The delivery was done under general anaesthetic; mother and baby were put to sleep in order to avoid any contact. The child was afterward entrusted to adopting parents. Nadine went through teenage years experiencing a fear of death, with suicide threats and suicide attempts, the origin of which she found only in re-living her birth. Even though this information was available, and her

adopting parents knew it all along, they remained unaware of the emotional impact of these events on the child.

A child has a high potential for learning and transformation; for example, when guided in the expression of their emotions with empathy, they can regulate their emotional states through play. They need to be supported by their parents to work it out; they can learn how to create a happy ending to their story in an emotional and relational dimension by experiencing sufficient recognition. They can connect with their emerging humanity and develop a strong feeling of security, empathy for themselves and others – loving and trusting in life. This process connects with the developmental stages described by Pamela Levin: the child becomes a human being among human beings in every dimension when they get the emotional and cognitive information they need (Levin 1982; Clarke and Dawson 1998).

> Emerson (1998), an American therapist, born by caesarean, developed a specific technique for supporting the emotional expression of a traumatic birth through very simple movements and appropriate empathy.
>
> This is also the intention of various psychomotricity practices. In French-speaking countries, 'psychomotricity' is a term used to define specific activities offered to children to develop various abilities linked with the body: the purpose is not to achieve a desired physical outcome but to promote a holistic experience; movement is considered as a direct result of an internal process of perception and management of emotions and experiences. A psychomotrician may for example invite children up to the age of eight to play with tunnels, cushions, explorable constructions in order to experience body sensations close to their birth experiences; to help them find a better way and build confidence. A precise observation of the child's behaviour will discover what is needed to help the individual move more freely. Through play, free movement and non-verbal processes, unconscious and body memory are supported.
>
> Consequently, psychomotricity is a way to revisit the individual's early story and, if teachers and sports trainers were also trained with that perspective, educators could bring about a deeper social, cognitive, relational and emotional development of children

In a sixth grade programme, the teacher organizes a descent into a cave as a speleological activity. This activity symbolizes birth, particularly when there are some narrow parts; it de-stresses the body and the mind because it is lived-out in a group, is accepted and experienced as play. The process is supported by adults, aware that what is being experienced is not a sporting achievement but an unconscious crossing of a story in our personal as well as familial origins.

Finally, the *root of self*: This can also be explained from a Jungian perspective; what he defined as the sense of self, and the process of individuation and emergence of the self. This process is linked with memory and data coming from the spiritual essence of each individual. This is also what urges the individual to question the meaning of existence.

TN: Do you relate this to physis, which Berne described as a force for life and achievement?

JG: Yes, in the sense that there are aspects of the self that are used in self-expression, self-actualization, self-esteem and identity. We might regard a young person as fully 'under construction' for 25 years, during which time they process material many times – 'As much as they need to', to use an affirmation from the Cycle of Development. What remains unresolved or unanswered is 'stored' within the body – in anticipation; these are the 'frozen' elements. Regarding the 'As many times as needed' affirmation, a practitioner or parent only needs to be around a six-year-old child asking 'Why?' a hundred times a day, to know that 'as many times as needed' exceeds the number of times that an adult needs a piece of information!

As well as these 'roots' there are five 'laws' to take account of when exploring resolution through constellations.

1 *Life continues*: Life has a biological strength, above everything else, that pushes life to recycle itself; it is a well-spring. And life goes from top to bottom: it comes from parents, and parents give it to their children; later on, children will pass it on to their own children. Parents give life, warmth and freedom; they also provide, in a less conscious way, the consequence of their actions: this establishes belonging and allows individuals to take their rightful place among the generations. Again, this is physis in action!

2 *The older system has precedence over the younger system*; but the younger system has a priority in terms of needs.

Respect is due to the ancestors, and first priority is given to the youngest's needs: in TA terms this involves an awareness of the essential hungers for stimulus, recognition and consistency (structure).

3 *The child is always innocent*; whatever their age, they are not responsible for the 'games' that they start: only when the game is playing out, and repetition becomes conscious, do they become responsible. Parent and child conversations can include restoring communication, such as: 'I didn't know I was doing it . . . I see now the consequences my actions have on myself and others . . . I am sorry . . . I love you'. Naturally this requires adjustment in relation to the child's age and stage of development.

4 *In life there is a tendency to balance taking and giving*. This is what Steiner's stroke economy (1971) is about. If I receive and accept 'warm fuzzies' from my friends, colleagues, my lover – then my wish will be to give as well: to balance the relationship, and even to give more. If I receive and accept 'cold

pricklies', the tendency will be for me to give back something similar. The task is to give more 'warm fuzzies' and fewer 'cold pricklies'. The balance is then re-established and will not degenerate.

Two examples:

> Taggers have put graffiti in a lift; they have been found out, and the town council has asked them as a means of amends to make a fresco in the lift: they must paint the fresco, and the town will pay for the supplies. The 'repair' removes the 'debt' and is now evened out positively.
>
> And a mother takes her neighbour's children into her home every day after school. They do their homework before going back to their own place. Over ten months of helping out in this way, this mother asks the neighbours three times if they would look after her own sons; they refuse. After these three requests, she stops taking their children to her place. She understands that a balance will never be achieved; rather than collecting 'negative stamps', she decides to stop.

5   *In a system, everyone deserves a place*; no one is excluded. We can see the connection here to permissions and injunctions: does the child have permission to belong, or to be themselves, or to be important? Are these permissions conditional, or even withheld? This is directly linked with the 'self-root' and the fight/flight behaviour connected with traumas. It can affect people at a deep and unconscious level.

> A father and a mother came to see me about frequent fights between their two daughters. They had four children: one son with disabilities, the two daughters, and a younger son. Presenting the children with soft toys, I noticed immediately that the eldest daughter kept looking at the ground. I turned towards the mother and asked her whether she had had a miscarriage. She answered that she had had a miscarriage at about three months of pregnancy. I placed a representative of the dead child who had biologically existed, both for his parents and his brothers and sisters, among the other representatives of the family. In this family there were five children, five places occupied by five individuals. Now there was a place for that lost baby and nobody could discount it.
>
> The first daughter had been unconsciously furious and was fighting with the second daughter for occupying this place. The parents were instantly relieved and remembered various confirming events; when the two daughters realized what was happening, the second one understood the reason why she found it so difficult to know who she was and had resisted complying with others' wishes. Part of her self-root was occupied by the energy of the fragmentation.

A final example illustrates these five laws:

> Recently John, one of my students in family constellations, mentored a three-year-old boy, Sandro. Because of his violent behaviour it was sometimes impossible to deal with Sandro in the classroom: his teacher couldn't bear it anymore. People use the word 'violence' when talking about Sandro: in fact he expresses himself like a forty-year-old man – if we consider the level of his rages, his anger, and even his strength and physical attitudes.
>
> John is a teacher, and usually mentors children in his school individually. He had tried to work with this child using a technique close to bonding, and had been violently rejected. Sandro was going to end up in a specialized learning environment if a key to his behaviour wasn't quickly discovered. His challenging behaviour only appeared in the classroom, never at home.
>
> At this point, Sandro's mother told John about the boy's father; John asked to see the father together with his children and wife, and then asked him to tell his own story as a child. John was surprised to notice that throughout the whole interview Sandro behaved like a child in his play and interactions.
>
> The father told his story: when he was fifteen days old, his mother left with another man and his older brother, leaving him alone at home. She knew that her husband wouldn't come back for three months as he was on a military mission; she was therefore giving up Sandro's father to certain death. Luckily the father came back, as he had been injured, and found the abandoned baby.
>
> Three-year-old Sandro says, 'But Daddy, you would have been dead?'
>
> 'Yes' says John, 'Your daddy would have been dead'.
>
> 'And I would still be here?'
>
> John told him, 'You would maybe have been there with the same mummy, but your daddy wouldn't be your daddy, because he would be dead'.

A child's curiosity is blocked when there have been prohibitions around asking questions because of moral pains (Tisseron 1999). For a sensitive and clever child like Sandro, the injunction was especially powerful, as it related to a question of life and death.

In this example, we see that Sandro immediately comes back to being a child, being curious and asking questions, and the permission or validation is given by the father in presence of the whole family. We may notice connections with epi-script and 'hot potato' theory (English 1969). There are many such examples with children under four years old; if trauma is not dealt with, it has the potential to become integrated as part of a personality trait. The child doesn't stand in a good place and cannot consider the world or others as trustworthy. We can see the very beginning of script formation in a child within their familial history, known but not named by adults, transmitted from unconscious to unconscious; in this case from the father's C1 to the child's P1.

TN: How do you work and encourage parents to interact with their children; to heal these traumas?

JG: These healing principles bring life back into a system, restore the sense of enabling life to exist at its full creative and relational potential, and they are directly connected to the five fundamental laws:

- Account for facts: what is, is.
- Those who carry a dramatic fate in the familial history firmly require that their descendants let it stay with them; their story and all its consequences.
- Take life as it has been given; and apply oneself to do with it something good for oneself.
- Acknowledge that I am the little one; and that I am innocent.
- Acknowledge that I am the big one; and that I am responsible, and that all the consequences of my actions belong to me.

My own work has shown me that the more educators and parents normalize this process, the more it can be integrated by the child. Constellations can enable practitioners to be aware of the processes that capture life itself, in all its complexity: a loyalty to ancestors and to their dramas.

14

MATHEMATICAL CALCULATION PROCEDURES AND DRIVERS IN ACTION IN THE LEARNING ENVIRONMENT

Cesare Fregola, Italy

Introduction

This chapter reports on the qualitative results of the experimental phase of a study to examine the links between children's learning experiences associated with two-digit division and the transactional analysis concept of drivers. I present results obtained from a process using a questionnaire developed during a prior phase of research. These are combined with undergraduate student observations of the children, drawings produced by the children, and teacher observations on permission transactions used.

Study objectives

The aims of the research were to:

- investigate how different mathematical calculation procedures for two-digit division, with increasing levels of difficulty, might activate drivers (Kahler 1975) with different levels of intensity;
- explore the impact on the children's learning results of permission transactions used by teachers.

The research context

This paper reports on one part of a research process that has been developed over a period of about seven years and concluded in 2010. The heuristic phase ran from 2003–2005 and involved development of a questionnaire, and included pictures and a structured interview guide, plus a grid and associated training in direct observation of driver behaviour. In this phase, four 4th year primary classes (98 children) and two 3rd year classes (46 children) were involved.

The experimental phase, which is the focus for this paper, ran from 2005 to 2007, during which experiments were carried out according to the following procedures:

1   Administering evaluation entry tests.
2   Administering driver questionnaires.
3   Starting up the didactic interventions, which included five activities in sequence. These were courses in class and study of drivers in action by means of the observation grid for: division with successive subtraction; division with the repeated addition method; division with the traditional method; division with simplified traditional method; division with traditional method.
4   Administration of final examinations and production by each child of a drawing of themselves during the test.
5   Organization of recordings and observations in order to indentify suitable describers and relations between the data. In the experimental phase, four 4th year primary school classes were involved with a total of 93 children.

The diffusion phase ran from 2008 to 2010 and relates to the presentation of the first qualitative results and diffusion of the research.

The theoretical background

In terms of learning mathematics there are a number of structural characteristics which include the processes of abstraction, generalization, transfer (Gagné 1985). In addition, learning involves the method of representation using specific codes defining a language that requires an evolved and complex formalization process (Fregola 2010: 57–63). These characteristics become organized through mathematical language, rules and constructs, and in turn provide a basis of a mathematics didactic influence at both cognitive and meta-cognitive levels. This creates an evolved ability of thought, either of procedural or declarative knowledge (Gagné 1985), requiring mechanical and elaborative activities. This is often the case where previously mastered know-how has to be reconfigured using the capacity for understanding, intuition, analysis, synthesis, decision-making and problem-solving (Resnick 1987).

The aspects relative to the emotional sphere are connected to a potential fear of mathematics and a common conviction that mathematics is a subject for a chosen few who are gifted with remarkable intelligence. My interest in this study is to explore whether it is possible to intervene on some emotional/relational experiences which are connected to the history of each child and prevent, facilitate or influence the learning process of mathematics and motivational aspects.

Bloom (1979) starts with the supposition that every subject matter can be understood by focusing on the quality of instruction, and that this considers both cognitive and affective-interactional variables. Bloom separates affective suppositions from cognitive ones and demonstrates, by means of transversal and longitudinal studies, that there is a component of variability in scholastic progress given by such suppositions. Emotions and feelings often cause frustration, and do not always steer the learner towards planning sufficient effort in order to achieve learning objectives in mathematics. Rather than being a resource for motivation, feelings of fear, which might arguably fuel a defence from danger, threats or anger which might drive finding the solution to those dangers and threats, instead reinforce common convictions about the learner in learning mathematics, which typically comprise notions about mathematics itself, the maths teacher and the teaching:

- individual learner's inadequacy and inability
- inaccessibility of mathematics
- inadequacy or incompetence of the teacher and their teaching.

In the didactic relationship there is a risk of perpetuating a vicious circle among these three factors, which intensifies and impacts on the motivation for learning mathematics. If one enters 'fear of mathematics' or similar feelings into a search engine, there are about 2,500,000 findings. Alternatively, it might be expected to find others experiencing joy in relation to successful learning. Instead there is a kind of 'syndrome of the man in disguise' (Novellino 2003); a syndrome that affects students who are skilled in maths, and which makes them feel like supermen: intelligent, but also alien.

The fear of mathematics has been the subject of numerous studies which tend to identify the source as earlier, negative, unsuccessful experiences. Tobias (1993) introduces the expression 'Maths Anxiety', which refers to:

- the fear of making a mistake (one of the most important factors reported by students)
- the method of reinforce/punish used by teachers
- partial results attained by students
- the myth that (once again) the ability to learn is a special gift that cannot be affected by the method of learning.

From the point of view of social communication this consequently instils an adaptation of students, teachers and parents to a model of behaviour which tends to make the children justify themselves and yield to their lack of ability. Anne Siety (2003), a psychopathologist and a specialist in the psycho-pedagogy of mathematics, focuses on the emotional aspect of mathematics and its consequences on the individual. The block in mathematics is not always caused by failing to understand the subject or a problem, which might simply be resolved with an explanation and work; the entire world of mathematics remains relentlessly closed, and this can result in panic or something more serious which is based on fear. Siety argues that the origin of this fear is in a student perception of mathematics as something unpleasant and incomprehensible, since anyone who does not have a good head for maths will never be able to do it. From a constructivist perspective, such convictions are the fruit of a continuous process of interpretation of reality, co-created by children, which develops with an implicit purpose to give sense to experiences with mathematics. Op't Eynde (2002) describes the convictions of students relating to mathematics as those subjective conceptions which are possessed implicitly or explicitly by students, who regard them as real and continuing to influence their mathematical understanding. Schunk and Lilly (1984) emphasize the influence of self-esteem on results and performance in mathematics; perception of their own ineffectiveness causes pupils to lower their motivation for – and effort in – mathematics.

In terms of linking ideas about learning maths and emotional experience to transactional analysis, two concepts were regarded as especially relevant: drivers and permission transactions. Kahler (1975) described drivers as behaviours that last from a split second to no more than seven seconds and reinforce an existential position of 'I'm only OK if . . .' He linked this to Berne's (1972: 344) notion that our script is 'driven' by repetition compulsion, so that drivers are microscopic repeats of our overall life pattern. Crossman (1966) identified permissions as transactions that effect a change in the direction of the recipient's behaviour. Meanwhile, Steiner (1971) referred to a permission as an attempt to realign the recipient with their original script-free state, while Woollams and Brown (1978) used the term 'permission transaction' to embed a message that 'It's OK to . . .'. Brook (1996) reviews the concept and provides a categorization of permissions into *affective*, *behavioural*, *cognitive* and *physiological*.

The results of the study

A report has been tabulated for each child showing: identification of the driver through the grid; the profile of the driver obtained by means of the questionnaire; the student's drawing of themselves; intervention of the teacher with the permission transactions; results attained.

Verbal behaviour

Some examples from the work carried out in the 4th year primary school supports the identification of drivers from an analysis of verbal behaviour:

1   'Mathematics is written in an exercise book with small squares and I like small squares because they help me to write well, neatly and precisely.' – Be Perfect Driver
2   'When I do division I can't find the number I need straight away and I start thinking that I am a bit crazy.' – Hurry Up Driver
3   'I try my best, but then everything seems so difficult, I have to try harder and then the numbers go missing and the sums never come out.' – Try Hard Driver

TABLE 14.1 Child 1

Observations and grid	Questionnaire and driver profile	Drawing of myself	Behaviour before intervention of the teacher	Intervention of the teacher	Learning results
Words: 'Of course', 'I'll do it again', 'I don't like it like this'	*Driver*		Becomes agitated when a new activity is suggested	Turned to the Normative Positive Parent	Attention time and functional concentration increased
Tones: well modulated			Concentrates on details and loses the thread	Transmitted confidence in pupil's ability: emphasized the correct results achieved and at an appropriate time	Accepts mistakes
Gestures: brings the hand towards the chin			Conscientious	Praised the moments of concentration on the process rather than on the activity and unessential details	Does not get lost in details
Positions: upright and well balanced					Accuracy means being able to deal better with the task
Facial expressions: severe				Gave permission to 'be worth something', even though something is still missing	More intuitive
Result: **Be Perfect**				Stimulated intuition	

Driver profile chart labels: Try Hard, Be Perfect, Hurry Up, Be Strong, Please People (scale 0 to 5.0)

TABLE 14.2 Child 4

Observations and grid	Questionnaire and driver profile	Drawing of myself	Behaviour before intervention of the teacher	Intervention of the teacher	Learning results
Words: 'come on', '. . . will you help me?', 'is that right'	Driver 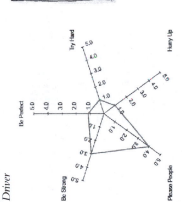		Keeps on asking for confirmation of correctness of operations	Encouraged to think about a single operation	Accepts and overcomes difficulties by discussing and asking for confirmation on the strategies adopted and no longer on the 'correctness of what s/he has done'
Tones: alternates between high and low			Easily changes method of attention	Pointed out the difficulties and mistakes of the child and discussed them with the child to make up for the prerequisites	
Gestures: taps fingers and fidgets with legs					Expresses feelings without expecting the teacher to confirm them
Positions: moves continually				Encouraged the child to express real feelings	At times is more connected to carrying out the task than getting approval of adult
Facial expressions: sullen, tries to catch teacher's eye					Faces criticism without getting offended
Result: **Please Others**					Depends less on opinion of others

4 'I now just let things bounce off me, even if I can't do division I think it's pointless worrying about it because lots of my schoolmates can't do it either.' – Be Strong Driver

5 'The teacher hasn't checked my maths exercise book, and I haven't done my homework because I only learned division for her sake.' – Please Others Driver

Relationship between learning results and drivers

The 'Be Perfect' driver is what caused the greater number of students to abandon or temporarily halt the test. The children with the 'Be Strong' driver – and this surprised many of us – on the whole achieved excellent results; that is to say, when anxiety is controlled one is more ready for mathematics. Less positive results were obtained in cases where, even though they had doubts or queries, children did not ask for, or did not want, help when the teacher approached them. The 'Hurry Up' and 'Try Hard' drivers were noticed to be more frequent during the standard procedures for two-digit division, and it was noticed that in ninety per cent of the cases with low percentages of failure, either one or both were present. Finally, regarding the 'Hurry Up' and 'Try Hard' drivers, there is not always a correspondence between observations in the field and results of the questionnaire, and this made us reassess the potential limitations of the questionnaire – while also deciding not to abandon it. The children with the 'Please Others' driver are those who asked for more explanations and assistance, even pointing out their own deficiencies.

Discussion

The research team is still working on these results, because we have felt it necessary to carry out a qualitative analysis of research done on a wider range of children and, above all, to train the teachers to handle the instruction course themselves. On the basis of the observations, we have implemented a course which aims at tackling, along with the teachers, the meaning of the drivers from a pedagogical angle; and we have noticed that it will be necessary to deal with teachers' drivers and their effect on didactic interaction. We have provided teachers with explanations about drivers and we have directed their attention to the fact that there is an internal process which characterizes drivers and involves very significant emotional characteristics. The work has enabled us to observe essential aspects that are relevant when creating environments for learning mathematics – and possibly other subjects. Competence in transactional analysis can be incorporated into didactic activity, and we might also consider the extent to which some of these competences should become an integral part of the basic training for primary school teachers. We feel that the method of managing the didactic relationship, and intervening at the right moment in emotional experiences, opens new perspectives for mathematical teaching and for teaching in general.

This chapter first appeared as an article in *The International Journal of Transactional Analysis Research*, 1.1: 30–9.

The questionnaire used with the pupils, and a complete set of Driver-profile pictures, can be found in 'Mathematical Calculation Procedures and Drivers in Action in the Learning Environment' (Fregola 2014).

15

WINNING WITH SILENCE

Educational journeys

Ferdinando Montuschi, Italy

Silence in school

Silence in class has always been a problem for teachers. Its maintenance is a continuing worry as it represents both the condition in which to carry out activities as well as the possibility to keep control of the class. This is the reason why the word 'Silence!' is so often repeated and it denotes a whole range of emotions: fear, anger, helplessness, the anger of frustration which is then followed up with by pitiful entreaties, threats, extortions, punishments. The request for silence can also be expressed non-verbally: the beating of a fist, a blow or more forceful objects on the back of a chair. The acoustic measurement of this 'request' could be a good test for detecting the importance the teacher attributes to the silence, but also to highlight the emotional drama experienced at particular moments.

Beyond these colourful and external signs, silence in the classroom is the most eloquent sign of a teacher's professional competence and educational ability because it is linked to the interest of the student and to what happens in the classroom, to the motivation of the activity that is unfolding and with the emotional and social relationships – occasional or permanent – experienced between students and teachers, and between the students themselves. It should be immediately noted that silence, in this context, is not a value in itself, but simply a guide, a sign that can help interpret what is going on internally for each person and at a social level, what is going on for the whole group. Similarly, when silence falls, it is not always completely negative and could be interpreted in the context of class life, specifically in the moment in which it occurs. The buzz of students working in groups, for example, cannot be considered as an inappropriate and untimely loss of silence; and the momentary, icy silence that follows a teacher's angry threat of punishment, cannot be compared to the positive silence derived from an interest of the whole class. Silence and its absence therefore, are not educational values or anti-values:

they are simply a guide for interpretation and along with the social context are a guide for governing, and above all for preparation or prevention. In fact, these interventions reveal the educational intent and the true skill of the teacher.

Building an active silence

Silence that is appreciated by teachers does not always coincide with the silence that appeals to students who can tend to perceive silence as one of the many school duties to respect. And when duty and pleasure are in opposition, an endless and unbearable tug of war begins between teachers and students leading to a risky game of power from which it is difficult to exit, particularly for the teacher.

Maria Montessori, who anticipated this risk, introduced a 'game of silence' in her schools in such a way so that the child experienced this duty as a shared pleasure, (Montessori 1966). It is a brilliant intuition which can be implemented in so many ways and has its primary principle the change in ego-state for both the child and the teacher. A playful alliance rather than a tiresome obligation to be maintained by both parties. No more heartfelt, desperate, angry requests for silence on the part of the teacher, not even boring, unjustified, unnatural demands – as seen through the eyes of the student – but a fun game. A game that motivates the winning of silence and paves the way for a peer relationship between teachers and students leaving a positive mark in the emotional and active memory of the pupils. Then, any reference to silence that follows will be something pleasing, as it will trigger a memory of a motivational and shared experience. Silence then becomes a useful tool for motivation, for self-expression, for the joyful and noisy manifestation of other moments.

Avoiding splitting and counter-positioning of duty and pleasure, between what makes sense for the teacher and what makes sense for students, keeping an inclusive and collaborative relationship between teachers and pupils – both in moments of silence and in those noisy expressive moments. This seems to be the most interesting educational achievement of the Montessorian approach. Her method is based on a child-centred approach, and at the same time the teacher's role and method remain equally central. Against this background, different concepts, different goals and different meanings of silence appear: one which enables the teacher to survive and to keep control of the situation; one in which the silence is shared between teachers and students and is characterized as common heritage and where no one is the sole owner; one in which silence prevents the split and counter-positioning of duty and pleasure; and, moreover, the operating silence characterized by the vital, expressive, joyful buzz consistent with the activity in progress and which, at the same time, respects those carrying out their work. The silence then begins to differentiate itself and show its many connotations. From being an absolute value, it assumes a value relative to the activity being performed, to the assumed attitudes towards silence both by ourselves and by others.

In the winning of silence, the many journeys that one can glimpse and choose range from the tiring, incomprehensible, mandatory silence perceived by the pupil as a duty – which corresponds to a strenuous, nerve-wracking effort from the teacher to obtain it – to industrious silence that is naturally maintained and is equally shared between students and teachers. We could say that educational silence is characterized by the ability to increase its meaning: it acquires a natural stability and structure, enables peer relationships, and ceases being a problem to resolve. However, we are faced with an objective that becomes ever more difficult to achieve as we move up to the more senior classes where the exhibitionist forms of adolescent behaviour and the ever more defiant power games – which, though, mask personal unease or a sense of inadequacy – are beginning to emerge both in life at school and more broadly.

Silence won over by the schoolchild

The schoolchild's need for silence matures in parallel with the need for self-expression and the desire to learn. Students who have not developed the need for silence instinctively create an ever-increasing noise. We are faced with the appearance of non-expressive, yet demonstrative and seemingly free beings. Pupils left alone by the teacher, without any particular guidance and without someone who controls their activity, certainly don't look for silence but rather the opposite, giving rise to anti-discipline, anti-rules, anti-school, anti-everything. This gives a tremendous push towards the illusion of freedom, of self-affirmation – revealing a poorly exercised need for power – which usually shows up in all sorts of disruptive ways and is accompanied by a desire for someone to bring an end to this empty and unsatisfying noise.

After experiencing the opposite of calm, a subtle and shy desire for peace and tranquillity begins to emerge. This is obviously not the way for peace and tranquillity to grow in its truest sense, but we can already understand, and help others understand, that its opposite is deceptive and does not guarantee the gratification it seems to promise. If children's desire for calm does not seem to be instinctive, it is true that gradually, playing with its meaning and the pleasure of living with it gives it a positive value. In this sense, the 'game of silence' can be an opportunity to discover its value and enable it to be seen not only as an external environmental factor, but also something that comes from within.

The child begins to notice that tranquillity has roots inside a person and is a feature of external social situations that can usefully be shared with others. In addition to understanding, the child may start feeling that silence is not only one of the many limitations that the school imposes on them, but is also an opportunity individually and relationally: each one of us can feel the presence of others within ourselves while still keeping quiet, and we can each play with our own ability for self control, with our own internal brakes, rather than just the instinctive emotional outburst of behaviour with no rules that is an end in itself. Ultimately, we can say that a child begins to test the value of silence with the expression of silence.

Creative teachers can invent many original ways to use the Montessori 'game of silence' in order to avoid it becoming merely a repetitive, mechanical and 'end-in-itself exercise. For example, you could give preliminary instructions for each person to spend that time individually. Once the exercise is ended, the teacher can ask everyone to describe the feelings they had, the images that came to mind, any sensations in their body, what was going on in their mind, in their imagination. All this can be part of a larger educational project focused on the teaching of feelings, mastery of one's body, education guided by the imagination, and so on.

We are not interested here in taking this route. It is sufficient to note that, even in these cases, the silence is not empty and not just an exercise in self-control; it can become a constructive and creative way that puts forward a positive approach to actively use the time through the silence. The goal is to discover that every person needs silence and that silence is necessary: therefore, it has to be gradually understood with all its various meanings.

The silence of the schoolchild who learns

The meaning that students engaged in learning give to silence can be revealed on entering a classroom where the class is carrying out a school activity in the absence of the teacher. At that moment, the silence – accompanied by whispers in low voices, such as when working in small groups – is the sign of interest, commitment, motivation, the desire to achieve an expected result given by the teacher; but this result only interests and satisfies those who are committed to achieving it. Chattering and whispering remain in the background and do not cause discomfort or indiscipline. On the contrary, the annoying increase in noise is a typical sign of transgressive anarchy, a false kind of freedom. Therefore, silence is not a result of education in itself: it is rather coincidental, the sign of attention invested in productivity and learning. The return of the teacher, in this case, does not change the situation, and they do not need to ask for silence. By contrast, when the teacher is forced to ask for it, the real problem is not so much silence as the motivation, the meaning and value that students give, whether to learning or their presence at school. In school learning, then, silence is only the external layer of a much broader and deeper subject. The task is to address those interests, motivations and processes through which reflection can also be obtained together with other results. With this perspective, we cannot consider silence as the student's responsibility, because their true responsibilities are different. The 'game of silence' can make sense, but the responsibility for silence represents a useless effort, a no-win game, one which can end up reassuring and gratifying the teacher but, in the eyes of the students, it's a sterile request, an adaptation to a nonsensical request for an incomprehensible gain which ends up increasing the stakes in order to reach an obscure goal with regards to their presence in school – at least for those students who only find interests and joy outside of themselves.

When there is no quiet in the classroom, one cannot simply blame students for indiscipline. The teacher can usefully ask themselves, 'What's not working – how come there is a vacuum which distraction and noise are trying to fill?' So, before inviting students to silence, it can be useful to ask oneself how to magnetize their attention, in the shortest time, in order to obtain silence without demanding it and, checking to see what conditions there might be, to anticipate that moment of recreating a sense of calm. Stillness must, therefore, be planned for alongside the teaching skills and combined with an educational sensitivity which allows the teacher to master the flow of time at school and the development of the student's learning processes. In this way, silence becomes a guiding signal that the teacher can use to guide their work and their interventions. However, the pace of school life does not only depend upon the teacher's initiative. There are challenging behaviours that require specific skills from teachers in addressing. In these cases, one can resort to the theory and techniques of specialized teaching skills; in any case, broadly speaking, a teacher capable of doing their job largely determines progress at school, even in the face of unpredictable lapses in the children's attention.

In general, then, silence can be considered as an emotional motivational state which has a useful variance of intensity in relation to the schoolwork that is taking place. The stillness of concentration, the thick silence full of wonder or interest in a moving narrative, can, at other times, have different meanings – and turn, for example, into an acceptable hubbub; a tension that ends with a legitimate expression of release in the face of an expected and hoped for success. Pedagogical insight and educational sensitivity will therefore turn silence, not into an ideal, but into a useful background to highlight differing moments of school life. The variations in different situations can be taken as an evolving sign, positive or negative. For example, group work by beginners – both with children and with adults – is often noisy at first and gradually, as the group matures in its ability to relate, it becomes quiet; voice tones are lowered as the fear of not being listened to or not being understood decreases. In this case, the gradual conquest of silence is the sign of a new confidence, of a more mature expressive ability with easier communication and social interaction.

The silence that fascinates those who speak and those who learn

Silence can be useful to teachers – but also to every speaker who addresses an audience – as an indicator of motivation, and its absence can be interpreted as lack of interest in the words that are spoken. This trivial observation reminds us that there is a significant link between the speaker and the listener. It is a dynamic that we can get used to noticing, and use very practically. For someone who speaks to a group of people, silence – or the lack of silence – can signal whether to deepen the investigation into the topic, or change the topic completely. Attention to these sometimes unpredictable moments can help the speaker discover their own communication resources, as well as identify useful topics and content for different types of listeners. With this perspective, the conquest of silence is a parallel process in terms of learning and the discovery of one's own powers of expression and communication. The silence of the cloister is not just for hermits, intimacy with nature and contemplation,

In reviewing educational and formative journeys for the individual, I would like to include one that might appear a little unusual; it brings us from the din of the city to the quiet of the cloister. It is a journey primarily undertaken by monks and by hermits who have felt the need to isolate themselves and, at the same time, to raise themselves up while not abandoning the world. In many aspects, this route can affect even those who are not interested in a radical choice of religious life, but who simply wish to be with themselves in a closer and more intimate way. We can immediately note that this does not mean escaping from the world, or giving up on social relationships. The monk, even the one who chooses long periods of reclusion and solitude, carries with him the whole of humanity in his cell, rather than being locked in solitary well-being which is nothing more than egoism. He enters into communion with God and with men, feeling them present in his thinking, in his feelings, and in his prayers. It is not by chance that the solitude of the hermit is prepared at length, based on the experience within religious communities where community life is experienced and positively lived with all its problems and all its difficulties. The solitude of the hermit, in this regard, is the highest point of social maturity. In the silence of solitude, the richness of sociability finds fulfilment. We are therefore in the presence of full solitude: full of what is vital for individualization and social life. Silence in this case acquires a value and becomes an essential condition rather than a backdrop.

The contemplation of the secret, mysterious world of nature enables a silence full of emotion and meaning, which favours unedited moments of expression and creativity. Feeling, thinking and judgement are immediate responses from the ego-states. Responses that can be translated and represented through words, images, sounds, colours, artistic creation in all its forms and in all its meaning. Silence, contemplation and creativity seem to trace and follow a coherent linear path which transforms the 'empty solitude' into a solitude which is full and rich with people and meaning, individual values of expression and social content. As the ancient Greek philosophers have taught, at the apex of multiplicity is unity, 'the One' that encompasses everything and is everything. Simplicity is, therefore, at the pinnacle of perfection. And contemplation is an educational journey which enriches and at the same time frees human beings to be close to themselves, and as close as possible to the others in that inner area of silence that gathers and unifies, valuing everything of significance.

The silence between escape and desire

A person flees from, and at the same time seeks, quiet. We flee from it when it is being lived in an empty way, when it is lived in solitude or isolation. We arrive at this when we are frightened of facing ourselves and when we consider the relationship with ourselves as unacceptable and even to be a source of suffering. The need to fill this void is immediately apparent, and we use whatever can be used to offer a response to that void: whether it be through the expression of useless or banal words, or listening to the mobile, or to loud music at full volume in a disco. In order to fill this emptiness, and even more to keep away from ourselves, we seek refuge in din and noise, in giddiness, in excitement and agitation. The opposite of this experience involves encountering the person willing to gain inner calm: a particular state which enables them to make contact with the deepest part of themselves and to live that exalting experience of inner intimacy from which new emotions, original thoughts, reconciliatory feelings and behaviours arise. The fear of silence is identified with the fear of loneliness; with that empty loneliness that forces the person to remain alone with themselves – a fear that we delude ourselves by overcoming by breaking the silence, diverting attention from ourselves – but the problem remains. It is here we can see that emptiness is not to be simply avoided or hidden. Rather, it must be earned so that we can be mentally and emotionally transformed in a privileged state of personal and relational well-being.

The path that leads from intolerable silence to a silence which exalts is manifestly long, because it is not about the external environment but the internal being and requires, in the first instance, a radical change in the relationship that we have with ourselves. The first step therefore consists of self-acceptance, valuing oneself unconditionally. Unconditional acceptance is not about avoiding one's own personal development but is about achieving this new state without the brakes of dissatisfaction, doubt, the sense of inadequacy, self-denigrating criticism. Self-acceptance means also accepting one's own positive development, one's life plan, the positive change of our own feelings and behaviours. The gradual achievement of self-acceptance brings out the need to remain ever more deeply with our own thoughts in a protected place in which the emotional, cognitive and relational space expands rather than narrows. In this solitude, where a full silence reigns, there is room for everything that has human value, for everything that enriches the inner person.

The route to silence is an experience of maturity, of integrating oneself with the natural reality and social life. True silence is not for isolating oneself or escaping but for meeting, in a new way and through a new noticing, those who have appeared as adversaries or as limiting and opposing beings. The long path to maturity and the attainment of inner silence thus lead to reconciliation with oneself and, soon after, to reconciliation with others. The religious 'Peace be with you: And also with you', becomes the true measure of love towards others, transformed from a binding duty into a fullness of expression; from a moral obligation to a joyful sharing. The silence that is lived internally opens up other unexpected avenues precisely because it is found on the opposite side of emptiness, of distressing loneliness, of the fear of abandonment, of the anguish of being with oneself. Silence reached as a purpose, as completeness, opens up the road to hidden meaning, to beauty not yet appreciated, to the value of unexpected intimacy with oneself, with nature, and with human beings – a well-being that makes it possible to stop oneself; to give up demanding, defending oneself, and planning actions that are defiant, disobedient, offensive. When stillness is obtained, one is alone and at the same time feels together with others, including those we have never met. For these reasons, education and self-education with regard to silence and stillness is more than just eliminating the noise: it aims to achieve an inner space after overcoming one's ego – a space from where no one is excluded and the prevailing, and more consistent, sentiment is the joy of existence combined with gratitude for belonging to life and being able to share it.

Operational indications

The path we have followed has taken a journey from school education aimed at children to the achievement of advanced formative goals for a person of any age. Silence has appeared as a continual and personal quest. Its character has taken on connotations that are always different. We have not dealt with the pathological silence of the child who closes themselves off, or with the adult who sometimes remains silent because they cannot find the words to express themselves or to reply.

We have rested upon silence in school life as a background and as a condition; the silence one can achieve to find the best conditions for learning, but also the silence that accompanies and reveals the interest and enthusiasm of listening, doing, and being creative. Silence in the communication process is an attainment, but also a language to be interpreted. Speakers who address an audience learn to interpret silence as a counterpoint to their words, as a significant sharing and as an element of interaction with those who are listening.

We have, in closing, determined the highest point that silence can reach and that can itself be reached: the experience of contemplation. We are in the presence of a total and all-encompassing experience that has the power to radically change a person. Contemplation is born from silence, but also has the power to build silence within every individual, quieting any sound, internal and external, even those in the background. Contemplation, as we have stated, is not the heritage of a few and doesn't only belong to those who have made a specific life-choice. First of all, contemplation means to be intimate with oneself, but also with everything that affects the senses: nature, objects, people and events, seemingly grey and insignificant daily life. It is at this point that we discover the extraordinary value of solitude and silence. Above all we discover that the person has the power to build silence, transforming the initial perception of emptiness and lack of meaning into an authentic attainment of fulfilment.

This chapter is a translation of 'La Conquista del Silenzio; Itinerari educativi' ('The Conquest of Silence: Educational journeys'), *Italian TA Journal*, 16/2007: 59–69.

PART 4

Educational transactional analysis

Adult learning and community development

INTRODUCING PART 4

Trudi Newton, UK

> There is not a more creative position, and more satisfying for those aspiring to create, than one of respected marginality.
>
> (Gianpiero Petriglieri 2010)

Transactional analysts know about marginality – Berne built it into our cultural script by his opposition to what he saw as an overcomplicated psychiatric system, and by his ability to stand at the edge of the establishment and observe, critique and challenge what he saw ... and live with the consequences. In his keynote address at a TA conference Montreal in 2010, marking the centennial of Berne's birth, Petriglieri explored how TA still holds a marginal position today in the world of psychology – how this is part of its value and significance (Petriglieri 2010). And, because every system has to have its margins, there are areas of respected marginality within the culture of TA itself.

This was highlighted for me by the response of a delegate on hearing Petriglieri's address, 'the legacy of "respected marginality" [. . . helped me] better understand my lifelong wish *both to be different and to belong*' (Landaiche 2010, my italics). And so it is for educational TA.

'Marginality' is a creative place, where we can look both outward and inward; new perspectives appear and gain attention in the ongoing dance between the fringe and the centre. That wish – both to be different and to belong – is illustrated in Berne's own training at the centre of the psychiatric and psychoanalytic establishment, followed by his chosen migration to the margins. There seems to be a similar tension in the TA community's recurrent dialogue between its desire for academic acceptance and respect for its radical origins; and in the discomfort sometimes felt within the TA world about it being not only a model for psychotherapy, but a *social* psychology that includes educators and organizational consultants within its commune. For me, this raises two areas to explore.

First, something that is characteristic of – but not unique to – the educational field. Many educators are led to use TA through their concern for disadvantaged, underprivileged or excluded learners. The readiness and accessibility of TA models for understanding what goes on in school, in adult education and in community projects; for sharing with learners or for designing teaching and intervention strategies, has a great appeal. There may also be an empathy and identification with the marginalized that some educators recognize from their own experience of being 'at the edge', and that may energize and compel a change in their practice.

Second, there is a real sense of excitement and liberation when we see the breadth of where and how TA is practised in different fields and in different cultures, and acknowledge and appreciate the range of ways that TA is informing social change and development.

There is a natural movement from describing TA as a social psychology to promoting its involvement in the field of social responsibility: the ITAA, for instance, includes a social responsibility network that aims:

> to achieve [a] goal of positive social change [by encouraging] transactional analysts to become actively involved in using their intervention skills and expertise to work cooperatively with community leaders in government, education, business organizations, and religious institutions.
>
> (Campos 2011)

Pearl Drego suggests that:

> Through the last three decades of its development, a sizable portion of the transactional analysis endeavour worldwide has been directed at social restructuring and bringing comfort to the victims of carnage, conflict, discrimination, and domestic violence. It is my guess that transactional analysts have critically confronted racism, colonialism, exclusivism, patriarchy, fundamentalism, domestic violence, sexual abuse, addiction systems, and tyranny more than therapists from most other disciplines.
>
> (Drego 2006: 95)

One of the means through which this confrontation happens is education in its widest sense. Educational TA is not just about working with children and young people, although working with children and young people is, of course, one of the key ways of initiating change in attitudes, expectations and hopes: the areas of adult education, professional training, community development, are also fertile ground for the insights of TA in its social psychology and social responsibility manifestations.

Before going on to introduce the contributors to this part and the ways in which they demonstrate this and relate it to TA theory, I want to mention a new aspect of the ego-state model, again derived from Drego, that extends the theory to draw attention to the altruistic qualities of people and the beneficent intentions of working with those whose socio-cultural context has damaged as well as nurtured them:

the task of the transactional analyst in this context is to heal and empower the Child in such a way that the best of ancestral tradition is transformed into a buffer against global stereotypes. We need a new updated ethnic Child who is guided by a healthy transformed ancestral Parent who integrates updated universal Parent values and is monitored by an Adult who carries responsibility for self and society [see Figure 1]. This updated Child must learn to identify with ancestral culture as well as with contemporary, eco-friendly culture.

(Drego 2009: 196)

She suggests that updating and integrating take place within *each* ego-state and *between* the three ego-states, and that this process engages the total personality in enabling helpfulness, responsibility, compassion, service and so on, to flow 'abundantly and easily' (2006: 99). In the 'updated and integrated' PAC model we find (and experience) Parent potency, Adult responsibility, and a Child with the security of inner freedom. 'Furthermore, as the intra-psychic attraction between ego-states deepens, so does interpersonal connectivity with others' (ibid.)

Drego's earlier work on the cultural Parent has been a vital source for educators; it is an outcome of her work with women in rural India and with children marginalized in school. She shows how Berne's three aspects of group, organizational, social or national culture – the etiquette, technicalities and character – are carried in the Parent and determine individual and group responses in relationships, encounters, new experiences, learning, in any and all situations (Drego 1983).

How does the thinking and practice of educational TA meet these needs across diverse societies and with different age groups? There are many examples in this following part. Two key concepts that provide a linking thread are *symbiosis* and *learning imagos*.

FIGURE 1 Integrated altruistic ego–states (adapted from Drego 2006)

Learning imagos

Do adults learn differently from children? Ideas about this vary, and *andragogy* (Knowles 1973) is a regularly quoted concept which suggests that adults learn from experience, motivated by need, and that their learning is self-directed and life-focused. Very often, school experiences may inhibit rather than inspire learning in later life. Transferential relationships with teachers, tutors or trainers may be the result, exacerbated in societies where there is, or has recently been, a strong hierarchical structure.

The learning imagos model (Newton 2003; 2014) presents the various underpinning educational philosophies (Elias and Merriam 1995) as 'group's group imagos' (Clarke 1996), showing the unconscious negotiation that results in a common belief about what goes on in a learning group – how the teacher and learners are perceived, what metaphors describe the beliefs the group holds about learning and teachers/learners, what is approved (stroked) or disapproved (discounted), and – most importantly – what the contract is that holds the group together and defines its aim and purpose. The Bernean group imago model is fully explained in Rosemary Napper's article on leading learning – in which she also discusses the different roles leaders may take in the various types of group (Chapter 16). Here is a brief summary of the philosophies or styles of education:

A *liberal* (or traditional) learning group often 'fits' with our cultural – and actual – experience of being taught, with a teacher who is the 'expert' and novice pupils, and a focus on imparting knowledge and information. This is, in many ways, our 'default' model; but there is another much older way of learning, that of imitation and apprenticeship: as *technological* education, this is a behaviourist style with the tutor an assessor, teaching according to objectives and checking criteria in students' work. An extreme version of these two is *dogmatic* education, a rigid system where students' success is gained through compliance. *Progressive* ideas, on the other hand, take account of adult learners' life experience and commitment, using these as the ground for learning. The *humanistic* approach promotes student-centred learning, the development and nurture of each person's holistic growth through education – which can become somewhat individuated. A more politically and community focused model is the *radical*, which removes the teacher–pupil distinction and proposes that we learn from one another – that education is the 'practice of freedom, the means by which men and women deal critically and creatively with reality and discover how to participate in the transformation of their world' (Shaull 1984: 15).

Barrow (2009: 300) refers to the first three of these styles as 'schooling'; placing all six styles on a continuum (Table 1). On the right are the three more recently developed, potentially transformative ways of teaching and learning. We can say that the three models to the left are knowledge-focused, and those to the right are person-focused, and therefore grounded in life-experience as the source of learning and growth. Each of these learning styles implies a different contract about teaching and learning, and about how people see each other and relate to one another. They are summarized in Table 1.

TABLE 1 Learning imagos

	Dogmatic	Technological	Liberal	Progressive	Humanistic	Radical
	↓	schooling	↑	↓	transformation	↑
	knowledge	–	–	–	–	person
contract for	reward	assessment	information	support	nurture	mutuality
leader as	guru	instructor	teacher	guide	enabler	animator
learner as	in need	malleable	empty	committed	growing	equal
imago						
strokes	obedience	competence	thinking	vision	development	empowerment
discounts	person	flexibility	experience	own needs	community	information

Why does this matter? By becoming aware of how 'what we do' influences the outcome for learners, we can propose contracts, methods and metaphors that suit the purpose of any particular learning experience and address the potential transferential relationships between teachers and learners. The learning models are not a hierarchy – each has a place – the skill lies in combining personal preference with appropriate application to circumstance and desired results. 'Continuing reflection on philosophical issues in adult education [. . .] develop[s] methods of critical thinking, aids individuals to ask better questions and expands the visions of educators beyond their present limits' (Elias and Merriam 1995: 206).

In her extensive overview of 'learning to lead learning', Rosemary Napper tells how she travels worldwide training people in TA. She is alert to the potential transferences onto leaders of learning, and describes seven areas of attention that promote healthy development and autonomy for both leaders and learners. These include a full explanation of Berne's group imago theory that underpins the learning imago model above, as well as considering leadership roles and the hungers that are part of human psychology – and will appear in the stages of any learning programme. Her personal story of discovering, and then integrating, TA in her own learning and in her professional life is the ground for her illustration of how different TA concepts link and support learning programmes – the 'givens', and potential risks, of leadership roles, hungers, and transference; and the 'solutions' – contracts, emergence, and meaning-making through an understanding of learning and script change.

In the following three chapters, Jan Grant and Rhae Hooper in Australia and Marina Rajan Joseph in India illustrate three ways of integrating TA in adult education and training. Grant, from a humanistic perspective, relates recent developments of the classic concepts of ego-states and script to current thinking in adult education theory. She draws parallels between several structured, cognitive theories, aimed at improving skills in teacher effectiveness, and shows how these are enhanced when underpinned by the understanding and relational ingredients that TA brings to the table. As a counsellor as well as an educator, she identifies with Carl Rogers' belief in the common goals of education and therapy: self-knowledge and personal growth.

In the following chapter Hooper, a trainer in the corporate context, is interested in the links between research on trainer effectiveness from two different sources, one in therapy and one in education. She shows how these two pieces of research, from different academic fields, come to similar conclusions about what is needed from trainers in order to create a ground for adult learning. With her long experience of the corporate environment and the many constraints it can put on the training process, she shows how TA philosophy and principles, and an understanding of straightforward TA models, support and are supported by the research findings. In a way, she moves the training environment along the continuum, from its essentially technological focus to a more progressive, experiential approach. Is it enough, she asks, for the trainer to be warm and have a well-organized programme? The deeper understanding of *why* the attributes identified through research are so crucial helps the trainer develop self-awareness and professionalism, as well as providing a wonderful platform on which to base learning.

While Grant highlights theory, and Hooper research, Rajan Joseph centres her chapter on the practice of training in the specific context of medical education. In a traditional teaching situation, with all its familiar expectations, she takes a classic – though not too well known – idea from Berne, that of 'therapeutic operations', and fluently demonstrates how it can be transposed into the learning environment. Her argument is well worked out and, again, persuades us that, like all Berne's developments in TA theory, it is based in human experience and social relationships, not on academic hypotheses or 'big words'. Her goal, again like Berne's, is always to strengthen the Adult and so to counteract any lingering symbiotic invitations from students to teachers or from teachers to students.

Symbiosis

Symbiosis is another key idea in adult and community education. Ordinary grown-up people, wanting to learn, may nevertheless hold an unconscious perception, carried over from childhood, that the 'teacher' knows everything and the 'learner' knows nothing. The teacher has all the power and the learners are powerless and expect to be 'done to', without taking any responsibility for their own learning. They then discount their Adult experience, and may repeat 'old' Child patterns of 'not understanding' or playing 'stupid'. The teacher may get stuck in feeling responsible for everything and 'doing all the work'. This is symbiosis in action.

In working with many different groups of educators, from parent-education to university lecturers, I have found that symbiosis is instantly recognized and pounced on as a descriptor of family, school or academic life. As Joseph writes about her work with medical students, constantly and uncritically inviting students' critical thinking and 'expanding the Adult' moves everyone out of the symbiosis.

Tomoko Abe shows how, in her description of her work with the parents of children in kindergarten, symbiotic relationships can be embedded – not just in learning, but in a culture – unquestioned, and affecting the whole of family life and, consequently, social and political life as well. Her careful and detailed story of how she enables her students to regain their sense of themselves as independent, autonomous individuals (who can, in turn, promote a similar sense in their children as they grow up), is a microcosm – or even a fractal – of the application of TA in analysis of challenging situations and designing for a healthy future.

In the final chapter of this part, Karen Pratt gives a wonderful overview of the scope of her involvement in diverse learning groups in South Africa. The ancestral symbiosis and entrenched attitudes that have defined SA society for generations are now confronted by a new 'rainbow nation' politics and a drive to pride in the national heritage and potential, as well as a continuing critique. This shows up in many areas of life, and most clearly in education. Karen chooses OK-ness as the basis of her interventions, an OK-ness that takes account of differing 'levels' of social development (and differing cultural Parents) as illustrated in the spiral dynamics model. Supported by good contracting, this approach opens up fresh possibilities for all her students. As she writes elsewhere (Newton and Pratt 2015), one student from a development programme for disadvantaged young people, now fulfillingly employed as camera operator in a film company, said 'I am like this because of what you thought of me. You helped me believe in myself'.

This student, and those quoted in other chapters, are all engaged in *becoming* as well as learning as a result of their encounters with TA. That is what makes this a creative place to be.

We can all value our respected marginality, enjoy the dance between fringe and centre, and the chance both to belong and to be different.

16

LEARNING TO LEAD LEARNING

Rosemary Napper, UK

'This learning is different!' This comment comes from many participants over my past 30 years of training teachers, trainers and facilitators within a broad palette of adult learning. My quest for an underpinning theoretical base for high-quality adult learning was slowly resolved when I came across transactional analysis. My own learning story may help to illustrate my passion for co-creating spaces where all of us can learn.

A learning-from-life story

Reading under the bedclothes by torchlight added an illicit thrill to the learning which accrued from looking at my collection of PG-tips cards, *Dandy* comics, *Look and Learn* and frowned-upon Enid Blyton stories. I attended several mediocre schools and gratefully remember the occasional good teacher who made learning a real pleasure and around whom I felt inspired to expand my mind. The university lecturers who posed questions in their monologues – interspersed with rather good jokes – provoked knowledge which remains with me today. The women's consciousness-raising groups, where heated arguments flourished, impacted my attitudes enormously, and in these cooperative ventures I learned that some sort of leader always emerges and makes a difference. My three-times-failed school French motivated me to travel Latin America with my 13-year-old daughter to prove whether or not I could learn another language, leading to lively debate with didactic Cuban teachers in my pidgin Spanish about how real learning happens.

I was determined that I would never end up working in education – the rebellion of an only daughter of a primary school teacher and a university lecturer. I worked in advertising when adult literacy schemes were beginning, and naively decided that in my spare time I would enable others to know the joy of being able to read and write – and quickly came to realize that political, economic, psychological and social class barriers ensure there is forever an illiterate 'shadow' in the British population, showing how our social construction of reality is alive in a system that had successfully provided me with learning while at the same time depriving others of the tools to learn with.

A motorbike accident and a broken leg sent me to convalesce in Brazil where my father was teaching in the mid 1970s. Brazil was suffering from raging inflation and, as my savings began to run out, I realized that if I could teach I might earn money teaching English. Back in London I used the last part of my savings learning to teach English as a foreign language: a revelation! I came across contemporary ideas about how people learn, the value of an underlying structure, the vitality of interaction, the importance of learning outside the classroom, and the creative possibilities of techniques to support learning – most of which had been missing from my formal learning journey so far. So, I serendipitously fell into a career in adult learning – beginning with coordinating services to teach English to immigrants and refugees in the UK and then Australia. I rediscovered the political, social, economic and psychological factors which inhibited people's capacity to deal with institutions, culture and language. I learned so much from those I was teaching: the group of middle-aged professors, tortured refugees from Chile – who every Friday afternoon would send the teacher out of the classroom while they discussed her performance using a Marxist analysis, then called her back in to give their assessment – changed my views on the value of feedback forever!

I quickly realized that creating an environment in which people can choose to learn is quintessential – the emphasis is on learning, not on teaching. I discovered that only 7 per cent of adult learning projects take place in a classroom; most learning is informal (Tough 1971). Some understanding of the variety of ways in which people learn is hugely important, and the role of the person leading a learning environment is to create the conditions where learning can occur for everyone – inviting a culture where quality learning is valued and facilitated.

Transactional analysis as a framework for considering my learning

In my learning journey, I realized that subjectivity shaped my search for learning and meaning-making. And I relished the sharp thrill of creating a new meaning – a different attitude, fresh thought, or nuance of feeling – through intermingling my subjectivity with that of others. While fumbling towards this self-understanding, I came across transactional analysis again.

Earlier, I had not been inspired by three circles and the terms Parent, Adult and Child presented in a reductionist style. This experience was different – a work-funded residential escape from the daily grind on a 'TA for Managers' programme, with experiential learning of a coherent set of TA maps – 'topological' maps showing the key communication features in the workplace and in the political shenanigans of the organization; 'geological' maps providing a structure to understand myself to a depth that years of psychodynamic counselling had not plumbed – with applications to individual psychology, organizations and education. I was engaged! I was on a learning path which continues to inspire me a quarter of a century later. Now, I train others in many countries around the world and, in particular, train TA trainers and supervisors to bring life to the inspirational maps of TA.

Seven key aspects for a leader of learning

How can TA 'maps' inform and inspire a trainer leading their training programme, whatever their curriculum focus? Seven maps are highlighted here as core for creating the conditions for deep adult learning:

1   *Role theory* (Schmid 1994, 2008) – for assessment and curriculum design
2   *Hungers in learning and for leadership* – Berne's (1972) ideas about motivation linked to stages of programme development (Levin 1982, Napper and Newton 2014)
3   *Leadership* (Berne 1963) – and the inevitable transferences onto leaders
4   *Group imago theory* – Berne's (1963) psychological theory of group development
5   *Emergent process and 'soft' contracting* (Sills 2006) – for sufficient structure and safety
6   *Experiential learning design* (Kolb 1984) combined with accounting levels (Napper and Newton 2000, 2014) and positive dimensions of scripting (Newton 2006)
7   *Learning as meaning-making* – a shift in the frame of reference (Schiff 1975; Mezirow 2000) and scripting as learning (Newton 2006; Tosi 2010).

Recognizing roles

Training is a category of education focused on the learning and development of a person in relation to a particular role. When training trainers and facilitators, I am concerned with the development of their professional roles as particular types of educators. If they are involved with leadership development programmes then they are focused on the expansion of leadership capacity and roles of their participants within their organizational worlds. Assertiveness training may be concerned with participants' professional roles, such as in the workplace, and also their private roles with family and friends (Schmid 2008). Training psychotherapists is about developing the individual in their singular role as psychotherapist, whereas training a TA counsellor focuses on a range of roles including facilitator, advisor, mentor, coach, guide, supporter as well as therapeutic counsellor.

When training transactional analysts my concern is for their professional expansion in their chosen field, with a capacity to self-process regarding their own private roles, and to consider the impact of – and roles within – wider social systems. Role theory (Schmid 1992, 2008) is helpful in considering the scope of any training programme and in differentiating my role as trainer from the participants' roles as learners.

Schmid defines a role as a consistent pattern of feelings, thoughts, a perspective on reality, behaviours, and a specific set of relationships. This definition provides a structure both for training needs analysis and curriculum design. Figure 16.1 below shows these aspects from the 'inside out' to differentiate different roles as slices of pie (the whole self) and indicate how the feelings, thinking and perspectives on reality are not visible to an observer. This is a useful way to define 'personal' – part of the internal world of the individual (rather than the private world).

Newton (2003) and Napper and Newton (2000, 2014) developed ideas about how different philosophies shape learning theories and thus group formation, stroking, learning activities, and associated trainer roles. Barrow (2009) posited a continuum of these roles from 'right' to 'left' (in a literal, not a political sense). Using role theory, it is apparent that each trainer type is different in terms of: internal feelings and emotions; philosophical thinking and learning theories; perspectives on being a learner or a leader of learning; the contexts in which learning happens; how to use different behaviours and learning activities; how to relate to different types of learners and other stakeholders.

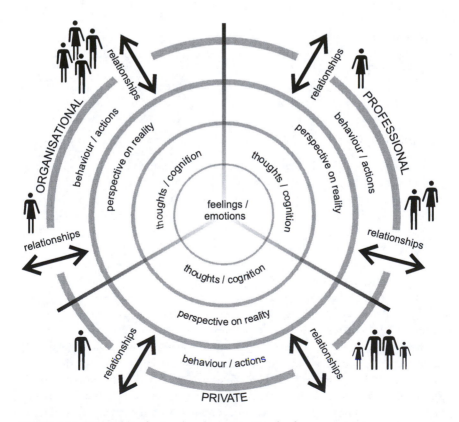

FIGURE 16.1 Private, professional and organizational roles

For example:

Guru – keynotes, lectures and didactic approach in formal settings, relating to learners as a group

Teacher – inputs with Q&A and a liberal approach in traditional educational settings, mostly relating to groups and occasionally focusing on individuals

Instructor – structured practice and demonstrations, a competence-based approach, assessment of individuals without building a group dimension

Facilitator – eliciting and categorizing into existing frameworks, a humanist approach focusing on differences between individuals and aiming for group support

Enabler – providing a forum for exploration and reflection and creating new frameworks, with an emphasis on belonging and co-creation

Animator – provoking disturbance to the frames of reference and being alongside learners as they collectively work these through and create change together.

Here I use the term 'leader of learning' to cover these six differentiated roles, which are often generalized under the umbrella term 'trainer'. It will become apparent that I favour some roles more than others: how about you?

Hungers – for learning and leadership

In *What Do You Say After You Say Hello?* Berne (1972) was explicit about the psycho-biological hungers, which he suggests are inherent and so describe a theory of motivation. He outlined seven hungers overall – appetites of individuals that need to be 'fed' in order to survive and thrive. These hungers require a healthy diet: however, if starvation threatens, with any of the seven an unhealthy diet is sought. Such motivations and responses co-create the learning culture and a wise leader of learning is aware of how to be alert to, and respond to, different appetites and 'proclivities' within a group (Berne 1963: 117).

> *Contact hunger*: a warm welcome impacts individuals and the group alike. In Brazil it is common for all trainees, whether early or late, to kiss each member in a learning group – whether or not they have previously met! – and there is a noticeable ease in these groups. Contemporary neuroscience indicates there are at least thirteen senses (Cirneci 2012) and that the 'sniffing out' which such greeting rituals encourage provides opportunity for the pheromonal sense to size up one another – these less obvious senses are part of how we unconsciously communicate. Moving around and pairing up in the initial stages of a learning group creates an environment where such checking out can happen. If unmet, contact hunger can lead to withdrawal in the group and game-playing in the breaks. This hunger is sometimes linked with the Being stage in Cycles of Development (Levin 1982): usually the beginning stage of a session or programme, involving clarifying who's who.

Stimulus hunger. The physical learning environment, the paperwork, the furniture arrangements, as well as the learning activities, the content and the trainer, can all provide stimulus. Blu-Tack and small toys can provide stimulus for the fingertips – more synapses are aroused and learning is increased if we 'fidget'. Too much stimulus can be overwhelming for some, while others may racketeer due to their higher level of stimulus hunger. Transactions are a key way to feed this hunger. Opportunity for withdrawal as well as space to be raucous within the same learning environment can be valuable. This hunger is linked to the Doing or exploring stage (Levin 1982) of a programme, investigating who we are in the group, and checking out the group leader.

Structure hunger. Levels vary from person to person. An emergent programme might provide too little for those with a high level, especially in the early stages of learning. A rationale for the emergent design can support them, alongside some 'ritual' time structuring. This may be too much for those with low structure needs, and so optional reading materials might provide balance. Inviting questions from pairs or triads is another way to respond to the need for structure. In Germany it is usual to present the 'thread' which will run through the programme. This hunger is linked to the Thinking developmental stage, and can involve clarifying the contract and analysing needs.

Recognition hunger. The need for strokes – whether conditional or unconditional will depend on the individual. If positive healthy strokes are not gained, the appetite will be gratified by seeking negative strokes. In the earlier stages of a group, strokes from the leader are particularly sought after. All opportunities for transactions are stroke-laden; so short lecturettes, with plenty of opportunity for discussion and other activities. This is linked to the Identity stage of development (Levin 1982); as a group gets underway, individuals begin to differentiate. Activities such as standing on continuums – or imaginary lines across the room – to describe learning needs, history, preferences or roles, help the differentiation process and provide opportunities for strokes.

Incidence hunger. A need for excitement – constellations, rehearsals, participants' 'show and tell', sharing out the leading of the group, coaching in pairs or triad work, all are ways of responding to the varying levels of excitement needed by different people. Jean Illsley Clarke memorably says 'Beware of time' with small group work; if left too long, pairs or groups finish their task, become bored and begin to play games to recreate excitement. This hunger is connected with the Skills stage of the cycles of development (Levin 1982), so opportunities for participants to experiment in the learning design can mean that unhealthy incidents are less likely.

Sexual hunger. This may be a variation on the hunger for incidence and stimulus or, taking a more Freudian perspective, could be a hunger for creativity. Learning groups where there are possibilities for participants to take leadership, to develop their own projects, demonstrate their learning in relevant ways, and so on, can satisfy this appetite! This is linked to the Integration stage of development; action planning for the future is an aspect of such creativity.

Leadership hunger. Berne stated that people have a hunger for leadership (1963: 216). Linking this with what he says about group imago, this means knowing who the leader is, the boundaries of leadership, and seizing opportunities to test its authority and potency, and maybe to take it over. Berne writes of parents being the joint leaders in the family system (1963: 86). As they progress, learning programmes provide opportunities for both challenge and opportunity in the unfolding group imago and the transferences on the leader.

Leadership in the learning culture

Both *Principles of Group Treatment* (Berne 1966) and *The Structure and Dynamics of Organizations and Groups* (Berne 1963) contain deep understandings about leading groups. In contemporary terms, leading a learning group involves the trainer using their presence (i.e. cathecting their structural Adult ego-state), both in holding the group boundary and in containing the unconscious processes of participants within the context of the group imago as it develops.

The named trainer, whatever their specific style, is the overall responsible leader – and the participants' perception of the authority of this person is vital in enabling the psychological level of leadership and the vision for learning to occur at the early stages. Berne (1963: 144) considered that authority came both from the antecedents of the leader (their learning credentials), and from how they came to lead this particular group.

The nature of the membership of both the leadership and the participant group is significant in co-creating the authority of the trainer and the culture of the group. There are psychological implications for the learner and the trainer, depending on how membership occurred, and whether this is usual/unusual. Berne identified six categories of membership (1963: 324):

- *Obligatory* – 'sent' or drafted: genuine motivation needs to be invited and the participant given the opportunity to leave if they wish.
- *Accidental* – through heritage, or arriving by mistake: may need opportunity to stay and to find real motivation and again have the option to leave.
- *Conditional* – through achievement, promotion: may need a lot of recognition by both leader and other participants.
- *Voluntary* – self-selected: may have fantasies about how the learning programme will be and need reality checks.
- *Patronage* – invited: may have high or low expectations of the leader and the benefits of the training programme and grandiosity about their own contribution; need reality checks.

- *Representative* – through election, or delegation: may have mixed feelings or a specific agenda, and need to clarify boundaries, particularly about how to validate their learning to those they represent.

Decision-making is the realm of the effective leader. A flexible leader ensures that decision-making is increasingly taken by participants as the group develops, and individual preferences become increasingly recognized and appreciated; collectively a cooperative, collaborative culture is created by – and for – all.

The psychological leader inspires, and will hold and contain the evident zest for learning, the capacity to hold the unconscious as well as the conscious energies in the group (Winnicott 1965) and to contain the emotions and projections (Bion 1961) is crucial. Their disclosure of thinking and feelings in their trainer role provides a model for transparency for the learners in relation to their professional roles, and provides an insight into the humanity of the trainer.

Ideally the leader is one person harnessing all three aspects. However, if there is co-leading of the group, one may be seen as the responsible or senior leader and the other two aspects will be split between the leaders, rather than seen to be delegated by the senior leader. Ongoing contracting between the leaders in front of the participants can help prevent this splitting by learners' P1, which might unconsciously be seeking to split mum and dad into Persecutor and Rescuer and so be the poor Victim learner – enacting their schooldays learners' script with its unhealthy recognition patterns.

The 'character' or ambience of the group is co-created by all present through the interplay of the dynamics (the observable interpersonal behaviours Berne referred to as 'etiquette') and the structures (the tangible resources or 'technics'). The leader is initially key in shaping these dynamics and providing these resources. Once the invisible character of the culture is set, there is a time-lag with regard to culture-change. Such ambience will include varieties of OK-ness, and psychologically acceptable levels of recognition, drivers and games, which may be different from what is declared as acceptable.

In my experience, the length of time spent near the beginning of a learning programme in meeting each other and exploring the contract and the leader is invaluable. It makes for easier and speedier learning in the long run, and reduces transferential energies. This may mean challenging the 'hurry up' drivers of busy professionals, which prevent them from learning from one another through belonging.

Group imago – psychological differentiation

Berne's brilliant but little-used theory of group development clearly describes largely unconscious psychological constructs and provides insight into what the leader needs to be holding and containing at different stages. Berne calls this the 'private structure' of individuals, focusing on the transferences and unconscious shifts which inevitably take place in all groups between members and with the leader.

The *provisional* imago uses the template of the original family group, maybe modified by later group experiences, and is how we fantasize a group we are about to join. Contact from the leader and information about the others and the purpose of the group may allay some of these unconscious projections – nonetheless as people arrive they begin to adjust these as-yet-unthought-about images. At this stage they are particularly anxious and concerned about the capacity of the leader to hold the group boundary. Warm welcoming of individuals, without taking a full frontal position in relation to the group, and setting up structures so that the anxiety about who is here can be relieved, are all enabling at this stage.

Only when some of the initial anxiety and *adaptation* of the provisional imago has occurred can the participants focus on checking out the leader and their capacities. This is the time for whole group introductions, the programme introduction by the leader and the initial group contract. Confidentiality is often asked for: a good opportunity to show my robustness as a leader when I challenge the reality and relevance of such an agreement. This immediately deepens the level of thinking and invites Adult, which is so essential for learning to take place.

Berne wrote about how we arrive in groups with our 'individual proclivities' (1963: 216). Providing learning structures where these can be recognized and appreciated is valuable at this stage. Again, it is a test of how tolerant the leader is, and how firm they can be trusted to be in declaring and holding the group boundary. Transferences onto the leader are central throughout the development of the group imago – the resilience to take in, recognize and appreciate, gently name, and put back these transferences is key to creating the conditions for a productive learning culture.

As the members and the group move to the *operative* stage of their group imago the challenges to the leader increase and allegiances and sub-groups form. There will be enactments between group members (perhaps unobserved and outside the group), in order to test the major unconscious question that each individual wants to know the answer to: what is the leader's imago of the group and how psychologically close or distant am I to the leader – as well as to the others? Although the enactments and challenges may seem to be with each other, there is usually a wary watchfulness of how the leader will react and a test of the consistency of OK-ness demonstrated by the leader.

Many groups get stuck at this operative stage – it is only if the transferences have been well managed, and the leader's imago revealed as perceiving the individuals as equal yet different, that there can be a shift to the next stage of the *secondarily adjusted* imago. At this stage there is professional closeness and a giving up of individual inclinations in order to get on with the group task of deep learning.

Tudor (1999) suggests that there are further stages – the next being *a secondarily adapted* imago whereby participants have learned that it is OK to own some of their proclivities and for there to be different levels of psychological distance, without dislodging the energy in the group task and cohesion. This is followed by the *historical* imago as people leave the group with a fresh imago or template of 'my group' – and perhaps some new members arrive and so the process starts over.

Handling transferences in the leader role requires awareness of the counter-transferential response, avoiding reacting to the transference. Recognizing and realizing this P2 or P1 desire, and filtering it through an Adult here-and-now understanding of the delicate evolution of the group and the individuals within it, is an art. Leaders will also have their own transferences onto, and identifications with, individuals and the group as a whole – which can muddle the mix! This is when supervision can help to identify the different levels of individual history, group process, culture and organizational influences. It is easy when working with a group to identify one or two individuals as absorbing energy, and therefore the issue or the leader as at fault. It is vital to remember that everything that happens in the group is co-created and part of a group phenomenon; it belongs to, and can only be fully resolved within, the group (Sills 2003).

Trusting emergent process

Meeting learners in the moment – and co-creatively collecting their needs and wants – is a high-risk way of contracting for a meaningful session design, relevant to the present context of participants. This process, whereby new meanings can emerge out of the inter-subjective space (Tosi 2010), involves a high level of unpredictability and uncertainty, and may be experienced as teetering on the edge of chaos – where creativity is most potent.

This way of working requires the protection and permission of a negotiated 'soft' contract at the psychological level. The contracting matrix (Sills 2006) describes the difference between 'hard' and 'soft' contracting. The level of awareness of participants in relation to the theme suggests a sequence: first clarifying and then exploring experiences as wants and needs in relation to learning, then building and developing, leading on to change. Such a contract is about both the content and process of the learning, and is usually the practice of a facilitator, enabler or animator.

I distinguish 'wants' from 'needs': the former are desires, whereas the latter are necessities – when walking in a hot desert, water is a need, a glass of wine a want! Focusing on real learning needs in relation to the roles the training is focused on is vital in terms of connecting with genuine motivations, and directed at the developmental stage of the learner. It may be useful to see needs in terms of the developmental stage being recycled by the learner, and then consider the needs of the previous stage to create optimum conditions for learning to support the developmental task (Levin 1982; Napper and Newton 2014). If a learner has joined a programme in order to develop their identity as a supervisor, for example, it may be useful in considering their need to begin with 'thinking' about supervision (the stage prior to 'identity') to ensure a good grounding and a focus on real needs, rather than with vague or idealized desires.

Many learners bring their deficits or confusions in relation to their role – that is: their 'wrong' feelings and attitudes; their 'lack of knowledge, understanding and way of thinking; their 'issues' in their perspective of their role; their 'inade-quacies' in skills and behaviours; their 'ignorance' about who to most effectively

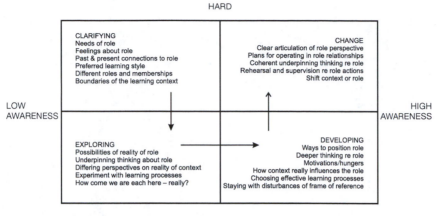

HARD

| CLARIFYING
Needs of role
Feelings about role
Past & present connections to role
Preferred learning style
Different roles and memberships
Boundaries of the learning context | CHANGE
Clear articulation of role perspective
Plans for operating in role relationships
Coherent underpinning thinking re role
Rehearsal and supervision re role actions
Shift context or role |

LOW AWARENESS — HIGH AWARENESS

| EXPLORING
Possibilities of reality of role
Underpinning thinking about role
Differing perspectives on reality of context
Experiment with learning processes
How come we are each here – really? | DEVELOPING
Ways to position role
Deeper thinking re role
Motivations/hungers
How context really influences the role
Choosing effective learning processes
Staying with disturbances of frame of reference |

SOFT

FIGURE 16.2 The contracting matrix

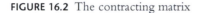

relate to. In itself, this exploration often results in growth, and the individual learner's focus on filling in gaps and shifting their frame of reference provides direction in the learning sessions.

However, such a negatively oriented entry into determining needs is likely to stimulate the fantasy-creating P1 to attend to idealized wants, rather than clarifying real needs. Inviting the Adult to recognize what might be useful strengths to build upon in their role, plus the context which the training is focused in, will lead to working with 'what is'. A focus on 'competence' has sometimes led learners and trainers to emphasize a deficit model rather than 'appreciatively enquire' about – and build upon – what is already working.

Using an adaptation of Sill's (2006) contracting matrix (Figure 16.2) in training programmes tends towards such appreciative inquiry into real needs:

While training a particular group of coaches, the use of this contracting matrix uncovered the realization that there were very diverse understandings about the role and purpose of coaches in relation to other roles. This led to an activity without 'right answers', whereby participants placed on the floor names of different roles in relation to each other and argued among themselves the nuances of their positioning until all were comfortable with what emerged. This led to further clarification of what competences each individual already possessed, and how these might be differently useful, with a changed perspective on their purpose and scope when coaching.

Experiential learning design

Enabling adults to reflect on the resonances, meanings and emotions of their experience is essential in moving towards a framework for a valid analysis – and to introduce new concepts. Embedding these realizations in such a way as to engage

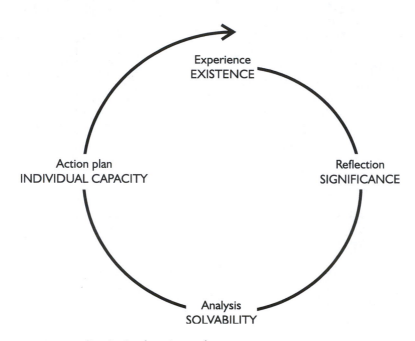

FIGURE 16.3 Continuing learning cycle

deep learning involves taking action and applying it to their future experiences – and then another cycle of reflection, analysis, action planning and new experience can take place (Figure 16.3). This process involves profound recognition of the existence and the significance of self-experience, and the potential to analyse – as well as the learner's own capacity to act on the options generated.

Levels of discounting and accounting (Macefield and Mellor 2005) add a dimension to the learning cycle (Kolb 1984). If I am present in my experience, my Adult ego-state takes note of the existence of my internal world as well as the external reality. I can then reflect on the significance of my observed and felt experience using my somatic Child (C1) and my intuitive Adult (A1), as well as my structural Adult (A2). I can then draw conclusions from my reflections and make hypotheses, both from my experiences and in terms of existing concepts, and so construct a model to make meaning and resolve my experience. On the basis of this model of reality, I can then make decisions and action plan in the light of my capacity. This is learning in action. As Newton proposed (2006), learning is scripting – and flexible script is the current story we have to make sense of our lives and our future actions.

Kolb (1984) explained how, sometimes, learning might not take place. He viewed concrete experience as *apprehension* and drew a vertical dimension with abstract conceptualization (analysis) which he labelled *comprehension* (both terms contain '-*prehension*', which means 'grab or grasp' as monkeys do tree-branches with their prehensile tails). In other words, operating in one or both of these dimensions 'grasps' at learning. Kolb suggests that it is the horizontal dimension between reflective observation and active experimentation which is transformative. This dimension brings about real learning.

This model therefore presents a design for emergent learning. In training, all participants have roles they are developing and deepening, and so have experiences to bring into the training space, and can reflect on what is significant about their needs in the context they operate within.

When I am open to the real learning needs that are emerging and becoming clarified in the group, I listen to my sense of what is significant and therefore valuable to pursue. For example, I went to a Training for Trainers third day with a plan about what I would teach – but what emerged from the reflection on the previous day was a desire to consider deeply how learning takes place and how it is hindered. We laid round carpets of different colours on the floor representing structural ego-states, and each person chose to walk or to point to where their learning through the here and now (structural Adult) was contaminated and hindered by past experiences (in the structural Child), or inhibited by messages from powerful and significant others from the past (Parent).

Learning as co-creative meaning-making

Human beings are meaning-making animals. We create meanings together, weaving in and out of our individual and intermingling pasts and presents. This view sees people as homonomous or interdependent (Salters 2006), rather than – or as well as – autonomous.

Learning requires attunement (Erskine 1998) from the trainer in order to generate a profound engagement between the learners, and the learner with the facilitator. Learning techniques can invite learners to connect their own experiences and meanings with the creativity of the process, which deepens involvement in the learning. New meanings often emerge retrospectively when there is such attunement – indeed this may sometimes be well after the learning programme is finished.

As a trainer I am changed through my meeting with the learner, just as much as the learner may be changed through their engagement with the programme and the facilitator. My own style verges on the provocative – learning is a disturbance to my frame of reference (Schiff 1975; Mezirow 2000). However, it is foolhardy to set up disturbing experiences as part of a training programme – these can ricochet in unexpected directions. A profound disturbance is a naturally arising phenomenon which cannot be engineered or designed. For each individual, what is disturbing at any one time will be different – and may be a positive experience as much as a negative one.

I use my Structural Adult, not only to 'helicopter' above the learning situation and identify patterns, but also to notice my own internal physiological emotional and intuitive responses to others and wonder – often aloud – what these unconscious responses may mean here and now. This can best be summed up as a relational approach: my wonderings often invite learners' musings, and it is this weaving of our different strands of meaning, our discovery of different nuances and differences in kind, which gives rise to profound meaning-making.

As an example, working as lead trainer with a transactional analyst assisting on a four-session counselling skills training for university students, my colleague was sufficiently disturbed by her experiences in training to create a poem for the final session, packed with levels of meaning, some of which only a transactional analyst will recognize:

Counselling conversations: shadow and light

I'll lend you my ears
To bend for a while,
We'll play a game of tit for tat,
Do ourselves proud
And conjure up a storm.

OR

We could sit, side by side,
And be ourselves,
We could agree
To pay attention
To what moves below the waves,
I could offer you my presence,
So you can test your own waters.
If our meeting is true
We will both be changed.

Rona Rowe

Creating the conditions for learning to take place is the focal task for the trainer. Contemporary transactional analysis provides in-depth maps of what this requires. It is a co-creative process, so I too am a learner in the training process.

Lifelong learning: a prison sentence, or a process of vitality?

17

REVISITING TRANSACTIONAL ANALYSIS IN ADULT EDUCATION

Jan Grant, Australia

Transactional analysis began as a model for therapy. However, right from the beginning, Berne opened his seminars to many different professionals and wanted transactional analysis to be generally accessible to people. Transactional analysis is a wonderful model for educators working both with children and adolescents, and adult educators. This chapter will explore several theories of adult education and relate them to two core concepts from transactional analysis: ego–states and scripts. The models to be covered are, first, Susannah Temple's functional fluency model (Temple 1999), which is related to Stephanie Burns' findings on what makes an effective adult educator (Burns 2009); script (Berne 1972) and current ideas on scripts, psychological life plans and the learning cycle by Trudi Newton (2006); work on generational script patterns by Michael McQueen (2012); and finally Richard Boyatzis' theory of self-directed learning (Goleman 2002), alongside the importance of physis.

Functional fluency and effective adult education

Let's start with ego–states. In his ground-breaking book, *Transactional Analysis in Psychotherapy*, Berne (1961) presents his three-ego-state model: Parent, Adult and Child. He talks of the Parent and Child ego–states as having an archaic quality, and the Adult ego–state as processing what is happening in the immediate situation. He also mentions different aspects of the Child ego–state, describing them as 'the natural and the adapted states' (Berne 1961: 12). Today there are many models of ego–states and this has sometimes led to confusion.

The first more recent theory I want to introduce is the functional fluency model devised by Susannah Temple (Temple 1999). Temple brings great clarity to the functional/behavioural model of ego–states. An effective educator has what Temple calls 'functional fluency', which she defines as 'the behavioural manifestations of the integrating Adult ego-state' (Temple 1999: 164). She applies this to the modes of behaviour used by educators as they help people to learn. She emphasizes the importance of educators being engaging, empathic and effective communicators. An awareness of the need for functional fluency helps educators stay out of negative modes, using positive options instead. A functionally fluent educator will be aware of internal and external stimuli and will respond appropriately to what is needed in the moment. Increased autonomy for the educator allows for creativity and increases their energy.

In 2014, Temple received the Eric Berne Memorial Award for her work on functional fluency. She starts her wonderful *TAJ* article, 'Update on the Functional Fluency Model in Education', with the statement, 'Education involves relationships' (Temple 2004: 197). Indeed it does. The person of the educator is crucial; they need to be flexible, to use appropriate behaviours, to relate to different students and different contexts of learning, and to create effective relationships with learners. Excellent educators rely on the 'fabulous five' (Temple 2004: 200): structuring mode; nurturing mode; accounting mode; cooperative mode; spontaneous mode. They least use the other four: dominating mode; marshmallowing mode; compliant/

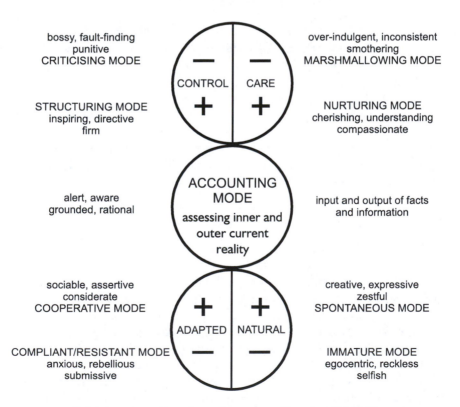

FIGURE 17.1 Behavioural manifestations of ego-states (Temple 1999: 168)

resistant mode; immature mode. An awareness of these modes is a great asset to educators.

Temple is clear that the functional fluency model is not a model of ego-states, rather a model of human functioning which draws from the theory of ego-states. Building on other theorists' ideas (Stewart; Heppel; van Beekum), Temple has used stacked squares to depict nine behavioural modes, as in Figure 17.2.

In connection with the idea of functional fluency, I want to introduce the work of Stephanie Burns. She has focused much of her career on teaching learning strategies to adult learners and has run a successful programme called 'Learning to Learn'. She has also conducted research into adult education and what makes the difference between effective and ineffective educators. She is clear about what makes a difference in educational outcomes for adult learners – it is the skill level of the educator (Burns 2009).

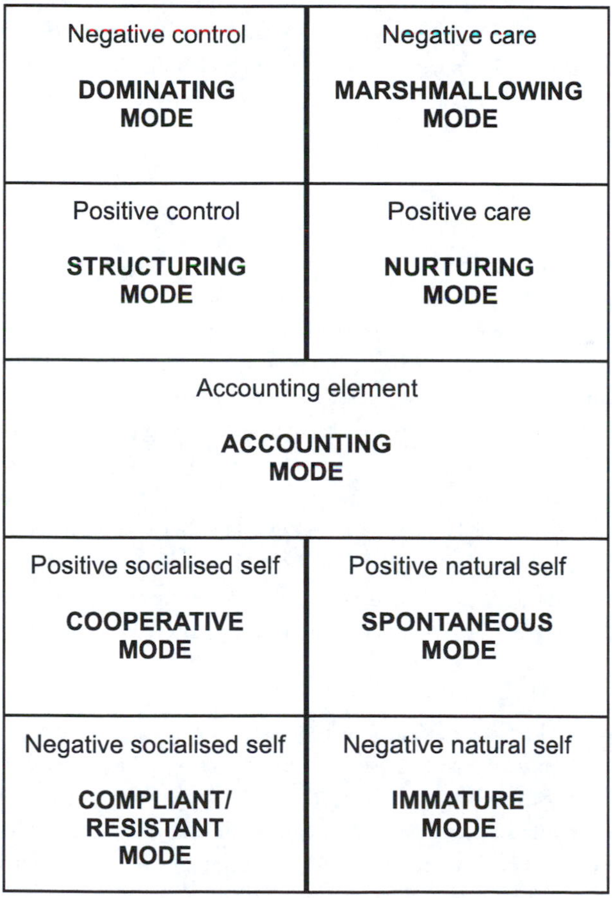

Negative control **DOMINATING MODE**	Negative care **MARSHMALLOWING MODE**
Positive control **STRUCTURING MODE**	Positive care **NURTURING MODE**
Accounting element **ACCOUNTING MODE**	
Positive socialised self **COOPERATIVE MODE**	Positive natural self **SPONTANEOUS MODE**
Negative socialised self **COMPLIANT/ RESISTANT MODE**	Negative natural self **IMMATURE MODE**

FIGURE 17.2 Nine behavioural modes of the functional fluency model (Temple 2004: 200)

She identifies three essential qualities and skills that typify excellent educators:

1   *Behavioural flexibility*: They have a range of characteristics they can call on, they are flexible (they can be firm, fun, straight, whatever is required for the context they are in), they are active, congruent and often continuous learners themselves (thus keeping them in touch with what it is like to be a learner). This is 'functional fluency'.
2   *Understanding the learner's perspective*: They understand what it is like for the learner. They know learning is challenging and sometimes arduous. They understand how learning can be tense as the brain changes and create a safe environment where learners can express their confusion. They understand that motivation can wax and wane. They protect the dignity and confidence of learners because they know their confidence can be fragile.
3   *Coherence*: They can explain things in a way that makes sense to the learners. Effective educators are clear on desired outcomes and help students by providing a clear sequence to the learning. New concepts are presented in manageable chunks. Both the content and the process are sound. Establishing a trusting relationship with the learners helps them to come on a learning journey.

She also adds two other important qualities:

1   *Ability to hold students' attention*: Effective educators can hold students' attention and be clear on the objectives of the class. We know how important this is for brain plasticity, which relies on being able to pay attention. Each session/class needs to have a 'set up': where the educator tells the learner what is expected, what the benefits of learning this material are and why it is important for them. This helps students feel relaxed enough to pay attention and to take in the new material.
2   *Participation*: They plan for learners to be actively involved. People need to engage with the class and materials. Learners need to be able to try things out in a safe setting and receive regular feedback on how they are doing. Helping learners to identify the evidence of learning is effective so that they can see that learning is occurring. Learners need to have a choice in how they participate.

Stephanie Burns' PhD research looked at student motivation and what occurs for students who complete their goal, as opposed to those who do not. At the beginning of a course, students' motivation is high. They are typically positive and excited. This is because they anticipate how good they will feel at the end. She says that the next time they are likely to feel like this is at the end – that is, students who are persistent enough to get there. Along the way, students' motivation will wax and wane, and they will feel a variety of emotions: anxiety, frustration, stress, anger, boredom, guilt and shame.

She found that students who succeed and complete their courses use three unique, cognitive strategies to cope with the negative emotions they experience. These are:

1   Don't think (about what you are feeling now): when beginning a new activity/subject, they don't think about how they are feeling in that moment – which is likely to be anxious.
2   Do think (about how you will feel at the end): they do think about how good they are going to feel at the end when they have achieved their goal.
3   Just start: rather than procrastinating they just start, whether that is doing an assignment or reading their textbook.

I have found it helpful to teach these three cognitive strategies to adult learners. Burns talks about the understanding that outstanding educators have of students' negative emotions, and how they can support students through the periods of low motivation and teach them that this is a natural part of learning (Burns 2009: 75).

Scripts and learning life-plans

Now, let's turn our attention to scripts. Berne defined script as, 'An ongoing program developed in early childhood under parental influence, which directs the individual's behaviour in the most important aspects of his life' (Berne 1972: 418). In her seminal article, 'Script, Psychological Life Plans, and the Learning Cycle', Trudi Newton (2006) reviews notions of scripts and script formation from Berne's original rather deterministic view to recent more natural views of 'script as a normal, necessary human process of making meaning' (2006: 186), and to co-created notions of script. The need for permission to make our own meaning is emphasized. Newton summarizes the debate and newer thinking in this area with four main points:

1   The child is active in the script formation.
2   The script is co-created.
3   The context in which the script is created is much wider than the immediate family.
4   The script is formed in a particular culture.

Following Cornell (1988), she makes a distinction between 'psychological life plans' and 'life script' (Newton 2006: 187). Psychological life plans are seen as a normal, healthy process of creating stories to guide a person's life. These can be updated as needed. Thus this is a non-pathological process that is open for revision. Life-script, however, may be limiting or self-defeating.

One way of understanding psychological life plans is to explore the widely used model of learning: the learning cycle (Kolb 1984). Learners are continually experimenting with new behaviours, reflecting on their experiences, thinking about new ideas and planning for how to implement them.

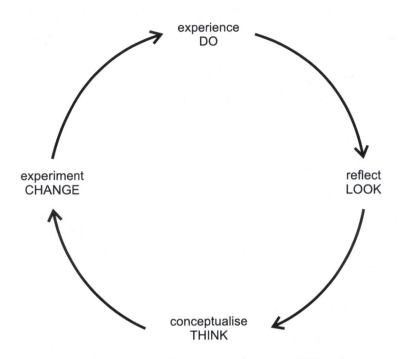

FIGURE 17.3 The learning cycle (Napper and Newton 2000: 1.6)

Our behaviour is changed as a result of reflecting on, and drawing conclusions about, the experience. Changed behaviour results in a new experience – and so the cycle starts again or, more accurately, becomes a spiral where each loop forms another stage in the learning process of 'do' (something), 'look' (at what happened), 'think' (about the implications) and 'change' (what you do next time) (ibid.), see Figure 17.4.

This is a two-way process, not a one-way adaptation of behaviour to the environment – behaviour also shapes the environment.

The well-known theorist of cognitive development, Jean Piaget (1971), focused on the active tendency of humans to develop their knowledge over time. He saw learning as an inter-play between the individual and the environment. He describes two important functions in human cognition: assimilation and accommodation. Assimilation is fitting new information into existing schema; transactional analysts see this as script in action, where experiences that do not fit with existing beliefs are discounted and experiences that reinforce script beliefs are taken in. Accommodation is changing the schema in order to include new information or creating entirely new schemas; the latter is updating the script and creating new narratives, based on new experience and knowledge. Piaget saw intellectual growth as the growing use of accommodation.

Newton also refers to the co-creative approach of Summers and Tudor (2000), who developed the 'script helix' to show the range of people influencing a person's

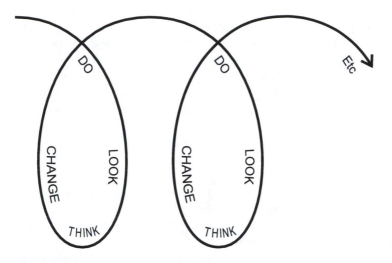

FIGURE 17.4 The learning spiral (Napper and Newton 2000: 1.6)

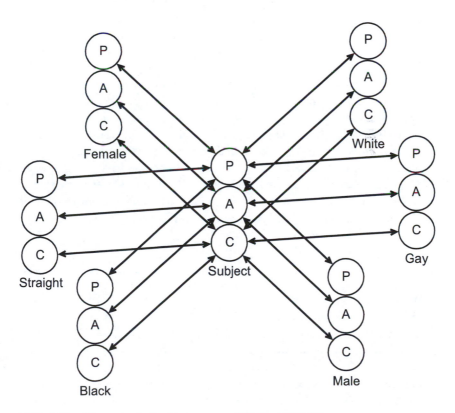

FIGURE 17.5 The script helix (Summers and Tudor 2000: 34)

script. They identify the influences of race and culture on a person's script and grapple with the post-modern concept of dominant and non-dominant narratives. Examples are a black child growing up in a predominantly white culture and a gay or lesbian person navigating a predominantly heterosexual world. This co-created story is constantly open to change and they state: 'the script matrix becomes a co-created series of matrices, rather like a constantly changing helix of relational atoms, spinning around us, by which we tell, retell, and reformulate the stories of different influences on our continuing development' (2000: 34).

In order to explore this further, I want to introduce the idea of generational learning styles. I discovered a gem of a book: *The New Rules of Engagement*, by Michael McQueen (2012). Perhaps something that transactional analysts have tended to overlook is the influence of generational differences on script formation. These differences will show up in the learning environment.

For transactional analysts, the idea of generational differences in script formation would combine points 3 and 4 of Newton's four main points. This means taking into account certain sociological factors that affect each generation differently. While each generation may be impacted by different historical events and technological changes, the overriding human need for contact and connectedness remains the same. For educators, it is imperative that we can de-construct our own expectations (partly derived from our generational scripts) and get into the world of our students. It is hoped that an understanding of generational script issues enables this process.

A 'generation' is defined by McQueen as, 'the entire body of individuals born and living at about the same time who share similar ideas, problems and attitudes' (2012: 10). Each generation is profoundly affected by the social milieu of its time. Many factors need to be taken into account: the socio-political climate of the time, the financial climate, the cultural climate, major historical events and the social norms of the time. An Arabic saying (quoted in Bloch 1964: 23) captures the essence of this: 'People resemble their times more than they resemble their parents'.

Adding generational theory to our understanding of scripts can be illuminating. McQueen describes generational theory as, 'the area of sociology that deals specifically with mapping, classifying and understanding the characteristics of different generations and how the gap between them is expressed' (2012: 14). He identifies five generations:

The Builders	– Early 1900s to mid-1940s
The Baby Boomers	– Mid-1940s to mid-1960s
Generation X	– Mid-1960s to early 1980s
Generation Y	– Early 1980s to late 1990s
Generation Z	– Late 1990s to . . .?

For me personally, a woman in my sixties, the Builders refers to my parents' generation, the Baby Boomers to my generation, Generation X to my children, Generation Y to many of my students, and Generation Z to my grandchildren.

For the first time in history, four generations may be in the same workplace or learning situation. In the college where I teach, we have students from eighteen to seventy. This means that in some groups we are working with three generations at once. As learners, these students bring very different experiences, attitudes and expectations.

For the purposes of this chapter I will concentrate on Generation Y – the reason being that this group is the one I hear many educators complain about, these being educators who come from among the Baby Boomers or Generation X, two generations before. Let's look at what influences have been affecting the script decisions of each generation, and may be causing the problems. I can only talk from the perspective of my own culture (I am Australian), but my guess is that these differences resonate for the developed world.

The Baby Boomers

In Australia, post World War II was a time of stability, full employment and prosperity. Things that had a huge impact on this generation were television, the war in Vietnam, and the introduction of the birth-control pill. Traditional roles for men and women were challenged. People born in this generation tend to believe they can do anything, are optimistic, have a good work ethic, are loyal employees, focus on their career path, believe in the good life, like clear steps to a defined goal, and work well in teams.

Generation X

This was a time of more uncertainty. Personal computers came in, divorce increased dramatically, single-parenting and step-families became more common, women re-entered the workforce, multiculturalism was introduced in Australia, and people sought work/life balance. The AIDS epidemic struck. People born in this generation tend to be cynical, self-reliant, individualistic, they like flexible work structures, they multi-skill, set their own priorities, and need recognition and feedback.

So what is so different about Generation Y?

This generation is the best-educated, well-travelled and tech-savvy generation. Their mantra is 'instant'. Parenting styles tended to be child-centric, with a strong emphasis on self-esteem. The term 'helicopter parenting' was introduced to describe parents forever hovering over their children. This generation tends to have confidence, be ambitious, know their rights and feel entitled. They relate without face-to-face contact; technology is their norm. They are continuous learners, and tend to be transient in their careers. Perhaps surprisingly, they have a strong social conscience and sense of civic duty (largely because of the access they have to information).

McQueen (2012: 48) gives a wonderful chart, based on the work of American generational expert Eric Chester, which summarizes the key differences across three generations:

TABLE 17.1 Generational differences (adapted from McQueen 2012: 48)

Topic	Boomers	X-ers	Gen Y
Wealth	I'll earn it	I don't care that much about it	Gimme or I'll take it
Role models	Men of character	Men and women of character	What's character?
Loyalty to employer	I'll work my way to the top	This could lead to the top	If I can't take Saturday off, I'll quit
Justice	Always prevails	Usually prevails	Can be bought
Education	Tell me *what* to do	Show me *how* to do it	Show me *why* to do it
Respecting elders	Is automatic	Is polite	Is earned not assumed
Personal debt	Only if I have to	If I really want something	How much can I get?
Change	Dislike	Accept	Demand
Technology	Ignorant of	Comfortable with	Masters of

McQueen identifies eight 'new' rules of engagement for connecting with Generation Y and what they need as learners:

1 *Focus on building relationships.* Temple reminds us that education is about relationships (Temple 2004). This generation is hungry for relationships. Power and control will not work with them. They are looking for role models who are authentic and interested in them. Taking time to get to know them and letting them get to know us is time well spent. 'Relationships are the foundation for engagement with this generation' (McQueen, 2011: 126).

2 *Use matrix learning.* 'Matrix learning' means putting context around content. With its access to the internet and instant information, this generation needs to know the relevance and connectedness of what they are learning. They want to know the answer to one important question: Why? Why do they need to know about what we are teaching them and how is it relevant to their future?

3 *Focus on outcomes.* How we measure performance and output is very important to this generation – why we do things the way we do (outcomes), rather than what we do to achieve them (process). Members of Generation Y are very focused on outcomes, but not on red tape and unnecessary structure. They value flexibility. They hate too many rules.

4 *Adopt a facilitator role.* Generation Y has more information than any previous generation. The challenge is to know what is relevant and connected to the

outcomes they want. A good facilitator knows how to use questions and experiential learning methods. Using open-ended questions that help the learner explore what they know, and what they want to know, can be very powerful. Good facilitators also make space for self-directed learning.

5   *Give regular positive feedback.* This generation has been raised on positive feedback, and they appreciate affirmation. Negative feedback is often difficult for them to hear, and they can take it very personally. Therefore, when negative feedback is needed for growth and learning it must be given in a timely fashion, be specific and focused on behaviour. It must be delivered calmly, and in a way that reaffirms your faith in the person, by telling them how they can do it differently.

6   *Set short-term, challenging goals.* As this generation has grown up in a fast-paced, constantly changing and technology-driven world, they require frequent, short-term goals which are reviewed regularly, and targeted projects. Large goals need to be broken down into specific, achievable, smaller goals.

7   *Use stories.* Stories are a powerful means of teaching and learning. Postmodern in their thinking, this generation is not interested in what is right and wrong. They are interested in what works, and stories are a wonderful medium to show how principles work in a particular context. This allows the listener to attach their own meaning to the story. Think back to the first rule here: take time to build a relationship with your students. Delivering information for the sake of information will not work, but if you can share your background, your history and your stories, you will engage them. You become relevant for them. Good stories are memorable and fun.

8   *Go for commitment, not compliance.* This generation has the reputation of being free agents. Rules and regulations do not go down well. Rather than aiming for compliance, aim for commitment. When asked 'Why', by students, this is our opportunity to create buy-in: if they can see the reason to commit they will. If they can see what's in it for them, they are encouraged to commit. With their strong sense of civic duty, doing things in the service of others is desirable. They want to make a difference. If you can show them how their participation in community projects will make a difference, they are likely to want to get involved.

Physis and self-directed learning

I want to end by introducing Boyatzis' model of self-directed learning. This learning model was developed by Richard Boyatzis during three decades of work in leadership development, working both as a consultant and as an academic researcher (Goleman 2002). It equally applies to leadership in organizations, and leadership and facilitation in an adult education setting. It is a change model and requires an understanding of the change process. This process relies on an intentional willingness to develop or strengthen aspects of who we are and who we want to be.

The model denotes five discoveries, each involving some discontinuity (2002: 110). Each discovery can be used as a tool for change. The steps are not smooth or orderly, but do follow a sequence with each step requiring different amounts of time and effort. This is a lifelong, recursive process of growth and adaptation. As new skills are practised and embedded they become part of our new 'real self' and the cycle starts again. The steps are as follows:

1   *My ideal self*: Who do I want to be?
    Having a sense of vision (who you want to be) evokes passion, hope and motivation. This is important because it helps to sustain you through the difficult parts of the journey.
2   *My real self*: Who am I?
    Knowing who you are, being able to make an honest appraisal of yourself is crucial. This requires honesty from oneself and honest feedback from others. It means assessing your strengths: what you already do well; and your weaknesses: areas for improvement. Some qualities will fit with your ideal self, and some will be gaps that need to be worked on.
3   *My learning agenda*: Building on my strengths and reducing gaps.
    From this reflection and appraisal, a change agenda can be formulated. This needs to be a detailed plan of action that builds on existing strengths, builds new skills to fill in gaps, and moves closer to your ideal self. This plan needs 'to feel intrinsically satisfying' (2002: 111) and fit with your learning style and the context of your life and work.
4   *Experimenting with new behaviour, thoughts and feelings*: This means practising new behaviours, trying them out, seeing what happens, and reflecting on the outcomes and what feels right for you – and what does not. It means laying down new neural pathways until mastery is achieved.
5   *Developing trusting relationships that help, support and encourage each step in the process*: This cannot be done alone. You need others to help identify your ideal self; appraise your real self: both strengths and gaps; to set a learning agenda; to experiment and practise new skills. Others may see things you do not. Others can affirm strengths we do not own, point out gaps we do not see and tell us when we have made positive changes.

Relationships are the context in which change occurs: 'Without others' involvement, lasting change can't occur' (Goleman 2002: 111).

I relate the premise of this model, an intentional willingness to work towards who we want to be, to the idea of *physis*. Berne defines physis as 'the force of Nature, which eternally strives to make things grow and to make growing things more perfect' (Berne 1957: 68). He explains physis as part of normal maturation (1957: 80). He also introduces the aspiration arrow to the script matrix (1972: 128) to emphasize this life-force.

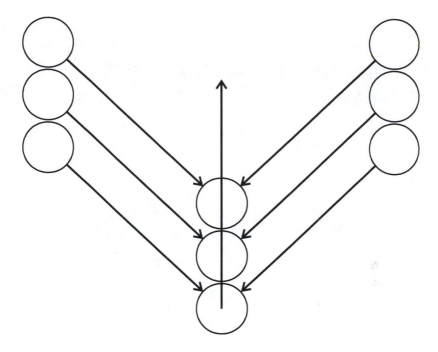

FIGURE 17.6 The aspiration arrow (adapted from Berne 1972)

Conclusion

Boyatzis' fifth point is crucial to adult education. The context of supportive, trusting and honest relationships is vital in supporting learners' physis and enabling them to achieve the outcomes they want. Learners need safe opportunities to practise new skills with honest feedback, both affirming and constructive. They need others to witness their growth, to challenge blind spots that they may not see in themselves. At the beginning of this chapter I said that transactional analysis started as a model for therapy; I believe that the goals of therapy and the goals of education are similar: self-knowledge and personal change. Transactional analysis offers educators a wonderful framework for understanding themselves and their students. Functional fluency, script change and physis underpin the models for adult education and to me this is the epitome of the I'm OK – You're OK life position.

18

TRAINING IN ORGANIZATIONS WITH TA

Rhae Hooper, Australia

My life as an educator started more than 35 years ago when I was a product specialist in the computer industry, working for one of the biggest international computer companies at the time. Little did I know then that, in training people to use specific computer equipment and programs, we closely followed the Kolb method of adult learning, (Kolb 1984). I would introduce or demonstrate a specific subject; the trainees would do what they had just been taught. If it worked, they would reflect on it and move on; if it didn't work, it would be reviewed and they would have another go. Within this process the students would be assessing the application of what they were learning.

In this chapter I will explore the central role an effective leader plays in the delivery of education in a corporate training environment. Regardless of the subject matter being taught, or how the attendees apply themselves, research clearly shows that the effectiveness of learning outcomes stems primarily from the competence of the trainer (Gage 1972; Lieberman, Yalom and Miles 1973). This competence lies in key areas of the trainer's skill as a presenter and in the presentation itself. It is always more than the trainer's expertise on content and subject matter.

The skill and talent of an effective educational leader goes to the heart of the philosophy of TA; it involves authenticity, spontaneity and intimacy. Transactional analysis theory supports trainers and empowers them to be effective leaders of training groups within organizations. To illustrate how this happens, I will also use two pieces of research, one undertaken by group psychotherapists Yalom, Lieberman and Miles, and a second by leading educational psychologist Nathaniel Gage.

Although conducting their research independently, both investigators explored group leadership and adult learning concepts. I will link the results of this research, show how it is supported by TA principles, and explore the application of theory and research in terms of planning, conducting and reflecting on training.

Experiencing and reflecting

American educational theorist, David Kolb, stated that learning is the process where-by knowledge is created through the transformation of experience (1984: 38).

As my career progressed, I would often use the Kolb model to inform my work as a trainer. When I moved on to train in sales, support and marketing fields, I became more interested and involved in the people skills side of training. Whereas I had been a technical expert, in these new departments I didn't need to be. Moving from computing, where I was expected to be an expert and knew what would happen when a variety of things were tried, I was now delivering training programmes for soft communication skills, written and designed to be taught in a specific format with little opportunity to try different approaches.

One of my strengths has been to take a subject and apply it to situations and examples, painting pictures and drawing from experience – and I was keen to capture the essence of that in my new role. With the introduction of the personal computer I had decided that I would not be going to bed with a reference book for the rest of my life so that I could keep up with the latest software and hardware changes. I set about looking for some psychology studies that would assist me in the new training I was undertaking. I discovered an educational trainer in Sydney – Jan Grant – and have not looked back, personally or professionally.

As a trainer in the corporate environment, TA informs my knowledge, training, experience, professional and personal growth. Over the years, my application of TA to any training course I have written and delivered has greatly benefited the learning for the attendees and the delivery experience for me.

Concrete Experience:
Having the experience
(Feeling)

Active Experimentation:
Trying out what has been learnt
(Doing)

Reflective Observation:
Reflecting on the experience
(Watching)

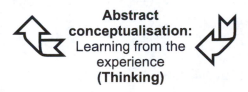

Abstract conceptualisation:
Learning from the experience
(Thinking)

FIGURE 18.1 The learning cycle (derived from Kolb 1984)

It has been my experience as a corporate trainer that businesses in the sector commonly require short training courses (one to five days), sometimes with follow-up days over a period of a few months. Mostly, this training involves employees from the same company. Sometimes attendees come from the same department, while at other times participants are working in similarly ranked positions from different departments across the company. With the restrictions of time, non-voluntary attendance, and company obligations, it is essential to use facilitation and training techniques that maximize both employee and organizational benefit.

Given the challenges associated with delivering quality content in short time-frames, and considering the issue of compulsory staff attendance, the trainer is faced with the task of ensuring that the best possible adult learning environment is achieved through a high level of engagement, and meaningful, time-efficient activities are delivered with energy and enthusiasm, coupled with content that is pitched at the right level for both the attendees and the company. In the great majority of cases the company is expecting certain prescribed learning outcomes to be met, and it is incumbent on the trainer to ensure these objectives are achieved.

The attendees at company training courses are all adults employed by the company. From that perspective, they are expected to make informed decisions, are paid by the company, and are also expected to perform appropriately to their position status. It is with this in mind that I combine TA concepts with the findings of two pieces of independent research on group leadership.

Transactional analysis – a practical frame for trainers

Eric Berne, the founder of TA, moved away from conventional psychiatric theory and practice and based the foundations of TA on his belief that clients inherently know what is wrong, what they need to do to fix it, and that they are capable of doing so if given the appropriate information and tools. He wanted TA to be accessible to everyone, not just psychiatric or therapeutic professionals. This seemingly simplistic TA philosophy is actually very deep and complex.

It is this fundamental TA philosophy that I believe underpins the findings in both Yalom *et al.* and Gage's studies, particularly that meaning and attribution (Yalom 1973) and indirectness (Gage 1972) are critical for successful training. When provided with the right space and information, a person can make what meaning they will for the change they want to achieve.

During my years training adults, working in the corporate sector and studying training, management and therapeutics, it seems to me that TA philosophy and principles have underpinned many other popular models of psychology in use today. I will share how TA supports and is supported by the research, and how I use TA to contract, prepare, plan and facilitate short training courses for the corporate sector.

Underlying principles of TA in education

The main concepts of TA focus on a theory of personality, interpersonal communi-cations, ego-states and group systems. It is founded on three basic beliefs and principles:

- Everyone is OK.
- They can think for themselves.
- Anyone can change.

When a training course is designed and delivered based on these principles, and the trainer inherently believes and behaves with those three values integrated into their approach, it optimizes outcomes. The trainer takes up a position which gives attendees permission to be at the training, to think for themselves, participate, make mistakes, learn and allow change. In this framework, the trainer provides protection for those experiences to happen, and is potent in their facilitation (Crossman 1966).

This is particularly important when the attendees are all from the same company. When they leave the training room, participants return to work with each other as peers, subordinates and managers. Trainers need to be potent in their approach so that they remain in an I'm OK – You're OK position and autonomous. With the best intentions of staying in the I'm OK – You're OK position, it may not always happen, and other TA concepts can be used to actively reinforce the process, most helpfully: ego-states; contracting; strokes; games; drivers. These concepts also address the findings of the research I discuss later in the chapter.

The research

I will now turn to the two seminal pieces of research which provide a backdrop to my thinking about the key requirements for delivering high quality training within a TA framework. Both were conducted with groups wanting to learn or make changes, and both produced outstanding findings that were similar in philosophy and meaning.

From psychotherapy to group leader qualities

Yalom, Lieberman and Miles studied the effectiveness of psychotherapy encounter groups with the dual objective of determining the validity of claims that they can change behaviour and personality factors, and in addition which modality of group psychotherapy was the most effective. TA was one of a number of models researched in the study.

The findings led researchers down another path: a significant finding was that the effectiveness of the group leader was a key element in the effectiveness of the therapy group, regardless of the model of therapy used.

The research emphasized the significance of factors that contribute to effective leadership. They found that the greatest impact on the group's learning and capacity for change hinged on specific leadership styles and behaviours of the trainer.

- *Emotional stimulation* – the ability to be challenging and confronting and actively modelling personal risk-taking and self-disclosure.
- *Caring* – offering support, affection, praise and protection as well as warmth, acceptance and being genuine.

- *Meaning attribution* – possessing strong capabilities in explaining, clarifying, interpreting and providing a cognitive framework for change, and for translating feelings and experiences into ideas.
- *Executive function* – strengths in setting limits, rules, norms and goals through managing time, pacing, stopping, interceding and suggesting procedures.

The key findings were that the most effective leaders rated high on *caring* and *meaning* attribution qualities and moderate on *emotional stimulation* and *executive function* qualities. Too much or too little emotional stimulation and executive functioning were associated with poor outcomes, and the same applied to low levels of caring and a low level of meaning attribution. Meaning attribution was found to be the most important quality for success in the group; it is the meaning the learner makes of an exercise or activity that is most important, not the exercise or activity itself. Therefore, the trainer has to come prepared with some useful models and have the skills to help process the participant's learning.

Educational leader qualities

Unlike Yalom *et al.*, Gage, an educational psychologist widely known as one of the founding thinkers of modern research on teaching, conducted research directly intended to determine the effectiveness of leaders of adult learning groups. Gage's research revealed that effective leaders had to have four essential qualities for success:

- *Warmth* – they tended to speak well of people, to like and trust rather than fear others and tended to establish warm relationships.
- *Indirectness* – they let people discover things for themselves and were willing to refrain from sharing everything they know, even when it would be 'good for people'.
- *Cognitive organization* – they hold clear behavioural objectives in mind and divide learning into orderly steps, offering appropriate data in response to questions and clearly conveying what they know and what they don't know.
- *Enthusiasm* – the most effective leaders have an innate enthusiasm for people and the subject matter.

Quite independently, on different research topics, the findings in these two pieces show remarkable similarity. While different language is used to describe these findings, they can be matched. For example: warmth and caring; cognitive organization and executive function; meaning attribution and indirectness.

I am particularly impressed with the synergy given my training in TA, which has its roots in psychotherapy, and my chosen application – education. These two pieces of research emerged from those two fields.

Based on the significant findings of these two pieces of research I have designed a form for trainers to use (see facing page), to assess where they believe their developmental stage is in relation to their current leadership skills. This is intended

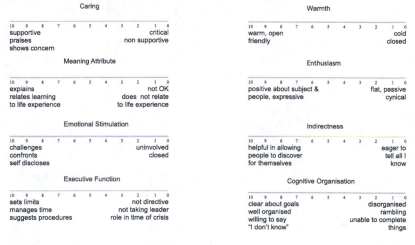

Your leadership qualities

Rate your leadership qualities by circling a number for each of these qualities.
Keep this scale and rate yourself again at the end of this course.

Yalom, Lieberman & Miles (1973) study indicated that Meaning Attribution, Caring, Emotional Stimulation and Executive Functioning were the qualities of Effective leaders with the most effective leaders rating HIGH on Meaning Attribute and Caring and MODERATE on Emotional Stimulation and Executive Function.

N. L. Gage (1972) study found that Warmth, Indirectness, Cognitive Organisation and Enthusiasm were the qualities found in the effective leaders in adult groups.

Caring

| 10 | 9 | 8 | 7 | 6 | 5 | 4 | 3 | 2 | 1 | 0 |

supportive / praises / shows concern — critical / non supportive

Warmth

| 10 | 9 | 8 | 7 | 6 | 5 | 4 | 3 | 2 | 1 | 0 |

warm, open / friendly — cold / closed

Meaning Attribute

| 10 | 9 | 8 | 7 | 6 | 5 | 4 | 3 | 2 | 1 | 0 |

explains / relates learning / to life experience — not OK / does not relate / to life experience

Enthusiasm

| 10 | 9 | 8 | 7 | 6 | 5 | 4 | 3 | 2 | 1 | 0 |

positive about subject & / people, expressive — flat, passive / cynical

Emotional Stimulation

| 10 | 9 | 8 | 7 | 6 | 5 | 4 | 3 | 2 | 1 | 0 |

challenges / confronts / self discloses — uninvolved / closed

Indirectness

| 10 | 9 | 8 | 7 | 6 | 5 | 4 | 3 | 2 | 1 | 0 |

helpful in allowing / people to discover / for themselves — eager to / tell all I / know

Executive Function

| 10 | 9 | 8 | 7 | 6 | 5 | 4 | 3 | 2 | 1 | 0 |

sets limits / manages time / suggests procedures — not directive / not taking leader / role in time of crisis

Cognitive Organisation

| 10 | 9 | 8 | 7 | 6 | 5 | 4 | 3 | 2 | 1 | 0 |

clear about goals / well organised / willing to say / "I don't know" — disorganised / rambling / unable to complete / things

FIGURE 18.2 Your leadership qualities

to assist in identifying areas for improvement, and can also be used to facilitate feedback to the trainer by course or workshop attendees.

Bringing the research and transactional analysis together

I want now to examine these findings along with TA, and to show how they apply to the provision of quality training programmes in the corporate sector. Yalom *et al.* found that the most effective leaders rated highly on meaning attribution and caring (with meaning attribution being the most important). Indirectness, in the Gage research, was the most strongly preferred attribute for the learners. The indicator on the Gage research that matches caring is warmth.

Meaning attribution and indirectness

Meaning attribution is described as the provision of a cognitive framework for change. This can be in the form of an explanation of the content, or new material being presented on the course. It also lies in the clarity of explanations, effective use of diagrams, flow charts and audio-visual materials. It encompasses the linking of all elements of the course to provide a framework for change.

Incorporating the translation of feelings and experiences into ideas is another key feature of meaning attribution, and this is best achieved through reflection and review following relevant parts of the course. It is particularly important to allow time for review after experiential exercises and activities so that meaning attribution can be achieved through thoughtful consideration of what has just happened in the group activity. All of this lies within the philosophy of TA – that people can think for themselves, and everyone can change.

During training, attendees complete a variety of activities. These can include writing an action plan, recalling experiences and applying the new learning, completing questionnaires, taking part in role-plays and interviews. These activities may be performed on their own or within small groups. It is in the experience of doing the exercises or activities that new learning begins to take place. For this reason there needs to be sufficient time for the reflection and review of the exercise to enable the attendee to experience this, and to optimize self-learning opportunities. This requires the trainer to be utilizing functional fluency or integrating Adult (Temple 1999), giving the attendee permission to discover the learning.

It can often be a trap for new trainers to feel that they need to be the expert and to have all the answers. However, Gage's leadership quality of indirectness, where the learner discovers for him- or herself, involves the leader refraining from giving a direct answer. In this instance it is better to resist telling participants what the trainer knows, even if it is beneficial for them to know. It can also be an expectation of the attendees and their organization: if the trainer is deemed to be a leading exponent of a subject, it is expected that they will provide all the information.

Incorporating a variety of training methods, such as reading, writing, discussing, didactic training and experiential learning, using audio and visual tools, enables workshop attendees to harness their own learning style. During the process, the trainer needs to provide the time and space for the attendees to reflect, integrate and apply what they learn to their work and lives. For this reason it is critical that the amount of content delivered leaves enough time to allow for review at the end of activities. Correct timing and pacing are crucial; good content and time structure ensure this occurs.

It is also crucial that the trainer does not automatically answer all questions posed by the attendees. The trainer needs to elicit the questioner's thoughts as well as group discussion (or both) to enhance learning, to resist being the 'expert' and to avoid telling the attendees everything even if they think it would speed up the process. An added demand on the trainer is to hold the awareness of the overt expectation coming from the company and those on the course who are waiting to be 'taught'.

A training programme that has been tailored to the specific needs of a company with appropriate time to apply the learning will optimize both meaning attribution and indirectness.

Caring and warmth

The next two most important attributes found in both pieces of research were *caring* (Yalom *et al.*) and *warmth* (Gage).

TABLE 18.1 Meaning attribution and indirectness

Leadership quality	Description	Transactional analysis
Meaning attribution (Lieberman, Yalom and Miles 1973)	Explaining Clarifying Interpreting Cognitive framework for change Translating feelings and experiences into ideas	Structure Contracting Caring Including all learning styles
Indirectness (Gage 1972)	Encourages self discovery Refrains from telling everything they know (even when it would be 'good for people')	Time structure Nurture and support Caring and listening

Caring is described as supportive; is shown by someone who praises and shows concern, and is genuine. The trainer who rates well with this quality will display a genuine friendliness, welcoming participants as they arrive at the course venue, providing nametags and materials suitable to the course or workshop. Key skills include noticing and resolving confusion, taking questions and being supportive, and respecting differing points of view. From a TA perspective, this requires the trainer to use the *nurturing* and *accounting* modes (Temple 1999).

Offering praise and feedback appropriately in the form of strokes is also vital; in designing the course, the trainer will provide activities that account for all types of adult learners. There will be visual aids, didactic pieces, group experiential exercises, and opportunities for attendees to speak or raise issues and ideas.

Gage attributed warmth as being friendly and open. A trainer who has a genuine interest in people and their commitment to learning will exhibit natural warmth. They will be well grounded and comfortable, and also diligent in their role, open to new ideas. Change, and responding to possibilities proposed by the learners, demonstrates both spontaneity and authenticity.

By combining both of these research findings, catering for all learning styles and paying attention to respect, the trainer can create an atmosphere of caring and warmth by listening, praising, congratulating and offering suggestions – as presented in Table 18.2.

Executive functioning and cognitive organization

Executive functioning and cognitive organization relate to the management of material, administration, time and boundaries. Time structuring and contracting assist here, so the trainer is the secure base for the management of the training. The trainer needs to employ effective situational leadership without losing the

TABLE 18.2 Caring and warmth

Leadership quality	Description	Transactional analysis
Caring (Lieberman, Yalom and Miles 1973)	Supportive Praises Shows concern	Positive Nurturing Parent Strokes Listening
Warmth (Gage 1972)	Warm Open Friendly	Positive Nurturing Parent Spontaneity Authenticity Intimacy

potency of the learning, with both directive and supportive behaviour. For example, at the beginning of the course, the trainer may be more directive by explaining the agenda, leading a discussion on a new topic, closing down an activity in order to move on. During the course the trainer may be less directive as attendees work in their own groups (Hersey and Blanchard 1982).

Executive functioning is associated with the management of time, setting limits and boundaries, the norms of the group, the goals, and pacing and suggesting procedures. TA offers contracts, structure and accounting as methods to ensure these aspects are met. The research showed that too much or too little executive functioning is associated with poor outcomes. Good management of these functions will be seamless to the attendees, with the trainer showing care and warmth while still supporting the needs of the learners and balancing the time and content.

In a time-limited course, there may be a temptation for a trainer to be rigid about time boundaries, such as limiting opportunities for discussion. There may be so much content that there is little time to observe and reflect. In other circumstances, there may be little content or direction, and more time than is comfortable for the group to work on their own. It is crucial for the trainer to create agreed working rules with the group to achieve the objectives. The working rules at the beginning of the course may encompass such items as the time structure for the day, respecting opinions, having mobile devices on silent, managing side conversations, and so on. These ground rules, an agenda and objectives, allow the trainer to manage the process without being too rigid or too loose. A trainer who can assess the situation and move seamlessly with spontaneity and authenticity will provide a well-balanced programme.

With respect to cognitive organization, the trainer needs to have good preparation. This includes an agenda with the objectives as requested by the company, having all the materials, presentations, audio-visual material and workbooks ready and well organized. It is interesting that in Gage's research, the willingness to say 'I don't know' is repeated as part of the leadership strengths of both indirectness and cognitive organization. Perhaps it is the knowledge of what the trainer doesn't know that enables the better management of time and procedures.

TABLE 18.3 Executive functioning and cognitive organization

Leadership quality	Description	Transactional analysis
Executive functioning (Lieberman, Yalom and Miles 1973)	Sets limits Manages time Suggests procedures	Contracting Positive Structuring Parent
Cognitive organization (Gage 1972)	Clear about goals Well organized Willing to say 'I don't know'	Contracting Time structure Authenticity

While the course is progressing the trainer needs to be very aware of distractions, how much time has elapsed, when the breaks are. All of these factors ensure the balance of executive functioning and cognitive organization.

Emotional stimulation and enthusiasm

The research on emotional stimulation showed that this characteristic should feature in moderation. It is described as the ability to be challenging and confronting, and actively model personal risk-taking and self-disclosure. When trainers feel confident and comfortable in their own shoes, their authenticity and ability to display intimacy ensures this happens. The trainer needs to challenge the attendees to go that bit further, without driving them so far they feel de-motivated. An example of this can be in the objectives or goals determined after a topic or an exercise. When the attendee has to think of three actions they will take as a result of the exercise, it is usually thinking of the third one that challenges. Working in small groups to discuss those actions, ideas and beliefs can be further challenged.

Confrontations could include: addressing regular latecomers; when more than one conversation is occurring in the group; and any behaviour that detracts from the agreed 'ground rules'. Rigid and dogmatic beliefs can be challenged and confronted where it is appropriate for the learning experience. An effective trainer will also be open and self-disclosing within the boundaries of the course and the material being covered. It is important to remember that adult learners present with different stages and styles of learning.

Introducing a variety of methods in the exercises provides emotional stimulation. For instance, I change the seating arrangement in the breaks – from U-shape to boardroom, to classroom. This can cause concern, bewilderment and excitement in the group when they return to the training room, but it also offers participants the experience of different seating arrangements reflecting aspects of the course content on groups. Having people move and interact and do a variety of activities is stimulating, though trainers need to be mindful of not over-stimulating with too much presentation material.

TABLE 18.4 Emotional stimulation and enthusiasm

Leadership quality	Description	Transactional analysis
Emotional stimulation (Lieberman, Yalom and Miles 1973)	Challenges Confronts Self-discloses	Accounting mode Strokes Authenticity
Enthusiasm (Gage 1972)	Enthusiasm about people Enthusiasm about the subject matter	Positive Free Child Spontaneity

As found in the research, too much or too little emotional stimulation does not bode well for the trainer's effective leadership or the attendee's ability to learn or make changes. It is important that emotional stimulation is well regulated, checked and moderated and continuously being considered by the trainer.

Finally, *enthusiasm* from the research completed by Gage: the most effective group education leaders have an innate enthusiasm for people and the subject matter. In TA, this refers to spontaneity and the existential position of I'm OK – You're OK. Apart from natural enthusiasm, the trainer who is well prepared and well rested prior to the training has confidence about their own abilities, models genuine interest in the participants, and enthusiasm for the subject matter of the course. They engage attention and display an authenticity that resonates with the participants.

Summary

Facilitating training programmes in the corporate environment is a process in which the attendees and the trainer learn from each other. The studies by Yalom *et al.* and Gage, and their independent but complementary findings, demonstrate the qualities of an effective group leader and also provide a tangible structure for the incorporation of TA into a trainer's portfolio of learning.

The eight elements discussed provide evidence of what researchers found to be effective in gaining better learning outcomes in adult groups. For trainers, they are easy to understand and implement. Is it enough to be caring or warm, to have an organized agenda and plenty of activities for the attendees? A deeper understanding of why these attributes are so crucial can assist the trainer to behave more naturally and authentically. That is where I believe TA underpins and supports these results, enabling the trainer to have self-awareness and providing a wonderful platform from which to base the design and facilitation of a programme.

TA provides us with the means to check our own professionalism (Hay 1992: 12). I have chosen to highlight only those elements of TA that underpin the findings of Yalom *et al.* and Gage but, as Eric Berne declared, an occasional stroll in the park with transactional analysis will hardly reveal all its possibilities (Berne 1961: 234).

19

EDUCATIONAL OPERATIONS

A transactional analysis technique for educators

Marina Rajan Joseph, India

Introduction

The theory and practice of educational transactional analysis is rooted in the transactional analysis (TA) theory of personality, psychopathology and psychotherapy. TA educators are trained transactional analysts who strive to apply TA theory for educational purposes. They develop the educational theory and practice of TA by consistently applying the theory and tools in the practice of education, blending and integrating it with other educational theories and concepts, and maintaining the boundaries between other applications and the educational field.

The TA theory of psychopathology and its parallels in learning theory

The original 'Script Theory' espoused by Berne (1975) is that a baby in the process of growing up transforms their experiences to make decisions about self, others and life situations from their vulnerability and limitations, and leads their adult life based on these decisions; the sum of these decisions forms the 'script'. It thus explains that pathological scripts are caused by unhealthy environments of the newborn and the struggle for survival in such situations. Classically, TA psychotherapy focuses on these pathologies and their cure through therapeutic interventions. In addition, present-day transactional analysts give emphasis to the growth promoting elements in the script. William Cornell invites a broadening of the concept of 'script' and suggests the term 'psychological life plan' to be used to 'describe the healthy functional aspects of 'meaning making' in the ongoing psychological construction of reality' (Cornell 1988: 270–81). This understanding of script comes very close to Kolb's explanation of 'learning', defined as 'the process whereby knowledge is created through the transformation of experience' (Kolb 1984: 38). Learning is a process of creating knowledge, resulting from the transaction between social knowledge and personal knowledge (1984: 36). Knowledge results from the combination of grasping and transforming experience. Since the present understanding of 'script formation' in TA is that it is an ongoing process of meaning-making of experiences, it may be assumed that 'pathological scripts' are results of faulty learning. TA psychotherapy is cognitive and behavioural, and brings about healing by undoing the faulty learning and replacing it with better learning. Script cure may be understood as the practice of new learning with ownership.

Many aspects of TA theory have tremendous potential to be applied in educational practice. This chapter discusses, from the writer's experience, how the concept of 'therapeutic operations' (Berne 1964) can be used as tools by educators to achieve effectiveness.

The eight therapeutic operations of Berne

In identifying different types of transactions Berne defined an operation as an 'honest and direct transaction undertaken for a specific stated purpose'. An operation is called 'procedure' when it originates from Adult and is directed towards 'manipulation of reality' (1964: 48). Operations are said to 'reach highest development' (1964: 35) in professional techniques. Berne identified and listed eight 'therapeutic procedures' or therapeutic techniques to be used by psychotherapists and called them the 'therapeutic operations'.

The eight therapeutic operations in their 'logical' order, developed for work with clients, are: interrogation, specification, confrontation, explanation, illustration, confirmation, interpretation and crystallization (1966: 233–49). Berne classifies them into interventions (the first four) and interpositions (the last four). In describing the operations and instructing on their use, he explains that each of these operations is a tool for inviting clients into their 'Adult' ego-state. He conceived psychopathology (Berne 1961) as contaminated functioning of the Adult ego-state or exclusion of any one of the ego-states. So he developed these techniques for decontamination and strengthening of the Adult ego-state as his therapeutic method. Inviting a client to respond from their Adult consistently is a therapeutic intervention. Those operations used to strengthen the use of Adult ego-state are called interpositions. He listed certain other interventions which are also targeted at the Child and Parent ego-states. These operations and their use made TA therapy very crisp, effective and quick compared to other methods existing in Berne's time.

Therapeutic operations can be educational operations too!

Berne himself equates therapy to teaching (1966: 355). As I started learning TA, and later became certified as an educator, I wondered at the parallels between therapy and education. One of my most interesting observations has been about the use of the 'therapeutic operations' as 'educational operations'. Whoever may be the learners – parents, children or adults in professional learning – in all ideal teaching/learning situations the process is essentially that of strengthening the Adult ego-state. Hence an educator can be trained to use the 'educational operations' in teaching situations, just as a therapist can be trained to use them in therapy. They can be used one-to-one and in group teaching situations. These operations help learners to develop the use of their Adult ego-state and thus promote healthy development of personality. Hereafter I refer to them as 'educational' operations.

Using the educational operations

These examples are taken from my experience as a medical educator, and TA educator, supervisor and trainer. My project for qualifying in TA involved designing and implementing a curriculum to teach medical research methodology to fifth semester medical students. Initially the use of therapeutic operations in my sessions was not consciously planned. This gradually evolved as I started listening to my recorded interventions and reflected on my techniques. I became aware of a developing competence in myself. It slowly matured through the supervision I received. Today I practise these operations as an educator in different groups and in different roles and have found excellent results.

1 Interrogation

This is the first educational operation described by Berne. It literally means to ask a question, a technique used by many teachers who engage their classes in 'active learning' (Felder and Brent 2009). It is very helpful to begin a session with a question regarding what the students know, and to proceed from what they know. The student's response to this operation reveals the content of what the student has learned to think, or the content of their Parent/Child ego-states and how they use their Adult ego-state. A teacher can use this as one of the first operations in order to assess the presenting level of students, plan the session and structure the inputs. When used with awareness while working with students, this invites the Adult in the student to respond. Linda Hutchinson says about medical education, 'Learning depends on several factors, but a crucial step is the engagement of the learner' (Hutchinson 2003). In transactional analysis language, one way of engagement of the learner is probably by maintaining an 'I'm OK–You're OK' stance (Woollams and Brown 1978) and constantly communicating with the Adult of the student.

2 Specification

This is the operation intending to reflect to the learner what they have answered in response to the interrogation, so that they can listen to their own statement and are able to rethink or make changes. This response reflects to them what they have said and enables them to 'listen' to it, and often invites them to come forward with newer ideas, which I consider as evidence of their thinking process or their using their Adult ego-states. Specification promotes reflective learning.

3 Explanation

This is the operation used to clarify learning or introduce a new concept to be learned. The response from the students to my specification gives me an opportunity to use 'explanation'. Explanation often helps in focusing on the learning outcomes. This is also an important component of the 'collaborative research model' (University of Oregon 2010). In this model students' learning goals are clearly stated, both for students and educators, through formulating learning outcomes. When the learning goals are clarified, both learners and facilitators know what they have set out to achieve. This clarity and lack of ambiguity also generate transparency in the teacher–student interactions.

Interrogation invites the Adult, specification clarifies any contaminations, and explanation states the learning objective.

4 Illustration

This is an interposition, a tool to strengthen the Adult, used in education to reinforce or strengthen learning or the Adult insights developed by the student. For example, usually immediately after the 'explanation' I use an illustration to reinforce the learning. Often it is a pleasant anecdote from my first experience in a similar situation. This not only strengthens their insight, but often inspires them. Sharing the teacher's experience and enthusiasm for the subject is an effective method of motivating and inspiring students described in the effective teaching programmes (ibid.). I have often had experience of my students suggesting to teachers that they teach them from their experiences.

5 Confrontation

In education, this may or may not be used immediately after specification. Often it is used when students slip back into statements stemming from contaminations, or continue in their original thinking. Interestingly, many students have come to me to acknowledge how the 'confrontation' helped.

Reflection and discussion on the problem are encouraged by using this operation, leading to consensus in group exercises and learning activities. In the collaborative research model, coming to consensus over a specific topic or some aspect of the topic is an important part of creating a learner-centred environment (ibid.).

6 Confirmation

This is another interposition or technique to strengthen the Adult. In the educational scenario, this operation is regularly used when students come forward with their insights. Often it is positive responses like 'exactly' that affirm the insights. The confirmations of the learner's insights become self-affirmations for them, strengthening their Adult and helping them to use it again and again in similar situations.

7 Interpretation

Interpretation is an operation used by the therapist to shed light on the client's experience in terms of the psychological processes. In education it may be used to explain a difficult concept using metaphors and analogies. Pickett suggests how interpretations could also be elicited from the students (Pickett 1986). Interpretations are evident in all acts of writing notes in the student's own words, or elaborating a concept in the teacher's own words, and so on. Especially, the process of writing a literature review, analysis of research data applying statistical methods, and making inferences from data or writing a discussion of the results, is interpretative work. Interpretations are possible through use of the faculty to think, which is a function of the Adult ego-state. The more students use it in learning sessions, the better they are equipped to use it later in independent work.

8 Crystallization

This is an interposition, an operation that consolidates all the new decisions in therapy. In an educational scenario, the Adult learning from the session may be précised using this operation. I often use it at the conclusion of a session as a summary of its major messages. It could also be elicited from the student, like the use of interpretation. In fact it may be more effective when elicited from the learners. The facilitator may check whether any important point has been missed, and add it. This gives the students a directive to take steps to go on with the new found learning.

Other interventions described by Berne

It is interesting that other TA concepts, such as strokes, are also listed as interventions along with therapeutic operations by Berne himself (1966: 248). *Support* is considered as an intervention, in the form of strokes. Strokes are units of recognition, their target is the Child ego-state since desire or hunger for recognition is a transformation of the desire or hunger for stimulation. Stimulations to the senses are considered the motivation for living and growing in the child. Berne has also suggested that for the Adult ego-state to be freely available, the Child must be satisfied, or the Child's needs must be met. Stimulations or strokes are the needs for the Child to survive and grow healthily. Strokes used appropriately take care of the Child ego-state, whose 'proper function it is to motivate the data processing and programming of the Adult' (Berne 1961: 78).

I often give support by way of strokes, for example, by appreciating questions asked by students; sometimes just actively listening to what they have to say, or by enough space being created in all sessions for interaction among students. Some kind of physical activity, or an outing which gives positive physical experiences, also functions as strokes or stimulation. I have observed that this reinforces the learning.

Other interventions, reassurance, persuasion and exhortation, are therapeutic interventions to be used in specific and difficult therapeutic situations. Berne reminds us how they have to be used with awareness. Pickett has included them as 'Direction', a ninth therapeutic operation as defined by Erskine (Horne and Ohlsen 1982: 245–75). I think grouping them together as 'direction' is very appropriate, because their target is the Child ego-state and the objective is to direct the Child to motivate the Adult.

Exhortation is seldom used by me. I agree with Berne (1966) that 'exhortation' has the danger of not accomplishing the ultimate aim of therapy/teaching, which is empowerment of Adult in students and attainment of ability to live autonomously. While using the educational operations, it is very important that teachers are not too 'pushy' with students (exhortations seem too pushy!)

Choosing an operation

Which operation is to be used in a particular context depends on the objectives set for the session. For a teacher, who perceives education as a means for expanding students' awareness, it is a process of constantly inviting their Adult. All operations are excellent for this purpose. The TA educator must ask themselves the questions, suggested by Berne for therapists in relation to their clients, while planning their teaching content and in relation to the student group.

Berne's questions are (1966: 252ff):

1   What am I trying to cure the patient of (teach my student) today?
2   Has the patient (student) said or done anything which could form the basis for a therapeutic hypothesis (teaching plan)?
3   What is my hypothesis about his personality (the student's learning needs)?
4   How can I best validate it (my assumptions about the student's learning needs)?
5   How do I think he (class or group) will respond to what I say?
6   To which of his ego-states should my interventions be directed?
7   Actually, at the present moment, which of his ego-states is most likely to give the overt response to what I say?

Berne's sequential description of the operations does give a logical understanding of the dynamics of use of therapeutic operations and responses to them. As educational operations, they may often be not used in the same sequence in which Berne has described them.

Are 'educational operations' to be used or elicited?

It is noteworthy that the effective teacher not only uses the operation, but also elicits it from the students. Pickett says,

> Whether a teacher performs or elicits these operations depends on whether he or she wants to lead or follow the class. Maintaining a balance between leading and following in the use of therapeutic (educational) operations ensures that students do their share in the relationship.
>
> (Pickett 1986: 244)

When a TA educator is leading the class, they use the 'educational operations' as tools, to attune to the situation in the classroom and 'use' or 'elicit' each of these operations in appropriate situations.

How to use the educational operations

- *Concisely*: It is interesting to note that Berne recommended that these procedures be 'as concise as possible' (Berne 1966: 237), and be properly timed and tuned for best results. I found in my practice that, whenever I consciously use these operations, I am able to keep my words to a minimum, giving opportunity for the students to be more involved and also 'own' their class.
- *With awareness of the inherent power/potency of these operations*: I see here a connection between therapeutic operations and the concept of 'permission'. Invitations to use the Adult are permissions to think (Allen and Allen 1988). Berne also says that permission to think is most important (Berne 1975). I think Berne's instructions (1966) on use of the therapeutic operations to aspiring therapists, invites them to be aware of the power/potency in them. The same is true for educators, as teacher's permissions are very important for the growth of the student. It is recommended that an educator practise these operations with awareness of this potency.
- *Acknowledging the autonomy of the student*: Learning is an event that takes place only when the student wants to learn for sound reasons. Just as the final decision to get well is to be left to the patient (Berne 1966), teachers may leave the learning to happen at the pace of the student.
- *Being mindful of the mind–body connections (psychosomatic continuum)*: Learning becomes useful, or finds application in life, only when it happens at the core of the learner. The Adult functions in unison with the Natural Child at the core. The mind or psyche is at the core of the person.
- *With awareness of the teacher's ego-states and their nonverbal clues*: The awareness about nonverbal expression of ego-states and conscious practice of Adult behaviours including tones, gestures and postures, helps an educator to use the operations with objectivity and awareness of the classroom situations. This

also requires awareness of the internal processes of self, and observation of the behavioural response of students to the teacher's tone, words and gestures.

Learning is a very individual process that has to take place in the internal environment of the learner in their own time, doing everything required for learning, yet allowing learning to happen at the pace of the student.

Real learning is also an event to take place joyfully and willingly, with concurrence of the Adult and Child ego-states; otherwise learning may become compliance to the Parent of the teacher, resulting in a compromise on the autonomy (Berne 1964) of the student. Berne, in his writings on therapeutic operations, says the therapist may tell the patient when he is ready, but the decision to get well is to be left to the patient (1966: 247), and speaks of the dangers at a somatic level if a client is pushed towards cure. I think it is fair that educators also pay heed to this guideline to bring about effective learning experience.

When and when not to use the educational operations

- *To promote learning*: Just as therapeutic operations must be used only for the curing of the patient (Berne 1966: 251) the educational operations are to be used by an educator only to promote learning.
- *Never for the educator to feel smart*: They are never to be used in order for the educator to feel smart and show off their superior knowledge. This may happen if the operations are used from the Parent rather than the Adult. The non-judgemental tone of voice and attitude with which the operation is delivered is what decides whether it is an operation to help students learn. The same words used with a ridiculing tone (coming from Parent) might be for the teacher to feel smart rather than for helping the students to learn.

Benefits of using educational operations

- *Educational operations make classes interactive*: When I started applying educational operations in my work with medical students for teaching research methodology (epidemiology), the classes became interactive, students were more involved, and teaching became more effective in terms of producing expected learning outcomes. All educational operations facilitate two-way communication in the classroom. In discussing the common causes for students' non-involvement, one-way communication has been identified as very important (Bergquist 1975). Interactive teaching and learning processes have a great importance in the recent trends in medical education. In a review of randomized and non-randomized controlled evaluations of continuing medical education programmes employing different methods, it has been found that interactive workshops resulted in significant improvement in at least one of the major outcomes indicators. Some of the studies report significant improvement in patient care practices after interactive teaching programmes (Khan and Coomarasamy 2006). In the hierarchy of educational formats, interactive programmes are ranked high. The 'educational' operations generate structured interaction in a teaching process.

- *Educational operations give structure and order to the class*: Planned and conscious use of the 'educational' operations gives an effective structure to the teaching learning process in the classroom. Lack of classroom structure is one of the identified reasons for poor student involvement in class, which in turn leads to ineffective teaching and learning (Bergquist 1975).
- *Educational operations promote concurrent updating and continued learning*: Conscious use of the 'educational' operations by the teacher invites and strengthens the student's Adult. This ability to use Adult ensures a quality in their learning which enables them to be in tune with the dynamics of the everyday changes in the world and keep themselves updated. Most students are able to relate to the learning and translate it into work situations. I have witnessed this when I have followed up the same students in later sessions as house officers, post-graduates, and as responsible medical practitioners.
- *Educational operations promote self-reflection and reflective learning*: Specification and support are the most commonly used operations for holding discussions on learning experiences. I have noticed that this gives opportunity for Adult reflection and validation to the students for their internal experiences of learning. Reflective learning has been identified as a very important component of the 'collaborative research model' promoted in the Teaching Effectiveness Program by the University of Oregon (2010). In this model, the learners work together to explore issues relevant to research topics, create briefs focused on a common resolution with common claims and counterclaims that represent multiple perspectives, and then engage in a cooperative debate. Reflection allows students to take a meta-cognitive stance to their learning and is promoted at all stages of the research project.

Recommendations for application

- 'Educational' operations are useful tools for application in such fields of TA as educational and organizational settings.
- 'Educational operations' can be promoted for all the 'non-therapeutic' applications of TA: educational, organizational, mentoring, coaching and supervisory work.
- Every educator, trainer, coach, mentor and supervisor needs to be aware that conscious use of the 'educational' operations will enhance their potency and awareness.
- TA training should include conscious applications of 'educational' operations, since the TA learning process is similar to any other learning process.

- Use of 'educational operations' with conviction and awareness by educators will make them a significant force in bringing about effective learning outcomes, just like therapeutic operations happen to be significant among the 'therapeutic forces' in therapy.

Conclusion

There are many parallels between therapy and education. Berne's therapeutic operations are among the TA tools that have important educational applications. The given examples show how effective and powerful they can be. Educational operations can be applied and practised by following the same guidelines for practice of therapeutic operations. Berne himself equates therapy to teaching especially in therapy of adolescents, 'The situation can be decisively altered at the social level by explicitly setting up an Adult–Adult contract, whereby the therapist (teacher) offers to teach the patient (pupil) transactional analysis' (Berne 1966: 355). Just as Berne reminds therapists that it is no use trying to conceal from the patient the therapist's bias or prejudice in favour of health and security, it is good for educators also to be aware of their own prejudices, so that they do not force them on their students but help the students to blossom according to their own interests and choices. I find it interesting that the etymology of the word 'doctor', which commonly means 'the healer', lies in *docere*, which means 'to teach'.

20

PARENT EDUCATION AND TA

From symbiosis to autonomy

Tomoko Abe, Japan

Introduction

I held TA study groups for parents at three private kindergartens from 1993 to 2010. Children two to six years old attended the kindergartens before going to elementary school. These parenting classes were called 'Mothers' and 'Study Room for Moms'. Each was a 90-minute session introducing a TA theory and then thinking and discussing together in the group on the possible solutions to participants' problems. In the session, they first shared their problems, anxieties and hesitations about their child rearing and, later in the session, they became aware of some clues to help themselves. The group was a combination of sharing and discovery (Clarke 1998). I came across some common issues among the participants (mostly mothers). The issues represented their low self-esteem in child rearing or some discomfort from organizing a new family structure, which often seemed to come from symbiotic relationships with spouse, parents or parents-in-law.

In this chapter, I would like to share their processes of change and growth and show how participants gained autonomy.

The workshop culture

'Mothers' was the original name for these groups; later I changed the name to 'Study Room for Moms'. I asked the parents who wanted to register for the workshop to manage their own babysitting service for their younger children. Most mothers could not secure personal time because of taking care of their children; I really wanted them to experience their own time alone at my workshop.

At the beginning, I saw resistance from many participants but then, gradually, they began to accept the workshop culture (Berne 1963). Moreover, in the 'Study Room for Moms', the participants would manage their own babysitter or ask a family member to take care of their infants, although later I did not insist on the participants not bringing their smaller children.

I came to see a pleasant change and growth with the mothers who managed to be apart from their children and cherish their own time through the developing new culture. Even if we did happen to have an infant present, we managed a 90-minute workshop calmly and effectively with the kind support of members, and it seemed another group culture developed naturally.

The target group was any carers (father, mother, grandfather/mother, and anyone who has been concerned in child rearing) whose children belong to any one of three kindergartens. In terms of their financial situation, these participants are well-off. Kindergarten in Japan is one of the educational institutions and belongs to the jurisdiction of the Ministry of Education, Culture, Sports, Science and Technology. It runs from the morning to two or three in the afternoon. It differs from a nursery school, which takes care of children for long hours from early in the morning to late in the evening. The mothers who leave their children with the kindergartens mentioned here are mostly housewives. It was rare to have someone who works full-time.

The neighbourhood of these kindergartens is a residential area; some couples have their own homes, other couples live with their parents-in-law or their original families – or the in-laws and original families may live very close. We in the workshop very often came across the discussion topics of parents and parents-in-law.

Family has a very special value in Japanese society. In particular, the responsibility of the firstborn son is very heavy, both at the social and psychological level. At the same time, it is usual for a wife who is the mother of a firstborn son to be strongly aware of and affected by these social and psychological responsibilities.

In the three areas where the kindergartens were located, I could see a mixture of two different family groups – one that has lived in these areas for generations, and the other the new family group who has moved into the area after marriage to start a new life. The former get a high level of verbal and non-verbal pressure by their relatives and neighbours. On the other hand, the latter group have faced the difficulties in making new relationships in their new area, or faced loneliness and alienation in their new environment, being away from their familiar places.

To make matters worse, a wife does not get much practical support in child rearing and housekeeping from her husband, or in keeping contact with the in-laws. I have observed that wives or mothers in both cases have strong symbiotic relationships and have felt alienated, which made them lose their identities and sense of being themselves.

What participants can learn from the workshop

To unfasten the chain of strong symbiotic relationships, or move away from alienation, is one of my contract goals. In describing the concepts of TA theories with diagrams, this symbiosis can be visualized and understood effectively by TA beginners in order to feel autonomy.

In the workshop, I aimed to help the parents, not only to be aware of the existence of symbiosis, but also to get specific ways to release them from such relationships. When mothers recognize their symbiosis with husband or parents, they can get release from those relationships, and they also find the clue to solve their difficulties with their own children – which brought them to the workshop in the first place. They eventually find out and build better parenting – and spend a joyful kindergarten-hood together, transforming the relationship to parent–child autonomy.

Contracts in the workshop

Business contract

My contract was to work with the parents from the three kindergartens to reduce parental stress from child rearing. All the necessary charges were taken care of by each kindergarten. The expected result was the relief of the participating parents from their stress in child rearing. I was paid my transportation and my workshop fee every time from the administration offices.

The Three-Cornered Contract

1   The Contract between the kindergarten administrative office and me:

   –   To run one workshop from 10:30–12:00 (for 90 min.) on scheduled days of every month.
   –   To reduce some stresses of the parents from child rearing.

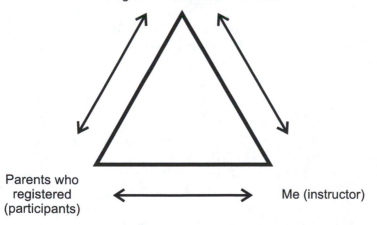

FIGURE 20.1 The Three-Cornered Contract (adapted from English 1975)

- Kindergarten provides the venue (on-site classroom) and facilities.
- Kindergarten invites the participants.
- Kindergarten pays the fees to the instructor (me).
- Kindergarten pays the miscellaneous charges such as copying handouts.
- This is part of the support programme for parents from the kindergarten and is considered a well-evaluated service.

2 The Contract between the kindergarten administrative office and parents:

- Kindergarten announces the workshop date/time via monthly-issued 'Newsletter' to attract the possible participants.
- Parents who would like to join the workshop apply by filling the application form in advance.
- Parents can attend the session without any charge.
- Parents are invited to attend the session alone (not with small children).
- Kindergarten does not provide a special babysitting/nursery service for younger siblings.

3 The Contract between participants and myself:

- Instructor is the responsible and effective leader of the workshop.
- Parents who registered will join the workshop as scheduled.
- Parents can bring their problem of child rearing and gain possible solutions.
- Parents will learn TA theories in order to think through their problems together.

Seating diagram

In the classroom we set chairs for the number of participants, plus mine, and a whiteboard. We also provided some toys and a futon quilt for napping for any younger siblings and babies (Figure 20.2).

Program

- Introduction: greeting by the facilitator, contracting and explanation of ground rules (see below).
- Sharing each participant's name and how they are feeling now, one recent happy memory and an issue they wish to discuss.
- TA theory of the day: facilitator presents one TA theory, prepared in advance, and the groups discuss how we can apply this theory to their own issues.
- Closing: each participant shares reflection in a short sentence.

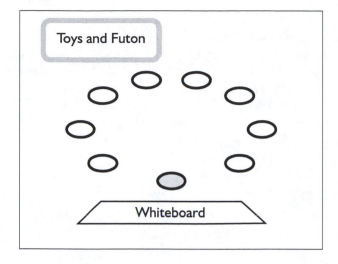

FIGURE 20.2 Seating diagram

Ground rules

These are agreed by the whole group, which makes the workshop a safe, effective and meaningful space. I always offer the following four ground rules and ask if they have any questions – and if my explanation was enough for them understand.

- Active participation
- Right to withdraw
- Mutual respect
- Confidentiality.

Active participation

- Focus the learning and experience here one hundred percent, without thinking of your children, other family members or housekeeping. Experience 'here and now.' Please come back (psychologically) to the workshop if you notice that you are thinking of something else.
- Even if you find that you have heard the same content from me somewhere else before, please keep your concentration on me and enjoy how I present it to you this time – if what I say is the same, be proud of your good memory. If you are aware that you are thinking of something else away from the topic we are dealing with, you may have a habit of thinking off-track even when you are with your children, family and friends. If you notice this, it makes a good start. I also say that being away from 'here and now' is called 'withdrawal' by group members who have already learned the TA theory of *Time Structuring*.

Right to withdraw

- I will focus on the topic of child rearing in this workshop. Therefore you will face many private matters such as your child, yourself (as mother), father and grandparents. It is your responsibility how much you would like to disclose about your family issues.
- There will be some occasions that I will ask you each a question. Although I would like you to participate actively, you can decide for yourself how much you disclose. Please say 'pass', like in a card game, if you would like not to answer the question and I will skip you. You may find you have a tendency to withdraw or 'pass' when the subject becomes particular matters such as money, academic background, sex etc – if you notice it, it makes a good start.

Mutual respect

- We tend to prioritize others in our daily life. We discount our own needs especially when it comes to child rearing and the matter of our family members. We often read the mood of others and think what we need to do to be good for them. Please prioritize yourself during this workshop. Do not hesitate to ask a question or say, 'I do not understand' or, 'Please repeat this again', until your needs get satisfied.
- We often need some patience in our daily life. Very often such behaviour is positively evaluated in Japanese society as being 'a good adult', 'a well-behaved person', 'a good housewife'. When we were little we were taught by grown-ups that we should not trouble a group's harmony by speaking up or that we must watch our behaviour. However, I welcome you to speak out as you wish in the workshop. Mutual respect starts from respecting yourself.
- We may notice in our daily life that we sometimes become very critical of others who do not behave themselves, and say to them, 'How dare you ask a question now!' or, 'How dare you repeat the same question!' We tend to respond severely if someone, without any hesitation, does what we forbid ourselves to do. When you start respecting yourself, you will find it an empowering change.

Confidentiality

- We promise not to disclose any private information which we have heard in this workshop once we step out from the classroom, whether in the place of work, schools or other situations.
- We may feel upset if we hear that private matters are spoken of somewhere else as rumours. If you really wish to say or discuss more about what you hear in the workshop, you have only one choice: that is to speak to the said person.

Please ask the person if they wish to hear anything from you; if they say 'yes', you can speak, but if they say 'no' you must accept not to speak at any level.

• Confidentiality makes this workshop a relaxed and secure place. I would like you all to understand this and cooperate together.

• If we have someone who says 'I am a talkative person, and I cannot keep confidentiality in our group', we must think carefully before we speak to the group during the workshop – because we cannot control others, but only ourselves.

After this explanation of the ground rules, I ask the group 'Did you understand each of the ground rules, and do you agree with them?'

It normally takes nearly twenty minutes to come to this stage of the lecture, and thus I would imagine that the level of the participant's concentration goes down by then. I tell the group 'Please stand up if you agree', then everyone in the room can see if others agree to the rules. This physical movement helps them to be aware of, to confirm and enforce their agreement visually – and at the same time make a shift in their energy.

This explanation of the ground rules may seem over-detailed; however I have found that participants learn how a secure situation may be created this way.

Sharing

In the opening, I ask the group to introduce themselves with their name, a recent happy occurrence, an issue they wish to discuss and a current feeling.

First of all, I ask them to introduce themselves with their full name, first and last names. It is often a Japanese custom to call a mother who bore a baby, 'Mother of (child's name)', both publicly and privately. I believe this is a discount of the mother's identity and an exaggeration of her role. In fact, some mothers remark, 'It's been ages since I introduced myself with my full name!', 'It feels good to call myself by my full name!'

It is extremely hard for Japanese people to express their feelings. We tend rather to express what we 'think' or what we should do. It often takes some time (or some exercises) for members to be able to express their feelings.

I suggest that participants, in order to explore their feelings, first ask themselves if it's feeling 'good', or 'bad', or 'fun', or 'not fun', without any reason or explanations. The group eventually learns to notice their feelings and express them in their own words.

I have them share their memories of a pleasant or happy events in the last month. This is a challenge to those who participate in this workshop with their 'troubles'. Sometimes the group finds it hard to share their happy events. Gradually, each participant becomes excited about choosing one and shares it with a big smile.

Although they bring and share their happy and pleasant events, some participants mention 'worrying issues' at this stage. I listen to these as much as time allows, then I try to give a hint how to apply the TA theories to each.

TA theory

After the opening, I explain a TA theory simply, deepening the explanation by using the content from their shared events and worries. In this way, many of the participants can find a clue to a solution of their own problems, even without detailed advice from me.

Explanations of TA theory applied in their daily life deepen their understanding; the group will remember to use that theory during the following month as their homework.

Closing

Approximately fifteen minutes prior to the end of workshop, we have a reflection in short sentences. Many participants have a relaxed smile on their faces; these are some of their comments: 'I would like to stroke my child, husband, parents', 'I would like to stroke myself' and, 'I feel released'. Their facial expressions have changed to pleasant and friendly – and it takes some time for them to leave the workshop room, as they stay and chat.

Five delightful cases

I will share five delightful cases with you.

The topic was TA philosophy

> After I explained the TA philosophy, one of the participants spoke up with tears in her eyes: 'It is delightful to know that I do have, and may have, my own ideas, expectations and hopes for my life! Up till now, I seemed to be exhausted when I just kept responding to my husband's expectations.'
>
> She was the type of person who always consulted her husband in a relationship of symbiosis. Once she heard the TA philosophy, she realized her real self. She practised little by little making her own comments, ideas and expectations. Then she managed to start a part time job.

Tears and happy smiles

> After she told us her name at the opening, Ms A could speak neither of happy nor pleasant events. She finally told us that she and her son cry together at the bus stop every morning, since her son could not separate from his mother and was not able to get on the kindergarten bus. She cried while she was telling this to us. I asked all the group members, 'Please raise your hand if you have experienced the same problem that Ms A has just shared with us', and more than half of the group members raised their hands with gentle smiles.

Ms A looked around at those hands and warm smiles, looked surprised for a moment, then said just one sentence: 'I am not the only one', and smiled fully. I asked 'What is happening to you now?' She replied, 'My problem is already solved'. This ended with many smiles and happy clapping hands from the group.

I explained briefly the symbiosis between mom and her son with a diagram, which helped the group to understand visually and reinforce their Adult thinking.

The topic was strokes

'I have forgotten how to stroke myself!' was the phrase one of the mothers said aloud.

The participants said that they got frustrated by the gap between their ideal and the reality, exhausted by unrewarding feelings from the endless housework everyday while they were taking the roles of mother, wife, and daughter-in-law for the sake of children, family members and in-laws. They took out their anger at their family members especially on their children, and thus many of them despised themselves and felt themselves in a vicious circle.

When I talked about strokes and explained about 'stroke yourself' from the stroke economy (Steiner 1971), the whole group seemed almost shocked by such simple and natural ideas. The group started sharing ways to stroke themselves, such as having a cup of coffee while reading a favorite book, working on handicraft, cooking, exercising, followed with many more ideas. The whole group went on freely and actively, inspired with their Natural Child.

Later on, participants told me with smiles, 'Simply thinking of these fun things to do would carry me away from a depression and frustration; it's magic!'

The topic was the symbiotic relationship

I explained simply the structural ego-state model and the definition of symbiosis. I also explained classic symbiosis, child-competitive and parent-competitive, with diagrams.

I asked the group to write down who takes what role in these diagrams. The participants imagined their relationship with their own family members – which made them understand, and laugh. At this point, we start to think of specific ways in which we can grow healthy ego-states.

The group discovered the importance of exchanging appropriate strokes and not over-nurturing or over-intervening – essential issues for child rearing.

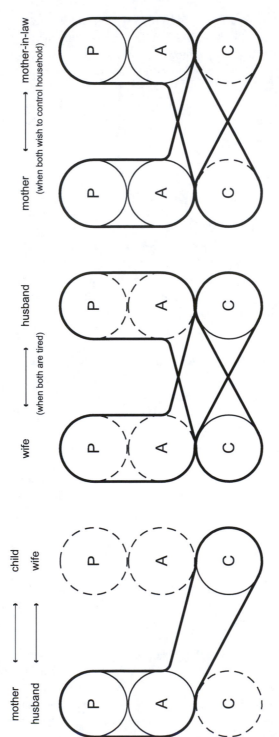

FIGURE 20.3 Symbiosis (based on Stewart and Joines 2012: 212)

(a) classic symbiosis; (b) child-competitive; (c) parent-competitive

Moreover, sharing and working together in the group made for healthy group dynamics and motivated feelings of autonomy among the group members. This group dynamic would affect their children in the kindergarten – the children showed their autonomy in the classroom as well.

The topic was frame of reference

I handed out one A4 sheet of plain paper to each person and said, 'Let's make a hole in this paper, wherever you like, and the size of the hole is up to you'. After everyone had made a hole in their paper, I told them to get into pairs to work with their paper: Each holds the paper in front of their face and one person at a time can say whatever they like to the other through this hole.

In this exercise, one person starts moving the sheet and speaking in order to deliver their voice well. It is fun at the beginning, but gradually the pair starts experiencing inconveniences. The group found that each person has their unique hole, which I relate to the theory of *frame of reference*. Two different holes trying to communicate with each other causes difficulty in hearing each other. The group realized that many spoken words would 'fall to the floor as they hit the surface of the paper'. This explanation makes participants understand and laugh.

At the end of the workshop, one of the participants said that she realized she and her husband had different frames of reference – which made sense. She smiled, and said that she would have a different reaction when her husband said something absurd.

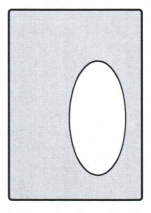

Person A   Person B

FIGURE 20.4 Worksheets for frame of reference

Lastly, I would like to introduce an episode that was shared by one of the mothers.

> Her elder daughter was ten years old, and one day she asked, 'Mom, when do you go to the next workshop?' When the mother responded, 'Why are you asking?' the daughter continued, 'Because you will be different right after the workshop, and I like you very much then'.
>
> I thought this was a real and good response for a daughter; this ten-year-old noticed the difference in her mother after visiting the workshop. I believe that Mom made some clear changes in the family relationship through learning TA. Unfortunately it would last only a few days!

Certainly everyone needs the time for practising. The workshop is a good opportunity to make not only mothers happy, but also the family. Maybe this is one of the reasons the group came to the workshop continuously.

TA Happy Cards – new tools to support mothers

My experiences with these parenting groups over twelve years show that if people get some kind of clue to engage and start functioning in Adult, they can avoid symbiotic relationships and get out from their scripts.

Based on the Oval Affirmation Cards (Clarke 1998) together with the concept of the Cycle of Development (Levin 1982), I created *TA Happy Cards* (Abe 2012), which contain 70 affirmation messages covering ten developmental stages. These short messages are affirmations for rearing children as well as calming adults; the card messages give parents ideas for stroking at any time, along with information about each developmental stage and its tasks. At the same time as parents read the message to their children, they can give it to themselves. The cards can be handled easily and do not take time; it is only necessary to put them in a convenient place in the home or office, and then pick one up and read it.

The cards are a playing-card size, in ten stages from 0: 'Maternity' to 9: 'Towards Death', each with a keyword and seven growth-supporting messages. Each stage has its own colour and, on the front, a picture of the 'stage' along with messages for nurturing, developing skills and new experiences.

On the reverse side are the keyword and a short sentence in small letters called an *anaboko message*. Anaboko means 'a hole' in Japanese – a metaphor for the negative message that you say when you get stuck or when you are in your script. I have found that it is pretty hard for some people to accept happy messages directly, even when they desperately need them. But people in trouble can identify these anaboko messages so easily that it is an eye-catcher to lead them to the positive message. To explain how the cards work, I give people this story:

> Life is often compared with walking one's road. When we are born, the road is not there, but by getting lots of caring and love from parents we start

constructing and walking our own road. The more we get the chance to receive nurture from parents, the more our road construction proceeds. However, sometimes we cannot receive the positive strokes we want, or we are simply not ready to receive the strokes our parents are giving us. At such times we cannot maintain our road construction, there are holes instead of smooth roads.

In the future, when we have difficulties with relationships in the family, at work or with friends, it seems we have our foot stuck into those holes and cannot move freely. The times we get stuck in such holes sometimes interfere with others, it's as if we cause a traffic jam.

We need repairs to our life road. *TA Happy Messages* which we needed at the beginning also help such repair. Just as a real road requires regular and serious maintenance, we also need regular maintenance, and serious repair when we experience difficulties in life. When we maintain our life road in good condition, we keep our autonomy.

How to play

You can use these cards as you like, but these are some of my experiences:

Pick up one for yourself, read it three times slowly to yourself or have someone else read for you; then exchange your thoughts and feelings if possible. This can also be an ice-breaker exercise when you start a group.

One of my clients started to read these cards to his new-born baby when she was two months old. The baby is now 18 months old, she carries the small box with these cards to her Daddy and asks him to read. She seems to know when her Daddy reads cards to her he has a big warm smile on his face. He said that he did not believe his daughter understood the meanings of the cards; however, when he saw and read the card she picked up, he became aware of himself, calm, and in his Adult with a sweet smile. So it is working.

One school counsellor shows the list of keywords to a student and asks if there are any keywords that help him to start talking. She finds that students, even their parents, will start to talk with the assistance of these cards. It is sometimes difficult to put into words what is in our minds, but these messages help us begin to speak.

Observations

It is not essential to know many TA theories or have a comprehensive understanding of those concepts in order to enjoy autonomy or getting out of useless, miserable situations. I believe that we as TA educators can do a lot to offer human growth and transition by giving people proper information and stimulating their Adult to function, which is what I call TA education. If they have more opportunity

FIGURE 20.5 Examples of Happy Cards

to learn and practise, and receive acknowledgement from others, they will experience autonomous and happy moments in everyday life.

It may be typical of Japanese culture that, through individual, social and cultural symbiosis, we often experience difficulties in our daily life. In this situation, it is very useful to have a tool to analyse and look at our own problem objectively.

To enable solving these problems – as in Berne's comment, 'A human being lives in search of being recognized' (Berne 1966) – stroke theory is a vital concept, not only for child rearing but for parents and personal growth. Parents who have been exhausted with child rearing, life and relationships with their surroundings, will recapture their Adult and then notice the need for strokes to Natural Child; and thus they can proceed to autonomy.

21

BUILDING COMMUNITY

Karen Pratt, South Africa

Introduction

Pumla is a community care worker working in rural Kwa-Zulu Natal (KZN) in South Africa (SA). She walks long distances to visit her patients with HIV-related illnesses; she struggles to feel her worth and find her voice and feels victimized by the system and by her manager in the organization.

Johan is a manager in a mining company in the north of SA, striving to be open to the diversity of cultures in the team he manages.

Sue is a teacher at one of the top schools in Cape Town, excited to be able to nurture and inspire young boys in her class.

Riyaad is a young dancer at a jazz dance school living his dream of being a dancer despite his poor background.

Andiswa is a young entrepreneur developing her consultancy and training business. She graduated top of her class in an entrepreneurial business diploma course.

Gadija teaches in a township school in Cape Town in the midst of sporadic gang warfare spilling over into the school and feels overwhelmed by the lack of resources and parental support and the aggression or indifference of her students.

Dave is an executive coach working with executive directors in one of the political parties in SA.

All of them get excited as they learn and explore the OK–OK communication model (Pratt and Mbaligontsi 2014) and TA concepts such as strokes and contracting. And I am ever in awe of what an immediate and practical impact TA can make on such a diverse spectrum of people. Frequently I hear the comments: 'It makes so much sense!', 'Now I know what I am doing', 'I know this stuff – now I can understand it as a model and have more choices'.

In this chapter, I will explore the model of Spiral Dynamics (Beck and Cowan 1996) as a way of understanding the different levels of awareness across the cultures in SA, and how learning is impacted. Using this awareness, I will describe how TA theory translates to practice in my work.

Background

South Africa is a country with a rich diversity of cultures and with twelve official languages spread throughout its nine provinces. There is still a large discrepancy in resources between different provinces and cultural groups – a legacy of the apartheid regime.

In terms of script, South Africans have internalized much of being either 'oppressor' or 'oppressed' in their cultural Parent (Drego 1983). White South Africans are seen as the oppressors and black South Africans as the oppressed, although there were many people in both groups who lived differently from the perceived roles. So although in theory we all live in a democratically free South Africa, each cultural group has their own etiquette, technicalities and character (Drego 1983).

'The more closed the parenting process, the fewer options will the child look for while growing up and the more the child will re-live the cultural Parent program of being oppressed or oppressing. This is the process that is shaken up by consciousness-raising and by those movements that work for a reversal of old structures' (1983: 226).

Consciousness-raising is part of the challenge and excitement of using TA in South Africa.

Cross-cultural transactional analysis

Mazzetti (2011) describes how Eric Berne visited many different countries, including India, Singapore, Thailand, Sri Lanka, Syria, Lebanon, Turkey and Bulgaria, and declared that TA seemed to stand up well cross-culturally. Mazzetti himself has used TA in various countries. He offers some reasons for the usefulness of TA across cultures:

- Contracting from a position of mutual OK-ness enables a TA practitioner to enter into the client's world-view in a respectful way and inquire into, recognize and respect multiple truths.
- Attachment theory has shown that across cultures people can form an autonomous attachment when there is an OK–OK relationship.
- Human beings share a common need for strokes and recognition. This is confirmed by our shared human biology – all people have similar brain biology, with the amygdala responding to fear and threat by producing hormones that shut down the pre-frontal cortex and logical thinking; with the reverse happening when people feel safe and acknowledged.

- Mazzetti discusses the importance of finding a balance between 'universalism' and 'cultural relativism.' A universalistic attitude believes that all people and cultures are the same, and hence the way to understand them is the same. The risk here is of ethno-centricism, where we believe that our way of thinking is the only right way. A relativistic attitude can lead to legitimizing everything from different cultures, including things such as gender inequality and other so-called 'traditional practices'. TA is universalistic enough to function in different cultural environments because it is rooted in common biology, and relativistic enough to be inculturated into different systems due to its base in OK-ness (Mazzetti 2011: 196)

Spiral Dynamics

A model that helps me understand the ongoing tension and flow between universalism and relativism is Spiral Dynamics (Beck and Cowan 1996). Salters (2011) discusses the development of Spiral Dynamics, its usefulness and connection with TA, and how it can be a tool to 'enrich the possibilities of working with individuals and groups by allowing therapists and/or developmental practitioners and their clients a deeper appreciation of their social context and cultural frame of reference' (2011: 265). Spiral Dynamics is one way of understanding the development of world-views or value systems within individuals and groups. It was developed by Chris Cowan and Don Beck (1996), based on the work of the late Professor Clare Graves. Each level can be thought of as: a world-view; a value system; a level of psychological existence; a belief structure; organizing principles; a way of thinking; and a mode of living (O'Grady 2009). Each person lives within a context and develops a set of responses which best help them to cope in that context. This forms the basis of our set of values and affects our behaviours, which in turn start to affect and change the environment. As the environment changes we develop a new set of responses and values. Each new stage is a reaction to the previous stage, which is then transcended and included in the new stage. Each value system reflects *how* people think, rather than what they think. The value system is the 'container' or the 'how' rather than the contents or the 'what'.

Beck and Cowan allocated colours to each level, see Table 21.1.

One group of people might display different levels at different times. I supervise coaches who work at a community project that teaches unemployed women entrepreneurial skills through developing a business of buying and selling clothing. These are some of the attitudes and behaviours that happen within this group, and the link with the different levels, see Table 21.2.

There are potentially more levels of the spiral emerging; we are not yet sure what the essence of these will be. Each level, beginning with the Beige level, alternates between *expressing self* values and *sacrificing self for others* values (Figure 21.1). Salters notes the flow up the spiral between autonomy and homonomy (Salters 201: 270).

People and groups in any of the first six levels are described as having first tier thinking – a person in any of these levels will believe that their way is the only

TABLE 21.1

Level	Theme	Mindset	Manifestations
BEIGE	Survival	Do what you must to stay alive	Hunter-gatherers, starving masses
PURPLE	Magical/traditional	Keep the tribe safe, observe traditional customs	Family rituals, shamans, blood oaths
RED	Powerful/egocentric	Get respect, do what you want	Feudal kingdoms, rebellious youth, epic heroes
BLUE	Authoritarian/purposeful	Life has meaning, enforce principles of right living	Codes of honour, Puritan beliefs, moral purity, divine control of the world
ORANGE	Achievist/analytical/rational	Risk taking self-reliance, competition, strive for success	The Enlightenment, corporate states, rational thinking, competition
GREEN	Humanistic/egalitarian	Belonging, dimensions of community, seeking harmony	Human rights movements, multiculturalism
YELLOW	Integral/ecological	Flexibility, self-responsibility, spontaneity	Systems thinking, integrative structures
TURQUOISE	Holistic/global	Experience the wholeness of existence	Intuitive thinking, global networks

TABLE 21.2

Purple	The first commitment is to the family and community – women will go into debt in their business so that they can help someone in financial need. They will prioritize using their savings to build a house for their ageing parent, rather than for themselves
Red	Some women become ruthless to get ahead on days set aside to buy new stock – hiding the best clothes, pushing others out of the way in order to get the best bargains
Blue	Others believe that right living and their religious duties are more important than their business and make choices about how to spend their time that jeopardize their growing businesses
Orange	Some women are motivated, eager to learn the techniques of running a business, analytical and strategizing for success
Green	Others will dream big and include others in their community in their plans. They will be conscious of the impact on the environment and operate in a sustainable way
Yellow/Turquoise	These women are highly successful, motivate others, think in terms of systems and long-term growth, and success for themselves and others

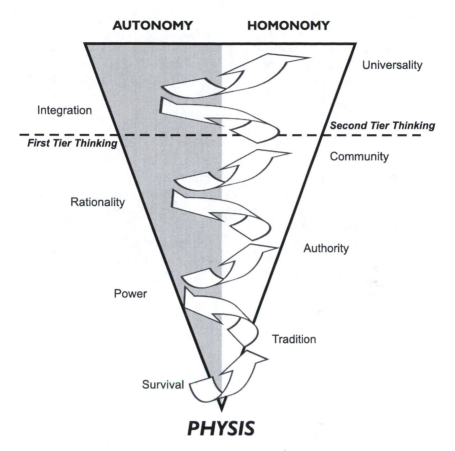

AUTONOMY **HOMONOMY**

Universality

Integration

Second Tier Thinking

First Tier Thinking

Community

Rationality

Authority

Power

Tradition

Survival

PHYSIS

FIGURE 21.1 Spiral Dynamics: autonomy, homonomy, and physis (Salters 2011: 270)

one that is valid. People in the last two levels are described as having second tier thinking – an ability to see value in all the levels without any one level being better than another. Second tier people will have transcended and included all the levels through which they have developed and be able to flow up and down the spiral as is most appropriate in each moment.

Change

First order change consists of people doing more of the same, with the belief that if something used to work, it should continue to work. Second order change is often unexpected, chaotic and paradoxical and requires a shift into a new dimension of thinking. This type of change is often unsettling and frightening at first. In South Africa, we saw the initial attempts to resolve the problems coming from the apartheid era driven by first order thinking. The laws were enforced, the country was shut down through emergency decrees, and more black people were put into homeland structures (Beck and Linscott 1991).

Second order change required a new way of thinking, and saw the imprisoned Nelson Mandela freed and becoming the first president of the democratic South Africa. Second order change requires a paradigm shift. Beck and Linscott describe Graves' six conditions for change:

1   *Individual potential for change – people's thinking capacity*: people may be open, arrested or closed to change.
2   *Relief from immediate problems*: create some relief from immediate problems to allow energy to explore the more complex problems.
3   *Discomfort from the status quo*: there has to be dissonance and a period of crisis before new thinking emerges. There must be a sense that old ways of thinking no longer solve the current issues.
4   *Insights into alternatives*: an understanding of what went wrong in the old system and what resources are available to create new resolutions.
5   *Barriers identified and resolved*: this often involves convincing other people to share the new-found insights.
6   *Endurance and consolidation*: the new way of being needs to be practised and become consolidated. Part of this stage is moving from the individual to the collective shift.

Drego (1983) describes an unhealthy cultural Parent as:

*   repeating old history
*   keeping things as they are as that feels safer
*   assuming responsibility for others that they could assume themselves
*   punishing new and untried behaviour
*   exerting power and control over others.

As we read these characteristics in the light of the Spiral Dynamics model, we can recognize Drego's 'unhealthy cultural Parent' characteristics describing first tier thinkers.

Becoming spiral wizards as TA educators

Beck (1991) used the term 'spiral wizards' to describe second tier thinkers. Newton (2006) describes how we all tell stories, using symbol and metaphor to create our version of reality. We create a narrative that gives meaning to the past, helps us cope with the present and predicts the future. Our script emerges from within our context and culture. We will tell stories of connectedness or separateness, depending on what is important in our community. Spiral Dynamics is another model for understanding how our script is created from within the dominant world-view and value system of the group. Each level of the spiral has its unique frame of reference (Schiff *et al.* 1975).

All learning is an opportunity to make new meaning (even of the past) and create new life-plans. Co-creative transactional analysis (Tudor and Summers 2014) proposes that we all participate in the co-creation of our reality. It is in the relationship of learning that new meaning emerges, not only in the content being taught.

Tudor (2011) describes empathy as playing a crucial role in co-creative work. He quotes Carl Rogers who defined empathic understanding as: 'To perceive the internal frame of reference of another with accuracy, and with the emotional components and meanings which pertain thereto, as if one were the other person, but without ever losing the "as if" condition.' Rogers (1975; 1980, quoted in Tudor, 2011: 40) also makes this powerful statement: 'Empathy dissolves alienation'. When people feel that they are really seen, the door is opened for new meaning to emerge.

Transcend and include

As people move up the spiral from first tier thinkers (the first six levels) to second tier thinkers (the last two and future emerging levels), the most significant aspect of this growth is that they have not only transcended the current level to the next level, but that they have included it as well. It is natural for people who are just emerging into the next level to push away practices and thinking from the level from which they are shifting. This seems to be a way of helping them settle into the new level, but it is important that this is a temporary occurrence, as the richness of each level is due to including all the experiences and thinking of the previous levels. So each emerging level holds a more diverse and richer pool of experiences that can be understood and appreciated. Another way of expressing this is that we hold an ever-expanding number of different frames of reference with which we can empathize.

There is power in the relationship of learning. This enables people to feel understood, safe and open to co-create new meaning. Sometimes our role as second tier thinkers is to help people hold the tensions of two seemingly contradictory levels. A young successful black business woman tells of how she transcends and includes the levels of her spiral of development: when she goes to visit her family in the rural area, the daily morning ritual is for the women to walk a long way to the river to fetch water. Instead of being impatient – she is used to stepping into the shower with instant hot water – she appreciates the opportunity for the sharing of wisdom and oral tradition between the women of the community as they walk to and from the river. She speaks of how these moments feed her when she is back in the city.

As TA educators, it becomes clear that our own ongoing inner development is crucial. When we keep learning and growing along the spiral, we are better equipped to continue to transcend and include our previous experience and show the characteristics of spiral wizards as described by Beck (1991):
Spiral wizards:

- think in open rather than closed systems
- live and work in sync with the natural rhythms and flow
- engage with ease across a range of different conceptual worlds
- have a diverse range of skills, resources and competencies
- are able to mirror all the levels and use each level in a healthy way
- can validate the best in each level
- can meet and relate to each person at their level
- are supported by personal work, reflection and/or spiritual practices.

Trudi Newton (2014) writes about professionals working in this way, as transactional designers. In Summers' response to Newton's article, he quotes de Bono (1992; cited in Summers and Tudor 2014): 'With analysis we are interested in what is. With design, we become interested in what could be'. It is this 'what could be' aspect of TA that makes it exciting and relevant to people wherever they may be along the spiral.

Enabling change

Do we have a right to imagine that another person should be at a different level? The word 'should' gives us a clue – if we believe that we co-create our reality, then we don't have a right to decide what is best for someone else. I believe that we can enable people to healthily express the level where they are, and at best nudge them to move.

I believe that the difference in the education process along the levels of the spiral is more about how the educator perceives, understands and relates to each learner – rather than a difference in the methodology. I will discuss some practical implications using some of the TA models.

OK–OK communication model

Temple (1999) used the phrase 'functional fluency' to describe the behavioural manifestations of the integrating Adult ego-state. She describes functional fluency as the capacity for intimacy, to decrease the likelihood of symbiotic transactions and increase the ability to respond flexibly and effectively using a wide range of ego-state manifestations. This model is equally powerful for TA educators, teachers, managers, and in fact all people who work with other people.

Using Temple's descriptions of the nine modes of behaviour, I have adapted the model, linking the five positive modes of communication with the healthy 'I'm OK, You're OK' life position (Pratt and Mbaligontsi 2014).

Dancing in the hoops

Using the OK–OK box to enclose the five positive modes of communication easily conveys the spread of options that people have in communicating. I demonstrate this using hula-hoops on the floor, and doing a dance with one foot in the Adult

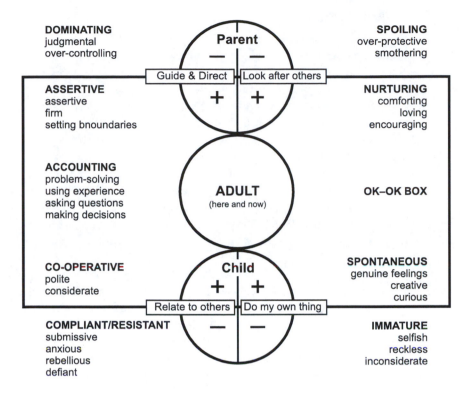

FIGURE 21.2 OK–OK communication (Pratt and Mbaligontsi 2014: 62)

hoop and the other toe tapping into structuring, nurturing, co-operating or being spontaneous, to visually demonstrate making moment-to-moment choices in how to respond. I demonstrate that when I step 'out of the box' into any of the four negative modes of dominating, marshmallowing, being compliant, or resistant, or immature, I move out of Adult awareness and into outdated ways of reacting.

As participants speak about consciously choosing to stay within the OK–OK box, they comment:

> 'I will stay in the control room.'
> 'Our team needs to keep asking ourselves if we are still in the red box.'
> ' . . . so I can dance in the hoops.'
> 'I can be powerful instead of having no voice.'
> ' . . . so now I know how I can manage my team in a powerful way.'

This model gives people in a group a common language. A director working with her team asked them the following question: 'What can I do that enables you to stay in the OK–OK box?' This was a wonderful way of doing the psychological level of contracting together, and making the potential covert agenda explicit (Hay 1996).

Empowerment

The realization of having choice powerfully impacts people. I work with an organization that engages with community health care workers to provide them with tools for self-awareness and self-care. TA forms one of the pillars of this work and gives them psychological tools to understand themselves and respond to others in a healthier, more enabling way. Carers speak of the compliant mode as 'no voice' – a place that they experience on a daily basis as they continue to live from their internalized cultural Parent, believing injunctions of not being valuable, worthy, or able to think for themselves. They learn that staying in their compliant mode unconsciously invites their manager to be in the dominating mode, and so perpetuates the oppression. They begin to discuss how they can move into the OK–OK box and find their power in the spontaneous mode to voice their feelings, and use the energy in this mode to advocate change. Community care workers earn a very low stipend, and have no official standing or stability in the work that they do. Their attitude was one of hopelessness and wanting others to change things for them. Now, many of the care workers have become involved in advocacy work to mobilize other carers to petition the government for recognition of their work, fair wages and benefits. Negotiations for recognized government posts for this work are well under way, with the carers themselves driving this process.

Many people in SA are involved in transformation through the vehicle of coaching and, almost without exception, coaches report that this is the model that makes most sense to their clients. After showing them the model and the OK–OK options, clients can readily see for themselves which modes they most use, and why they get some of the responses that they do. Without spending time explicitly teaching transactions, clients readily understand that communication from a mode 'out of the box' will invite a response also 'out of the box', whereas staying 'in the box' will invite others 'into the box' as well. Using this model is an example of a way of understanding interpersonal dynamics and making choices – it can be relevant for people across the spiral. People at different levels will have different values and ways of life that are important to them, but the common thread is relating from an 'I'm OK, You're OK' attitude, whatever one's values.

Crossing the line

A useful exercise to do with a group of people who teach, train or manage others, is to invite them to discuss, within whatever context they work, how they 'cross the line' between the negative and positive modes of the Parent, to encourage rather than discount others. In small group discussions, people discuss practical things they will begin to do to shift from dominating to structuring mode, and from marshmallowing to nurturing mode. There is often also a realization that they are in fact doing too much nurturing as a way of avoiding structuring. This model helps them see that managing others requires a balance of structuring and nurturing, and the ability to be flexible in each situation with each person.

Modelling OK–OK power

An important part of working with people as a TA educator is to live and model OK-ness. For some people, for example, the rural carers in KZN, this might be the first time they are experiencing respectful, OK–OK power. As a white facilitator, I was easily perceived as coming from the oppressor group, and the nature of being the leader of a workshop could invite them into their script – which would see me as dominant and expecting compliance from them. To create trust and openness to learn, I spent some considerable time at the beginning of each workshop in contracting in an OK–OK way. Some groups had very little command of English and I have only a smattering of isiZulu. I needed to be creative in how I showed openness and built connection and trust. My love of music came in useful, and I always had some local music playing as people started gathering for the workshop. Our eyes would meet – I would be moving in time to the music and they would smile and begin to dance as well. So both in non-verbal and verbal ways, I would slowly work to show mutual respect and build trust. I would demonstrate my belief that all people bring a rich life experience with them, and hold the belief that people will make their own sense of the models. In inviting role plays, people's own experience was brought into the room, and the TA models could readily be used to make meaning out of their own situations. There would inevitably be someone in the room who could translate and, even in role-plays in the vernacular, it was easy to sense the energy of the enactment and facilitate the discussion afterwards without necessarily understanding every word.

Contracting

Across the spectrum of people with whom I work, the three levels of contracting prove to be a powerful model. Hay (1996) and Napper and Newton (2000) refer to the three levels of contracting as being procedural or administrative, professional and psychological. I link these levels to a visual image of an iceberg, to represent that the procedural levels are explicit whereas the professional and psychological levels are deeper and more hidden.

In doing developmental work with managers from mining companies doing postgraduate management studies, what seems obvious in terms of contracting with their team is often an exciting new awareness for them. This is especially helpful with multicultural teams.

First, considering the professional level of contracting, managers realize that time spent explaining clearly each of the tasks and responsibilities with each member of the team helps to create structure and clarity. Managers often take for granted that their team will understand the implications of each task, and then grow frustrated when they do not see the performance that they expected. More importantly, they realize how important it is to address the psychological level and have the conversation with each person about how best they are going to work together. When this level of connection and relationship is cultivated, cultural differences can be understood and respected.

I use the following exercise to enable a team or group to explore the psychological level of contracting in a fun way. After discussing the three levels of contracting, I tell the group that they are going to do a 'speed dating' exercise: each person has two minutes with every other person in the team. The question they ask each other is: 'What do you need from me to bring out the best in you?' The limited time in each pair helps to focus each person to name succinctly what it is that would bring out their best. The question also focuses them to remember their best moments and prevents the temptation to recall past instances of difficult interactions with others in the team. The energy in the room is tangibly high as people begin to realize the value of asking these questions of each other, and listening deeply to each other.

In the context of working with the community care workers, authentic and thorough contracting sets the foundation for good learning. As mentioned briefly earlier, many carers have a script around discrimination and domination, especially when they meet a white facilitator. Many of them have been told what to do for most of their lives. To ask the group what their hopes and expectations are for the time spent learning together, is sometimes surprising for them. When they can articulate what they want, it creates a sense of their needs being heard and deemed important, and it invites people to be more engaged when the learning speaks to their needs, rather than imposes what others perceive their needs to be.

One of my most inspiring workshops was with a group of young dancers from a jazz dance school. I was contracted to address personal development with the group over four days. The manager had told me what she believed needed to happen. I was mindful of keeping an open and equal psychological distance (Micholt 1992) in the contracting, and arrived with no fixed workshop plan. I invited the group to take time in small groups to decide what would make these four days most worthwhile for them. As they discussed what they felt they wanted to learn and develop, the energy and the excitement grew. What they named as their needs was perfectly met by many of the TA models. I kept the programme flexible so that sometimes it was only when we were completing the learning around one topic, that it became clear what would fit best moving forward. I believe that this way of contracting and working honours the lived experience of each person, and offers learning opportunities where they are most needed – upholding one of the principles of andragogy: that people learn best when the learning meets what they most want to learn.

With all these examples, contracting helps to make explicit value differences and ways of being between diverse people and supports the relevance of TA across levels of the spiral.

TA educators as spiral wizards and transactional designers

As I have begun to mentor new trainers I have reflected on the various aspects of being an educator. I see it having four different aspects:

1   Focusing on the external environment and ensuring that it provides the best conditions for learning.
2   Knowing the content and how to enable people to make sense of it in their own context.
3   Understanding the dynamics of a group and how best to support the group at each stage of its development and growth.
4   Focusing on one's own inner world by taking time to reflect in supervision on one's own process during the work with others. And continuing to be mindful of ongoing inner work – the 'being' aspect rather than the 'doing' aspect.

Using the thinking of Spiral Dynamics, educators need to ensure to cultivate their ongoing development as second tier thinkers. This translates to a sense of living and modelling OK-ness in all conditions and contexts of learning. Sometimes people speak of being like a chameleon – being flexible and open to connect with people at their frame of reference. It means believing in and honouring one's own beliefs at the same time as honouring others who might believe differently. It invites us to connect on the fundamental human level, irrespective of our different scripts, cultures and experiences. It is based in the belief that each time we connect with somebody else, change and growth will occur in that relational space. And it delights in the fact that change and growth occur in both parties.

Conclusion

I have shared some of my experiences of using TA with a wide diversity of people in South Africa. How wonderful it could be if all those characters I introduced at the beginning of the chapter could understand and appreciate each other. Although they share a common humanity, there are many differences in their personal and cultural histories. If I imagine a day when all those diverse people come together; my fantasy is that through the common language and understanding of TA, they would be able to put aside their differences and be inspired as they shared their hopes, dreams and goals of making South Africa a thriving, enabling country in which to live.

As Berne wrote about 'saying hello' in *What Do You Say After You Say Hello?*: 'To say Hello rightly is to see the other person, to be aware of him as a phenomenon, to happen to him and to be ready for him to happen to you' (Berne 1972: 3–4). In Africa we speak of the concept of *ubuntu*, which is translated as 'a person is a person through other persons.' Archbishop Desmond Tutu describes it like this:

> A person with ubuntu is open and available to others, affirming of others, does not feel threatened that others are able and good, based from a proper self assurance that comes from knowing that he or she belongs in a greater

whole, and is diminished when others are humiliated or diminished, when others are tortured or oppressed, or treated as if they were less than who they are.

(Tutu 1999: 31)

How Berne and Tutu would have enjoyed speaking to each other!

22

EDUCATIONAL TRANSACTIONAL ANALYSIS

A retrospective

Jean Illsley Clarke, USA

Our final contribution in this collection is by Jean Illsley Clarke. Appropriately, Jean's chapter offers a retrospective on educational transactional analysis. For those involved in transactional analysis, Jean's will be a familiar name; in many respects she is the elder in educational TA, being one of the first and now longest serving trainer and practitioner in the field. We asked Jean to share some of the significant periods in the history of the field, her most useful TA models and general reflections on being involved in educational TA for quite some time.

Telling our stories

What is the story of your journey in the educational field of transactional analysis? Do you teach TA theories? Or are you a transactional analyst educator? There is a big difference. If you aim to be a TA educator, whether you are a beginner or a 'long-time always-learning-more' TA educator, your story is one worth telling. When the editors invited me to write this chapter, I asked, 'What do you want?' They replied, 'Tell us your part of the early story of the field of educational TA, and what you think is important about being a TA educator today'. So that's easy:

- Easy to tell, because I love the story.
- Easy to tell, because the journey has been so growth-filled.
- A joy to tell, because I have such high hopes for the future.
- Appropriate for me to tell, because telling our stories, and giving back, is a developmental task of my decade.

Telling our stories is an important life-task because it helps us keep ourselves centered and our cultures grounded. Find a way to tell your TA story and, remember, even when we think nothing appears to be happening, if we practice TA, growth is ever present. The story begins with a part about the psychological landscape at the time, followed by my part in the early history of education in the international transactional analysis community, and some examples of how it has grown since those early days. I will then share some thoughts about our methods, our frame of reference, and what it means to me to be an educational transactional analyst.

The winds of change

In the 1970s there was a craving for change, and TA was spreading across the United States like a wild fire. The dry grass that fueled the flames was people's hunger for growth, for more successful ways to interact right now, to create alternatives to years 'on the couch'. TA was not the only new theory. The breeze blew up and down the coastal state of California where new-thinking psychologists were inventing alternative therapeutic systems that challenged the entrenched Freudian theories. I am an educator, and I knew that the new theories needed to be examined and explored by educators as well as by therapists. I have a strong belief that every educator needs to know about several psychological theories, and to be thoroughly grounded in one.

It was a yeasty time. In many parts of the country it was easy to find a book or a class or a conference introducing the new theories. Psychologists, teachers, health care workers, business people and parents experimented with these new ideas. People were eager to learn new ways of relating with others and of understanding themselves. Each of these new models, in its own way, invited people to look at how their lives were going, to take charge, and to make their lives better. The theory that seemed to fit my needs, both intellectually and intuitively, was transactional analysis. Eric Berne's book, *Games People Play* (1964) and Tom Harris's *I'm OK, You're OK* (1973) swept at the forefront of the winds of change. People read them, and learned about transactional analysis, and wanted more. My history in TA is intertwined with the early history of educational TA.

In the beginning – my TA story

My husband Dick and I were sitting on a grassy bank beside a swimming pool reading *I'm OK, You're OK* (Harris 1973) aloud to each other. Happy swimmers' voices floated around us. Our children were young, and we were wanting better ways of parenting. The 'I'm OK, You're OK' book was helpful, but we needed more. We took a class led by a minister, an empathic clergy person who was excited about finding a new way of doing counseling with his parishioners. He was 'teaching TA', although essentially it was theory and tools for doing therapy. I knew there were ideas there that would help parents, but the ideas needed to be translated out of therapeutic jargon into parent language.

Russell Osnes, a frequent visitor at Eric Berne's San Francisco seminars, came to my town to introduce TA. Berne had died recently, but Russ brought many of the seminal TA thinkers to do workshops in my town, and my study of TA began in earnest. Soon I was not only riding the winds of change but had become part of the wind itself, always pushing to include educators in TA thinking. Russ was a therapist, but he understood the need for the role of educators, so I felt at home with TA. He encouraged me to continue my studies and become what was originally called a 'Special Fields Member' in TA. At an international conference in San Francisco, I quickly learned that there was no specific training program for educators, and that those of us regarded as being in 'special fields' were an assembly of people defined simply as non-therapists. There was a sense that this group didn't quite 'fit in'. This seemed to run contrary to Berne's expectation that people can think, which is typical of what good educators do: we help people think. Russ created a training program that was both demanding and rewarding, and I, Jean Wiger and Joanne Moses, both therapists but also both educators, began to create training programs for Educational Transactional Analysts.

Teaching transactional analysis theories

Looking back, I think the therapists at that time were so excited about trying out new methods and inventing new theories that they didn't have time to think about educational applications. Also, some expressed a concern that, if teachers learned TA, they would be doing therapy – and I considered this possible contamination. I believe that a genuine concern sprang from the awareness that, because TA was so easy to understand, it might be misused or perceived as a 'pop psychology'. While I shared the concerns of the psychologists, I understood that good therapy is often educational, and that effective education often has a therapeutic impact and can ease some of the old heart-wounds. I knew I could teach TA accurately. I deepened my knowledge and offered classes on the theories, classes that would now be framed as a TA 101.

It was not hard. At that time, if I could get a church to announce a class on TA in the Sunday bulletin, fifteen or twenty people would show up. The winds behind the wild fire were still blowing across pretty barren planes at that time and, as a trained educator, I felt clear about the boundaries between education and the practice of therapy, although I was uncomfortable as I watched a gifted therapist do some spot therapy at a workshop in an educational setting; I realized we may all need some classification on the boundaries between the specialties. Later, in my advanced TA training class, I focused on the boundaries and the differences in practices between education and therapy (Clarke 1981).

The parenting books

I learned valuable lessons at all those conferences with therapists, and I hope every educator has the opportunity to connect with practitioners in all of the specialties. However, I still wanted to create that book for parents! I was teaching several parenting classes and learning a lot about how parents learned at their best. They wanted to learn how to function better with their children without psychological diagrams, and without learning special meanings of words. So, on my fiftieth birthday, I decided to write the book.

Berne's decision to use familiar, plain English language – 'Parent', 'Adult', 'Child' – helped make his models easy to understand. As sometimes happens, a strength can also be a weakness: parents in the groups I was teaching often baulked at these labels. They said, 'I know about parents. I already am a parent. Just tell us what you are talking about. Use plain English!' Together, the parents and I settled on names for the three personality parts as the Nurturing and Structuring part, the Problem Solving part, and the Spontaneous and Adaptive part. The parents were satisfied, and we could get on with enhancing the healthy growth of all three parts in children, other adults, and ourselves. I was satisfied because the names helped us focus on the positive function of each ego-state. We learned about strokes, and stroking all three ego-states in our children and ourselves. Well, at first some of the parents skipped stroking themselves; it was too much like bragging. But they liked the impact it had on their children. Using positive functional descriptors of the personality parts kept us focused on what to do, instead of what not to do. It is important to teach TA to parents and to adapt it in ways that help them turn ideas into action.

I eventually did write the book, *Self-Esteem, a Family Affair* (Clarke 1978), and it is still selling, unrevised. Why? I believe it is simply because TA is helpful to parents. I wrote the *Self-Esteem* book to meet the needs of the parents I was teaching. They liked affirmations, visualizations and the concept of self-esteem (the belief that one is to act capably and responsibly, and to believe that one is loveable and to act that way). I had no idea it would lead to many more books, to *Growing Up Again*, with Connie Dawson (Clarke and Dawson 1998), to Leader's Guides, and most recently, the research-based overindulgence book, *How Much is Too Much?*, with Connie Dawson and David Bredehoft (2014).

TA goes global

The TA winds continued to blow. In the seventies, Americans were already spreading the word abroad, and people from other countries were coming to conferences in the USA to tell us what they were learning, how they needed to adapt in order to adopt, and what they needed from us. It was time to create a training and certification structure. In the early days, I am told you were certified when Eric Berne said you were certified. But Eric Berne could not be everywhere. I wanted to become a certified transactional analyst, so I joined the Training Standards Committee. I wanted to be sure educators would be included in the structure.

In many countries educators were making TA their own. In 1988, at a British Institute of Transactional Analysis conference in Blackpool, England, educational TA game designer Carole Gesme and I learned that the British were running full-day TA workshops for teachers, and that there were other countries in Europe where that was happening. We met educators who were as passionate about education as we were. I remember sitting in a bedroom at the Blackpool conference, where we shared stories about our adventures as educators in the TA world. Carole and I gave our hosts colored ovals, the *developmental affirmations* that Carole was creating. Our hosts gave us ideas, and hope and encouragement, and the start of great friendships. You already know the names of the people from England, Trudi Newton, Susannah Temple, Rosemary Napper and Julie Hay. They brought along a whole new wind of change. You have read their chapters in this book, and perhaps their other publications. It makes me smile to think of it.

Exciting educational adaptations were – and continue to be – created in many countries and languages. Sometimes a breeze brings news of one to me. An example – in Osaka, Japan, educator Tomoko Abe invented a game with cards and stickers (see Chapter 20). As preschool children played the game with their mothers, the children learned how to give appreciative strokes to their mothers and the mothers learned to give new positive strokes to their children. No lectures, no script questionnaire. Just a simple contract offered by the school: will you play this game each evening as a way to help your child? This education application is so elegant it still takes my breath away, and its winds continue to blow from one country to another.

We educators build on each other's work. For example, in *Self-Esteem* I published 'Four Ways of Parenting', an activity comparing positive nurturing and structuring to the less desirable 'criticizing' and 'marshmallowing'. Susannah Temple adjusted it to work with teachers. Rosemary Napper and Mark Price adapted it further, and Rosemary and Trudi Newton took it another step to become a helpful model for looking at ways the Parent ego-states discount and empower (Napper and Newton, 2014). Meanwhile, in *Growing Up Again*, Connie Dawson and I expanded the four ways to include all twelve parenting behaviors and put it on a highway. What a richness to belong to a professional group that is continuously developing new theories and adapting old ones.

Education comes of age

In July of 1995, I was informed that the international TA awards committee had chosen me to receive the Eric Berne Memorial Award. I couldn't believe it would be given to an educator, but my belief was out of date. On August 15 1995 when the award was announced, I was stunned. Before I could make my short acceptance speech the group of international transactional analysts of all specialties were on their feet and cheering. This group of very caring, highly intelligent people, who some years before hadn't seemed to notice parent education, gave their highest award to a parent educator! My major celebration is this recognition that parent education is important. We need all of our TA specialties!

Twenty years, 1975–95, seemed long – but that is not a long time in the history of the universe. Now, a couple more decades have passed and you have this book as evidence of the significance of the educational TA journey; educators hold high positions in the International Association of Transactional Analysis (ITAA); there are many books and articles, and many programs from many countries. Significantly, in 2004 education was chosen as the focus of a special issue of the *Transactional Analysis Journal* in which Newton and Emmerton provided the first comprehensive literature review in the field. Later, in 2009 the *TAJ* published another special issue on TA training in which the perspectives of educators again were strongly featured. The education specialty has become a recognized part of the ITAA around the globe.

What does educational transactional analysis look like?

I will offer a handful of methods which I associate with working educationally. Other people will have developed equally successful methods. Explore these examples, and think if any of them might be helpful if adapted for your work. I work with groups, but the methods offered here can be easily adapted by parent coaches for use with individual adults and children. Following a short description of the 'Planning Wheel' approach to curriculum design, I will then offer a few examples of ways I use TA theories in my profession as a parent educator. I will close with some thoughts about professional growth.

As educators, we are familiar with designing a curriculum based on our experience and academic training in educational methodology, and we add TA theory and methodology that helps us reach our goals. I design learning experiences by using the six step Planning Wheel, (Clarke 1998), because it reminds me to teach to what participants want/need, not to what I want to teach. Also, the wheel always brings me back to:

Step 1	Consideration of my underlying values
Step 2	Stating general goals, and . . .
Step 3	Choose specific behavioral goals. It reminds me to review the goals with learners and to adjust the content contract if needed. Always, the goals focus on empowerment, on helping people build on their strengths to meet here and now situations
Step 4	Make a plan of action
Step 5	Do the program
Step 6	asks me to evaluate the program in terms of Steps 2 and 3 Then look again at Step 1

Since most learning experiences are designed to invite people to change, either as a result of learning new information that is so meaningful to them that they make immediate changes, or by choosing new responses to something they want to have be different, 'the change triangle' (Clarke 1998) helps me design an activity that is a starting point for change.

Think about which position you like to take when you start to make a change. Remember that, if a change is started at any point and maintained conscientiously

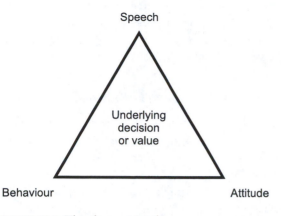

FIGURE 22.1 The change triangle

and consistently over time, adjustments in the other positions will follow. Listen to Julia's options from *Who, Me Lead a Group?*

> Let us say that you are leading a group on violence in society, and Julia has announced that she wants to stop spanking her child as a method of discipline. Julia can start to make this change in her life by altering her words, her attitudes, her behaviour, or her basic decisions. Julia may take the first step by changing the way she speaks about her child. She will say, 'Logan needs discipline,' instead of, 'Logan needs a spanking.' Or Julia could take the first step by changing her behaviour. When she feels like spanking Logan, she will send him to sit in the corner instead. She could examine her concept of discipline and change her attitude from a flippant, 'Spare the rod and spoil the child' to a thoughtful, 'It is my responsibility to socialize my child without using violence'.
>
> (Clarke 1998)

The middle of the triangle, *underlying decision or value*, includes script. Since helping people identify and change scripts lies in the skill set of the clinician or therapist, we educators invite learners to change behaviors, language, or attitudes – and the learner may or may not change an underlying belief or decision. That part is up to the learner. Our job is to set a range of helpful options that the learner can choose or reject.

Strategies that bring TA to life

Occasionally, it is effective to offer a piece of TA theory directly. However, since most adults prefer to learn by figuring out what they need to learn for themselves rather than by listening to a preacher/teacher, we often create indirect learning activities that invite people to think or perceive in different ways and then decide what they want to do about their new awareness. Here are some examples using common TA theories with the starting points from the change triangle:

Life positions, I'm not OK – They're OK (change behaviors)

Parents often indicate that they feel inadequate about their parenting. That's the 'I'm not OK position'. So, how to invite them to claim their OK-ness? Try this, for inviting adults who feel 'not OK' about their parenting skills to claim their OK-ness and to parent from their strengths:

After establishing ground rules that assure safety and the right to pass, place yourself to the group and ask participants to:

1 Stand and center yourself. Shake off any negative feelings. Be deeply centered.

2 Now consider the way you were parented. Step back and remember one thing – just one – that your parents did that didn't work well for you. Feel the feeling very briefly, shake it off.

3 Return to the center spot and regain your centered calmness.

4 Step forward one step and remember one specific thing your parents did that worked well for you. Capture that positive feeling.

5 Return to the center spot and enjoy that positive feeling.

6 Now consider ways you have parented. Step back one step and remember one specific way you have parented that you are not proud of. Catch your feeling briefly and then shake it off.

7 Return to the center spot and regain your calm centered place.

8 Step forward one step and recall one piece of parenting you did that worked well for your child and for you. Breathe in that good feeling.

9 Return to your centered spot and enjoy the positive feeling.

10 Remember that you have all these positions in you, and you can always choose which to use. In the future, if you feel confused, you can center yourself, step forward, grab the positive feeling, and think of what to do – or get help from others if you need it.

11 Ask those who like to talk while thinking to find a partner and share what they learned. In a class setting, it is up to each person to learn as much or as little as is helpful at the time. A curious teacher, like myself, would love to hear what each person learned – but in a personal assessment exercise such as this, it is none of my business unless people choose to share. I need to maintain a position of trust and respect. That would be different if this were a coaching situation with a different contract. This is an especially strong activity because it includes the auditory, the visual, the kinesthetic, and the visual/spatial learning style preferences. And it respects body knowledge, body wisdom.

Life positions, I'm OK – You're not OK (change attitudes)

A working group rejecting each other from the 'I'm OK – You're not OK', 'You're too old' or 'You're too young' position, can be invited into OK–OK by asking them to stand in a continuum by the number of years worked here. You fold the line into a 'V' shape. Ask each side to describe the strengths the colleague opposite them brings to the group. Ask people to identify a group task that can be better done by having input from the strengths of both.

Transactions (change speech)

The topic is teaching self-responsibility to children by taking ulterior messages to please others out of parental requests or demands: 'Eat your beans for mommy,' becomes, 'Are you finished eating your beans?' Using a list of examples, participants listen to both messages and guess which would encourage a child the age of theirs to feel responsible for self.

Games (change behavior)

Educators have many ways of handling game invitations. *The suggestion circle* is a versatile one. A participant who is initiating a game of 'Yes, but' or 'If it weren't for him', can be invited to move from complaining to thinking responsibly and acting in an empowered way by a suggestion circle:

> This simple but elegant intervention was taught to me by Otho Hestorly:
> The participant is asked to describe the problem in one sentence. Each group member gives their best suggestion, following the ground rules of 'no discounting the problem' and 'no violence'. The participant is asked to listen, take the list home, and choose one suggestion to try first. Everyone thinks, everyone learns. The leader is firm on the one sentence part, and the group learns the process.

Most groups of sixteen or less who know how to do a suggestion circle can do one in three minutes. This means five problems can be addressed in fifteen minutes, while a discussion will often take twenty minutes and address only one problem, and a game may go on.

Drama Triangle (change behavior)

The Drama Triangle is an easy choice when the parents are wrangling about an adolescent's misuse of his driving privileges – and taking turns in the Rescuer, Persecutor and Victim roles.

> A masking tape triangle on the floor has an 'R', a 'P' and a 'V' on the corners. After a brief demonstration by the educator, class members are invited to

stand on the corners, take the body posture of that position, and play out the conversation. There is usually a lot of good-natured laughter as they recognize the switches in the game. Then they practice stepping off each corner and flipping the kind of energy they felt on that corner. Rescuer moves to positive Nurture energy and body posture, and decides what nurturing behavior would be helpful. Persecutor moves to Structure, and Victim moves to Problem Solving.

Drivers (change behavior)

Learning about drivers is often helpful for a class of educators.

In the week-long facilitator workshops, where I have introduced more than a thousand teachers to TA, we learn about the constrictiveness of drivers by heaping shawls on a volunteer, one for each driver: Be Perfect, Try Hard, Hurry Up, Be Strong, Be Pleasing (I often add 'Get Mine Now', which, I'm afraid, is on the rise as a result of childhood overindulgence). Learners then cluster according to their familiar driver and identify what skills they learned when they were 'in' that process. For example, 'In my Hurry Up driver, I learned to act quickly', 'In my Be Perfect driver, I learned to pay attention to details'. Then they identify ways to use those strengths as a temporary strategy, instead of staying in the clutches of a driver. For example, 'This is a situation where confrontation probably won't work. I'll use some of my pleasing skills in order to stay connected while I figure out a way to be effective'.

Script

We educators will probably teach about script only when we are teaching TA theory. However, a thorough knowledge of script theory is a powerful tool in the educator's toolbox. Having a healthy respect for script, and knowing some of the script signals, triggers us to ask ourselves important questions:

A student is gallows-smiling about violent behavior; so do I address the smiles? How do I handle a blocking transaction, a tangential redefinition, or a first or second level discount? We make the best judgments we can based on our contract and the goals. Another important question is: when I catch myself engaging in some of my own script behavior, how carefully do I plan to practice what to do instead, next time?

Thoughts on professional growth

Students are often aware of when we are authentic, and when we are not. Therefore, it follows that half of our job as educators is to keep current on our subject matter and our craft, and the other half is to keep learning ourselves. Being life-long learners about ourselves, let us teach from that balance of mind and heart that lets us go beyond intelligence to our place of wisdom. I like these recommendations for professional growth:

1   Pay attention to current brain research. We recognize that children's brains are developing in response to the technology they use; therefore, our children will think differently than we do.
2   Be active in some professional organization.
3   Occasionally read a book by a sociologist, and connect what you do with the big picture. I'm currently learning from *The Accordion Family* (Newman 2012) about how expanded families and lack of jobs are impacting families and economies in six nations.
4   Periodically plunge back into the TA books that are the most challenging to you. I use *Tactics* (Napper and Newton 2014), which encourages me to keep growing, and Eric Berne's *Structure and Dynamics of Organizations and Groups* (1973), which for me is Berne's most difficult but richest book.
5   After each presentation you make, ask someone to tell you one thing you did well. You already know what mistakes you made – so, ask for strengths. Often, people will tell you about something you didn't even know you did. Good – Do that again – Go ahead! Expand, borrow, adjust and create: Be a strong part of the wind.
6   Every day, make room for laughter and joy!

The end and the beginning

The winds are still blowing. The generative energy of TA that started in San Francisco has spread, and the story of TA educators is being written in many countries and cultures. It seems like a long time since I first went to a San Francisco conference and learned about Special Fields. But, in the history of the world it is a very short time, and look what we have done! We – all of us!

I've been referring to TA educational books in English because I read only English, but I celebrate that there are TA books in many languages, and contributions from many countries. With many regional and local organizations, and many certified teachers and supervisors, the TA winds have truly gone global.

You know the story of how educators use TA in your country. Or, if you don't know, find the pioneers and start putting the story together. And, if there is no story in your country yet, you can start one. Imagine how future winds will blow!

My best to you; and thank you for sharing this journey with me.

AFTERWORD

Giles Barrow, UK

Our intention at the outset of this process was to step back from defining educational transactional analysis. We have resisted capturing or 'fixing' what the concept has to mean for all those who use and develop its theory and practice. Instead, we have an enthusiasm for seeing what emerges from the common endeavour of those leading the way in educational transactional analysis.

On reflecting across the contributions, a handful of concepts recurrently surface. The paramountcy of the live encounter, the significance of self-knowing, integrity of professional identity and commitment to co-creativity, would seem to permeate implicitly – and at times explicitly – all of the perspectives included in this collection, and, across all the regions represented, these themes associate strongly with educational transactional analysis. Yet we are reluctant to claim them as pre-requisites or exclusive fundamental principles. We assert our capacity for the 'creative indifference' referred to in our introduction, and have appreciated throughout this project how educational transactional analysis exists for now, anticipating that it will inevitably become something different again in subsequent stages of its development.

We are aware that there are consequences to our reluctance to tightly define educational transactional analysis. We have been open as to what our team of contributors has generated; we have encouraged individuals to offer what was uppermost for them at the point of invitation. In doing so, a number of themes have not been fully considered: readers from within the TA community may notice that there is little reference to supervision in the context of educational work or as part of the learning process. Others may be wondering whether more might have been offered in terms of research in the field of educational TA. Meanwhile, TA trainees may have been expecting a critique of the training and certification process from an educational perspective. Whilst this book touches on many theories and ideas outside TA, there are others which have been left for another time: environmental and outdoor education, eco-psychology and learning, the emerging connection between neuroscience and education, democratic schooling, are all themes which could have easily emerged from this process.

What we have wanted most as editors is to be sufficient to the task, and in fact 'sufficiency' is integral to our approach: on the one hand demanding utility, efficiency and intent, but also – for many involved in contemporary education and beyond – holding a subtle challenge.

Here's a final story to illustrate what I mean:

> I was invited to present a training day for a school at the beginning of a new term. The team of staff were feeling especially beleaguered. The summer results had not been especially good and an impending school inspection would bring inevitable criticisms.
>
> The person coordinating the training was keen for me to raise staff morale with an exciting programme for the day. As she introduced me, I stood to the side and watched the hundred or so faces eyeing me cautiously, as teachers can do at times. In her description, the host detailed in appreciative terms my qualifications, experience and qualities, finishing with a flourish declaring that it would be a really inspiring day.
>
> At that precise moment I had an internal sense of dread. It was connected to an unintended burden that came from the opening process: an unwelcome idealization; unrealistic hopes combined with a despair at knowing that neither they nor I would be able to completely meet such demands or expectations.

It was an experience typical of what Miljkovic and others have described earlier in this volume about the inter-subjective field in teaching and learning. The potentially destructive transferential/counter-transferential process was active; the dominant hegemonic dynamic explored by Shotton, with its competitiveness for 'who is most OK' – and who is not, was all set to activate. So, much of what our contributors have been describing – that can immobilize the educator through script-limiting beliefs and the absence of mindfulness, functional fluency or personal agency – were all there in that moment.

> Taking the stage, I offered thanks for the strokes. I then took a breath and simply said; 'My task today is sufficient to be only: to be sufficient for you in our work together'.
>
> I paused and took account of the response. It was the first time I had opened a presentation in this way. I was unsure of what to do next, so I asked them to consider what 'sufficiency' might mean for them? I shared with them my own internal process: that I could feel all of the expectations to be 'better than' and, simultaneously, doubts about my being 'good enough'.

Referring to 'sufficiency' opened up a possibility, an option that had not already been in the field. This demonstrates what we explored in our opening section, in which we emphasized how important it is for the teacher to introduce what has been previously elusive or unnamed.

> In bringing the concept into the process, something became unlocked. Discussions focused on the implications for the teachers of being equally explicit about being sufficient with their students. People offered thoughts about what the word meant for them; 'It means being authentic', 'I am enough', 'We are resourceful', 'I know who I am and can be open to who you might be', 'It means anything is possible', 'We are free!'

This is the encouragement of subjectification that Newton draws from the work of Biesta, in which individuals grow through the uncertainty of education.

It is not only the learner that undergoes change: my reference to sufficiency was forged in response to the encounter – they made me do it! I named what was important, and in doing so demonstrated a particular expertise, but we all made it important for that moment and, in doing so, increased our individual potency and the collective sense of purpose. Since then, I have used that way of being open to a group, and have had similar responses; and it has got me thinking about the significance of sufficiency and its function with reference to Biesta's notion of education as a 'weak' concept.

Essentially, sufficiency is a counter-cultural concept for educators caught in systems that prioritize measurement, preference exponential examination success, and render learning as a 'strong' concept. Being *sufficient* as an educator is an act of creative subversion – and educational transactional analysis offers a significant framework for understanding its psychological and pedagogic implications. So, in most respects our work as editors has been aimed at being sufficient; to be suitably resourced for the task, and to position ourselves alongside, 'in relation to', and not 'better than'. To build upon Jean Clarke's reference to the 'winds of change': to breathe something new into the educational transactional analysis story. To be hopeful, to be sufficient; sometimes, that's all it takes.

GLOSSARY

accounting   a function of the Adult ego-state, 'taking into account' all factors relevant to a situation, from both the external environment and internal Parent and Child input.

Adapted Child   one of the functional modes of interaction associated with the Child ego-state. It can be positively co-operative or negatively complying or rebellious.

Adult   the Adult ego-state which interacts with others from, and responds appropriately to, here-and-now reality.

affirmation   strokes which support people's need and ability to grow and develop; life-supporting messages linked to stages of development.

attribution   a defining message which tells someone they have a particular characteristic e.g. stupid, clever etc., so that the person believes this of themselves.

autonomy   a state of being in the present characterized by awareness of self and others, and the ability to respond spontaneously with openness and authentic expression of feelings.

Child   the Child ego-state, correctly a *set* of ego-states which hold the behaviours, thinking and feeling experienced during the various stages of childhood.

complementary transaction   an interaction in which the ego-state or mode addressed is the one which responds – hence on a transactional diagram the lines are parallel.

Compliant one behavioural mode of Adapted Child, in which a person does what is asked or expected without regard to their own needs, wants or thinking.

contamination Parent or Child ego-state content that a person mistakes for Adult.

contract a bi- or multi-lateral negotiated agreement between parties to bring about a mutually determined outcome.

Controlling Parent functional or behavioural mode of interacting with others which can be appropriately clear and limit-setting or inappropriately rigid and critical.

Co-operative a positive behavioural mode, one aspect of Adapted Child, in which a person works well with others from autonomous choice.

Critical a behavioural mode in which the person is domineering, authoritarian, rigid and/or critical.

crossed transaction an interaction in which the response comes from an ego-state or mode other than the one addressed; this may cause a break in communication which can be helpful if the interaction was previously 'stuck' or not beneficial.

cycles of development a theory of human development and learning which includes re-cycling of developmental stages throughout life.

discounting a process in which someone minimizes, belittles or disregards some aspect of themselves, another person or the situation.

Drama Triangle a way of describing and analysing psychological games; participants take on one or more of the three roles, Persecutor, Rescuer and Victim.

driver an unhelpful and apparently compulsive way of behaving under stress. There are five; Be Perfect, Be Strong, Hurry Up, Please People and Try Hard. Also known as working styles when the positive aspects are emphasized, e.g. high standard of work (BP), calm in a crisis (BS) etc.

egogram a histogram of ego-state behaviours which shows the comparative time and energy spent on each.

ego-state a consistent pattern of feeling and experience and a corresponding consistent pattern of behaviour.

episcript negative script messages that a parent passes to a child in the (unconscious) hope that this will release the parent from the effect of that message.

frame of reference our personal, overall world-view that we use to define ourselves, others and the world.

game (psychological game) a series of ulterior transactions which proceed to a predictable and familiar conclusion; usually results in bad feelings.

imago the picture we unconsciously carry in our heads of how a group we are part of will be, based on our early experience.

Immature negative behavioural mode of Natural Child in which a person exhibits egocentricity and disregard for others.

injunction a self-limiting part of the script which causes us to believe we cannot do something e.g. succeed, think, be important, be close to others; also known as *don'ts*.

life positions (windows on the world) four ways of seeing the world, related to perceptions of OK-ness in self and others. Also known as windows on the world as each offers a distinct perspective and excludes the others; also as *existential positions* because they are basic beliefs.

life-script (script) a set of beliefs and decisions made in childhood which continue to influence a person's life. Scripts include both self-limiting and self-protective beliefs and decisions; they can be updated as a person takes in new information, and they can be changed.

Marshmallow Parent a behavioural mode in which someone is over-protective or 'smothering' towards another person.

mode a behavioural aspect or manifestation of an ego-state.

Natural Child a functional or behavioural aspect of Child ego-state which can be spontaneous and creative or selfish and immature.

nurture a function of the Parent ego-state.

Nurturing Parent a functional aspect of Parent ego-state and a behavioural mode in which interactions are caring and supportive.

OK-ness the state of being in the 'I'm OK–You're OK' life position.

options choosing transactions and behavioural modes of response (rather than reacting automatically to stimuli).

Parent an ego-state which holds the thinking, feeling and ways of behaving derived from caregivers and other authority figures such as teachers.

permission a message that something is OK, e.g. to think for oneself, to be close to others, to trust, to experience feelings.

Persecutor a role on the Drama Triangle.

physis the drive towards wholeness and health – the life-force.

Rebellious a behavioural mode, part of Adapted Child in which a person resists demands and refuses to co-operate.

recycling the process of revisiting the stages of development experienced in childhood.

Rescuer a role on the Drama Triangle.

script see life-script.

Spontaneous a behavioural mode, part of Natural Child, in which a person creatively expresses themselves as they are.

stages of development series of stages in which age-appropriate developmental tasks are achieved, or not; there are seven, including recycling in adulthood.

stroke a unit of recognition, which may be positive or negative, and for being (unconditional) or doing (conditional)

stroke economy a set of social 'myths' or rules which limit the free and supportive giving and receiving of strokes.

structure a function of the Parent.

Structuring Parent a behavioural aspect of Controlling Parent in which someone interacts by providing direction, limit-setting and clarity of expectation.

symbiosis two people behave as though they have a single set of ego-states between them, discounting the other ego-states – hence 'symbiotic relationship'.

three-cornered contract a contract between any three parties in a situation; there may be other associated contracts.

transaction an interaction consisting of a stimulus and a response.

transactional analysis a system of theories, and their application, concerned with human development, personality, behaviour and communication, based on a philosophy of mutual and self respect.

triangular contract see three-cornered contract.

ulterior transaction a transaction which takes place outside the participants' awareness and dictates the outcome of the interaction; the component of games.

Victim a role on the Drama Triangle.

windows on the world see life positions.

Winner's Triangle a positive way of behaving in interactions; developed from the 'well-intentioned' aspect of the Drama Triangle.

working styles those aspects of drivers that enable people to maximize their positive features – excellence, endurance, enthusiasm, amiability and speed.

BIBLIOGRAPHY

Abe, T. (2012) *TA Happy Cards*, Osaka: Process Consulting.

Akkoyun, F. and Bacanfi, H. (1990) 'Sifat tarama listesinin Turkce'ye uyarlanmasi: TA ego durumlari olcekleri uzerine bir calisma', *Psikoloji-Seminer*, B: 637–43. Turkish adaptation of Williams, K.B. and Williams, J.E. (1980).

Alden, M. (1988) 'The Gossamer Injunction', *Transactional Analysis Journal*, 18: 321–4.

Allen, J. (1996) 'The Role of Permission Two Decades Later', *Transactional Analysis Journal*, 36: 196–205.

—— (2008) 'Permission, Protection and Mentorship: Their roles in psychological resilience and positive emotions', in Keith Tudor (ed.) *The Adult is Parent to the Child: Transactional analysis with children and young people*, Lyme Regis: Russell House, pp. 204–16.

Allen, J. and Allen, B. (1988) 'Scripts and Permissions: Some unexamined assumptions and connotations', *Transactional Analysis Journal*, 18: 283–92.

Arendt, H. (1961) *Between Past and Future*, London: Faber & Faber.

Babcock, D.E. and Keepers, T.D. (1976) *Raising Kids OK: Transactional analysis in human growth and development*, New York: Grove.

Bandura, A. (1997) *Self-Efficacy: The exercise of control*, New York: Freeman.

Banks, J. and Bird, J. (2002) *Emotional Needs: Achieving, behaving and learning in education (ENABLE)*, Modbury: The Modbury Group.

Barrow, G. (2006) *Distinctive Features of the Cycle of Development Model (CoD)*, Online. Available as download, 'Cycle of Development: An optimistic model': www.cracking behaviour.com/articles.asp (accessed 28 February 2015).

—— (2007) 'Wonderful World, Beautiful People: Reframing transactional analysis as positive psychology', *Transactional Analysis Journal*, 37: 206–9.

—— (2009) 'Teaching, Learning, Schooling and Script', *Transactional Analysis Journal*, 39: 298–304.

—— (2011) 'Educator as Cultivator', *Transactional Analysis Journal*, 41: 308–14.

—— (2014) '"Whatever!" The possibilities of adolescence', *Transactional Analysis Journal*, 44: 167–74.

—— (2015) 'Leadership and School Culture', in de Graaf, A., Thunissen, M., Cornell, W., Newton, T. (ed.) *Into TA: A comprehensive handbook of transactional analysis*, London: Karnac (not yet published).

Barrow, G. and Newton, T. (ed.) (2004) *Walking the Talk: How TA is improving behaviour and raising self-esteem*, London: David Fulton.

Barrow, G., Bradshaw, E. and Newton, T. (2001) *Improving Behaviour and Raising Self-esteem in the Classroom: A practical guide to using TA*, London: David Fulton.

Bauer, J. (2013) *Arbeit: Warum unser Glück von ihr abhängt und wie sie uns krank macht*, Munich: Blessing.

Beck, D. and Cowan, C. (1996) *Spiral Dynamics: Mastering values, leadership and change*, Oxford: Blackwell.

Beck, D. and Linscott, G. (1991) *The Crucible: Forging South Africa's future*, Boulder, CO: New Paradigm.

Bellah, R.N. (2011) *Religion in Human Evolution: From the paleolithic to the axial age*, Cambridge, MA: Harvard University.

Berardo, C. (2014) 'Alice in Writerland: Writing as a therapeutic tool and a way to understand adolescent needs', *Transactional Analysis Journal*, 44: 142–52.

Bergquist, W.H. and Phillips, S.R. (1975) 'Getting Students Involved in the Classroom', Online. Available at: www.cornell.edu/search/?q=getting%20students%20involved+site: www.cte.cornell.edu (accessed 3 March 2015).

Berne, E. (1947) *The Mind in Action*, New York: Simon & Schuster.

—— (1957) *A Layman's Guide to Psychiatry and Psychoanalysis*, New York: Simon & Schuster.

—— (1961) *Transactional Analysis in Psychotherapy: A systemic and social psychiatry*, New York: Grove.

—— (1963) *Structure and Dynamics of Organizations and Groups*, New York: Ballantine.

—— (1964) *Games People Play: The psychology of human relationships*, New York: Grove.

—— (1966) *Principles of Group Treatment*, New York: Grove.

—— (1970) *Spiele der Erwachsenen*, trans. Wolfram Wagmuth, Reinbeck bei Hamburg: Rowohlt.

—— (1972) *What Do You Say After You Say Hello?* London: Corgi.

Bettelheim B. (1976) *The Uses of Enchantment: The meaning and importance of fairytales*, London: Thames & Hudson.

Biesta, G. (2010) *Good Education in an Age of Measurement: Ethics, politics, democracy*, London: Paradigm.

—— (2014) *The Beautiful Risk of Education*, London: Paradigm.

Bion, W. (1961) *Experiences in Groups*, New York: Basic.

Bloch, M. (1964) *Apologie pour l'histoire ou Métier d'historien*, Online. Available at: http://classiques.uqac.ca/classiques/bloch_marc/apologie_histoire/apologie_histoire.html (accessed 6 March 2015).

Bloom, B.S. (1979) *Caratteristiche Umane e Apprendimento Scolastico*, Roma: Armando.

Bowlby, J. (1988) *A Secure Base*, London: Routledge.

Boyatzis, R. (2002) *Changing the Way We Manage Change*, Westport, CT: Quorum.

Brook, K.A. (1996) 'A Fresh Look at Permission', *Transactional Analysis Journal* 26: 160–6.

Burns, S. (2009) *Artistry in Training: Thinking differently about the way you help people to learn*, Online. Available at: www.stephanieburns.com/products/artistry_in_training (accessed 2 March 2015).

Çam, S. (1995) 'Ogretmen adaylarinin ego durumlari ile problem cozme becerisi algisi iliskisinin incelenmesi', *Psikolojik Danisma ve Rehberlik Dergisi*, 6: 37–42.

Çam, S. and Akkoyun, F. (2001) 'The Effects of Communication Skills Training on Ego States and Problem Solving', *Transactional Analysis Journal*, 31: 161–6.

Cameron, C. and Moss, P. (eds) (2011) *Social Pedagogy and Working with Children and Young People: Where care and education meet*, London: Jessica Kingsley.

Campos, L. (2011) 'Update on Transactional Analysis for Social Responsibility', *The Script*, 41(1): 5.

Choy, A. (1990) 'The Winner's Triangle', *Transactional Analysis Journal*, 20: 40–6.

Cirneci, D. 'How Findings from Neuroscience can Optimize Adult Learning with Impact on Training and Therapy', keynote address to EATA trainers' meeting, Bucharest, July 2012. Online. Available at: www.eatanews.org/ta-resources-and-links/ta-resources/#sthash.w1qapETS.dpuf (accessed 5 August 2014).

Clarke, J. (1978) *Self-Esteem: A family affair*, Center City, PA: Hazelden Foundation.

—— (1981) 'Differences between the Special Fields and Clinical Groups', *Transactional Analysis Journal*, 11: 169–70.

—— (1982) 'Self-Esteem, a Family Affair: A parenting model', *Transactional Analysis Journal*, 12: 252–4.

—— (1996) 'The Synergistic Use of Five Transactional Analysis Concepts by Educators', *Transactional Analysis Journal*, 26: 214–19.

—— (1997) 'Applied Transactional Analysis in Parent Education', *Transactional Analysis Journal*, 27: 7–10.

—— (1998) *Who, Me Lead a Group?* Seattle, WA: Parenting Press.

—— (1999) *Connections: The threads that strengthen families*, Center City, MN: Hazelden Foundation.

Clarke, J. and Dawson, C. (1998) *Growing Up Again: Parenting ourselves, parenting our children*, Center City, MN: Hazelden.

Clarke, J., Dawson, C. and Bredehoft, D. (2014) *How Much is Too Much? Raising likeable, responsible, respectful children: From toddlers to teens in an age of overindulgence*, Boston, MA: da Capo.

Cornell, W.F. (1988) 'Life Script Theory: A critical review from a developmental perspective', *Transactional Analysis Journal*, 18: 270–81.

Crossman, P. (1977) 'Acceptance Speech', *Transactional Analysis Journal*, 7: 104–6.

—— (1966) 'Permission and Protection', *Transactional Analysis Bulletin*, 5(19): 152–4.

Davies, L. (2004) *Education and Conflict: Complexity and chaos*, Oxford: Routledge.

Deakin-Crick, R., Broadfoot, P. and Claxton, G. (2002) *Developing an Effective Lifelong Learning Inventory: The ELLI Project*, Bristol: Lifelong Learning Foundation.

de Graaf, A. and Kunst, K. (2008) *Einstein en de kunst van het zeilen*, Amsterdam: SWP.

de Graaf, A. and Thunnissen, M. (2013) *Leerboek Transactionele Analyse*, Utrecht: De Tijdstroom.

Dekoninck, J. (1994) Unpublished Workshop Material, ARIATE: Paris.

de la Garanderie, A. (1984) *Le Dialogue Pédagogique*, Paris: Centurion.

—— (1987) *Comprendre et Imaginer*, Paris: Centurion.

—— (1988) *Tous les Enfants Peuvent Réussir*, Paris: Centurion.

—— (1991) *La Motivation*, Paris: Centurion.

Dennison, G. (1969) *Lives of Children: The story of the first street school*, New York: Random House.

—— (1971) *Developmental Psychology Today*, Del Mar, CA: CRM.

Drego, P. (1983) 'The Cultural Parent', *Transactional Analysis Journal*, 13: 224–7.

—— (2006) 'Freedom and Responsibility: Social empowerment and the altruistic model of ego states', *Transactional Analysis Journal*, 36: 90–104.

—— (2009) 'Bonding the Ethnic Child with the Universal Parent: Strategies and ethos of a transactional analysis ecocommunity activist', *Transactional Analysis Journal*, 39: 193–206.

Dryden, W. (2002) *Dryden's Handbook of Individual Therapy*, London: Sage.

Dusay, J. (1977) *Egograms: How I see you and you see me*, New York: Harper & Row.

Elias, J.L. and Merriam, S.B. (1995) *Philosophical Foundations of Adult Education*, Malabar, FL: Krieger.

Emerson, W. (1998) 'Birth Trauma: The psychological effects of obstetrical interventions', *Journal of Prenatal and Perinatal Psychology and Health*, 13(1): 11–44.

Emmerton, N. and Newton, T. (2004) 'The Journey of Educational Transactional Analysis from its Beginning to the Present', *Transactional Analysis Journal*, 34: 283–90.

English, F. (1969) 'Episcript and the "Hot Potato" Game', *Transactional Analysis Bulletin*, 8 (32): 77–82.

—— (1975) 'The Three-Cornered Contract', *Transactional Analysis Journal*, 5: 4.

—— (1977) 'What Shall I Do Tomorrow? Reconceptualizing transactional analysis', in Barnes, G. (ed.) *TA After Eric Berne: Teachings and practices of three TA schools*, Palatine, IL: Harper College, pp. 287–347.

—— (1994) 'Shame and Social Control Revisited', *Transactional Analysis Journal*, 24: 109–20.

—— (2007) 'Open Letter to Agnès Le Guernic', *Transactional Analysis Journal*, 37: 242–3.

Erickson, E. (1950) *Childhood and Society*, New York: Norton.

Ernst, F. (1971) 'The OK Corral: The grid for get-on-with', *Transactional Analysis Journal*, 1: 231–40.

Ernst, K. (1972) *Games Students Play: And what to do about them*, Millbrae, CA: Celestial Arts.

Erskine, R.G. (1994) 'Shame and Self-Righteousness', *Transactional Analysis Journal*, 24: 86–102.

—— (1998) 'Attunement and Involvement: Therapeutic responses to relational needs', *International Journal of Psychotherapy*, 3: 235–44.

—— (2002) 'Relational Needs', *EATA Newsletter*, 73: 5–9.

—— (2009) 'Art and Science of Relational Psychotherapy 2009–2010', unpublished notes, Nottingham Seminar Group.

—— (2010) *Life Scripts: A transactional analysis of unconscious relational patterns*, London: Karnac.

Faber, A. and Mazlish, E. (1974) *Liberated Parents, Liberated Children*, New York: Grosset & Dunlap.

Felder, R.M. and Brent, R. (2009) *Active Learning: An introduction*, Online. Available at: www4.ncsu.edu/unity/lockers/users/f/felder/public/Papers/ALpaper(ASQ).pdf (accessed 9 June 2010).

Fowlie, H. and Sills, C. (2011) *Relational Transactional Analysis: Principles in practice*, London: Karnac.

Fregola, C. (2010) 'Simulation Games and Emotive, Affective and Social Issues', in Piu, A. and Fregola, C. (eds) *Simulation and Gaming for Mathematical Education: Epistemology and teaching strategies*, Hershey: Idea-Group, pp. 57–64.

—— (2014) 'Mathematical Calculation Procedures and Drivers in Action in the Learning Environment', *Percorsi di Analisi Transazionele*, 1.1: 253–77.

Fregola, C. and Lozzelli, A. (2013) 'TA, Relationship with One's Own Learning Process and Strategic Studying', *International Journal of Transactional Analysis Research*, 4.1: 67–79.

Freire, P. (1975) 'Education for Liberation', paper presented at Ecumenical Christian Centre, Bangalore.

—— (1984) *Pedagogy of the Oppressed*, trans. M.B. Ramos, New York: Continuum.

Gage, N.L. (1972) *Teacher Effectiveness and Teacher Training: The search for a scientific basis*, Palo Alto, CA: Pacific.

Gagné, R.M. (1985) *Le Condizioni dell'Apprendimento*, Roma: Armando.

Gatto, J.T. (2005) *Dumbing Us Down: The hidden curriculum of compulsory schooling*, Gabriola Island, BC: New Society.

Gellert, S.D. and Wilson, G. (1980) 'Les Contrats', *Actualité en Analyse Transactionnelle*, 13: 4–9.

Goleman, D. (2002) *The New Leaders: Transforming the art of leadership into the science of results*, London: Little, Brown.

Gopnik, A., Meltzoff, A.N. and Kuhl, P. (1999) *The Scientist in the Crib*, New York: Morrow.

Gordon, T. (1974) *TET: Teacher Effectiveness Training*, New York: David McKay.

Gough, G.H. and Heilbrun, A.B. (1983) *The Adjective Checklist Manual*, Palo Alto, CA: Consulting Psychologists.

Gramsci, A. (1977) *Selections from the Prison Notebooks of Antonio Gramsci*, trans. Q. Nowell Smith (ed.), London: Lawrence & Wishart.

Green, A. (1990) *Education and State Formation*, London: Macmillan.

Grimm, J. and Grimm, W. (1984) *The Penguin Complete Grimms' Tales for Young and Old*, trans. R. Mannheim, London: Penguin.

—— (1986) *Les Contes*, Paris: Flammarion.

Hannah, S. (2003) *First of the Last Chances*, Manchester: Carcanet.

Harber, C. (2004) *Schooling as Violence: How schools harm pupils and societies*, Oxford: Routledge.

Harris, T. (1973) *I'm OK – You're OK*, London: Pan.

Hawkes, L. (2007) 'The Permission Wheel', *Transactional Analysis Journal*, 37: 210–17.

Hay, J. (1993) *Working it Out at Work: Understanding attitudes and building relationships*, Watford, UK: Sherwood.

—— (1995) *Donkey Bridges for Developmental TA: Making transactional analysis memorable and accessible*, Watford, UK: Sherwood.

—— (1996) *Transactional Analysis for Trainers*, Watford, UK: Sherwood.

—— (1997) 'The Autonomy Matrix', *INTAND Newsletter*, 5(1): 7.

Hellinger, B. (1998) *Love's Hidden Symmetry: What makes love work in relationships*, Phoenix, AZ: Zeig,Tucker.

Hellinger, B. and ten Hövel, G. (2001) *Constellations familiales: Comprendre les mécanismes des pathologies familiales*, Gap, France: Souffle d'Or.

Heppner, P.P. (1988) *The Problem Solving Inventory Manual*, Palo Alto, CA: Consulting Psychologists.

Hersey, P. and Blanchard, K.H. (1982) *Management of Organization Behavior: Utilizing human resources*, Englewood Cliffs, NJ: Prentice-Hall.

Hewson, J. (1990) 'A Heuristic Systems Model for TA', *ITA News*, 26: 2–5.

Holt, J. (1976) *Instead of Education: Ways to help people do things better*, London: Penguin.

Horne, A., and Ohlsen, M. (1982) *Family Counselling and Therapy*, Itasca, IL: Peacock.

Hutchinson, L. (2003) 'ABC of Learning and Teaching in Medicine', *British Medical Journal*, 326: 810–12.

Hyde, L. (2006) *The Gift: How the creative spirit transforms the world*, Edinburgh: Canongate.

Illich, I. (1972) *Deschooling Society*, London: Marion Boyars.

James, M. (1974) *Transactional Analysis for Moms and Dads: What do you do with them now that you've got them?*, Boston, MA: Addison-Wesley.

Jaoui, G. (1988) 'Les Permissions en AT', Paris: Unpublished Workshop Material.

Joyce, P. and Sills, C. (2009) *Skills in Gestalt Counselling and Psychotherapy*, London: Sage.

Karpman, S. (1968) 'Fairytales and Script Drama Analysis', *Transactional Analysis Bulletin*, 7 (26): 39–43.

Kelly, G. (1955) *The Psychology of Personal Constructs*, New York: Norton.

Khan, K.S. and Coomarasamy, A. (2006) *A Hierarchy of Effective Teaching and Learning to Acquire Competence in Evidence Based Medicine*, London: BMC Medical Education. Online. Available at: www.biomedcentral.com/1472–6920/6/59 (accessed 11 June 2010).

Kiltz, R.R. (2004) 'Berne and Buddha: A comparison of their fundamental concepts', *EATA Newsletter*, 81.

Kline, N. (1999) *Time to Think: Listening to ignite the human mind*, London: Cassell.

Kline, N. (2009) *More Time to Think: The power of independent thinking*, Pool-in-Wharfedale: Fisher-King.

Knowles, M. (1973) *The Adult Learner*, Houston, TX: Gulf.

Kolb, D.A. (1984) *Experiential Learning: Experience as the source of learning and development*, Englewood Cliffs, NJ: Prentice-Hall.

Krieger, W. (1989) 'A World Without Lifeguards', *The Script*, 19(4): 1.

Kupfer, D. and Haimowitz, M. (1971) 'Therapeutic Interventions Part 1: Rubberbands now', *Transactional Analysis Journal*, 1: 10–16.

Lakoff, G. (2014) 'Conservatives don't follow the polls . . .', interview by Z. Williams in the *Guardian*, 1 February. Online. Available at: www.theguardian.com/books/2014/feb/01/george-lakoff-interview (accessed 2 March 2015).

Lakoff, G. and Johnson, M. (1980) *Metaphors We Live By*, Chicago, IL: University of Chicago.

Landaiche, N.M. (2009). 'Understanding Social Pain Dynamics in Human Relations', *Transactional Analysis Journal*, 39: 229–38.

—— (2010) 'Reflections on the Montreal Conference', *The Script*, 40(7): 1.

Le Guernic, A. (2004) 'Fairytales and Psychological Life Plans', *Transactional Analysis Journal*, 34: 3.

Lepkowska, D. (2014) 'The Head-teachers Paying the Price of Failure', *Guardian*, 24 June. Online. Available at: www.theguardian.com/education/2014/jun/24/headteachers-paying-the-price-failure (accessed 2 March 2015).

Levin, P. (1980) *Cycles of Power: A user's guide to the seven seasons of life*, San Francisco: Self-published.

Levin-Landheer, P. (1982). 'The Cycle of Development', *Transactional Analysis Journal*, 12: 129–39.

Lieberman, M.A., Yalom, I.D. and Miles, M.B. (1973) *Encounter Groups: First facts*, New York: Basic.

Ligabue, S. (2007) 'Being in Relationship: Different languages to understand ego states, script and the body', *Transactional Analysis Journal*, 37: 294–305.

Lim, V. (2005) 'Unleash your Natural Leader', *Association for Management and Education*, 12: 2.

Linden, W. (1993) 'Meditation' in Vaitl, D. and Petermann, F. (eds) *Handbuch der Entspannungsverfahren, Vol 1: Grundlagen und Methoden*, Weinheim: Beltz, pp. 207–16.

Loria, B. (1990) 'Epistemology and Reification of Metaphor', *Transactional Analysis Journal*, 20: 152–62.

McCombs, B.L. and Whistler, J.S. (1997) *The Learner-Centered Classroom and School*, San Francisco: Jossey-Bass.

McCraty, R. and Childre, D. (2002) *The Appreciative Heart: The psychophysiology of positive emotions and optimal functioning*: publication 02–026, San Francisco, CA: HeartMath Research.

Macefield, R. and Mellor, K. (2006) 'Awareness and Discounting', *Transactional Analysis Journal*, 36: 44–58.

McQueen, M. (2012) *The New Rules of Engagement: A Guide to understanding and connecting with Generation 'Y'*, Sydney: Nexgen.

Marzano, R. (2007) *Wat Werkt op School: Research in actie*, Middelburg: Bazalt.

Maslow, A. (1970) *Motivation and Personality*, 2nd edn, New York: Harper & Row.

Massey, R. (1989) 'Systemic Contexts for Children's Scripting', *Transactional Analysis Journal*, 19: 186–92.

Mazzetti, M. 'Cross-Cultural Transactional Analysis', in H. Fowlie and C. Sills (eds) (2011) *Relational Transactional Analysis: Principles in practice*, London: Karnac, pp. 189–98.

Meighan, R. (1994) *The Freethinkers' Guide to the Educational Universe*, Nottingham: Educational Heretics.

Mezirow, J. (1981) 'A Critical Theory of Adult Learning and Education', *Adult Education Quarterly*, 32(3): 3–24.

—— (2000) *Learning as Transformation*, San Francisco, CA: Jossey Bass.

Micholt, N. (1992) 'Psychological Distance and Group Interventions', *Transactional Analysis Journal*, 22: 228–33.

Mietzel, G. (2007) *Pädagogische Psychologie des Lernens und Lehrens*, Göttingen: Hogrefe.

Moiso, C. 'Being and Belonging', *The Script*, 28(9): 1, 7.

Montessori, M. (1966) *Secret of Childhood*, New York: Random House.

—— (1991) *The Child's School: Montessori education in the primary school*, in P. Oswald and G. Schulz-Benesch (ed.), Freiburg: Herder.

Moreau, J. (2010) 'A Mythological View of Group Script', in S. van Poelje (ed.) *Keep the TA-O Torch Alight*, Utrecht, NL: Intact, pp. 29–46.

Nagel, N. (2009) 'Beziehung als Schlüssel zum Lernen', *Zeitschrift für Transaktionsanalyse*, 2009 (2): 128–41.

Napper, R. (2009) 'Positive Psychology and Transactional Analysis', *Transactional Analysis Journal*, 39: 61–74.

Napper, R. and Newton, T. (2000; 2nd edn 2014) *Tactics: Transactional analysis concepts for all trainers, teachers and tutors + insight into collaborative learning strategies*, Ipswich, UK: TA Resources.

Naughton, M. and Tudor, K. (2006) 'Being White', *Transactional Analysis Journal*, 36: 159–71.

Nelson, N., Amen, D. and Lemare-Calaba, J. (2006) *The Power of Appreciation*, Malibu, CA: Mindlab.

Newman, K. (2012) *The Accordion Family; Boomerang Kids: Anxious parents and the private toll of global competition*, Boston, MA: Beacon.

Newton, T. (2003) 'Identifying Educational Philosophy and Practice through Imagoes in Transactional Analysis Training Groups', *Transactional Analysis Journal*, 33: 321–31.

—— (2006) 'Script, Psychological Life Plans and the Learning Cycle', *Transactional Analysis Journal*, 36: 186–95.

—— (2007) 'The Health System: Metaphor and meaning', *Transactional Analysis Journal*, 37: 195–205.

—— (2008) 'Building the Virtual Village: Working with the social environment', in K. Tudor (ed.) *The Adult is Parent to the Child*, Lyme Regis, UK: Russell House, pp. 15–280.

—— (2011) 'Transactional Analysis Now: Gift or commodity?' *Transactional Analysis Journal*, 41: 315–21.

—— (2014) 'Learning Imagoes Update', *Transactional Analysis Journal*, 44: 31–40.

Newton, T. and Cochrane, H. (2011) *Supervision for Coaches: A guide to thoughtful work*, Ipswich, UK: Supervision for Coaches.

Newton, T. and Pratt, K. (2015) 'Educational TA Today: A dialogue between two TA educators', *Journal of the Japan Transactional Analysis Association*, 38: 5.

Nhat Han, T. (4th edn 2007) *Ich pflanze ein Lächeln*, Munich: Arkana.

Noddings, N. and Shore, P. (1984) *Awakening the Inner Eye: Intuition in education*, New York: Teachers College.

Novellino, M. (2003) *La Sindrome dell'Uomo Mascherato*, Milano: Franco Angeli.

O'Grady, T. (2009) 'An Introduction to Spiral Dynamics', Online. Available at: www.slideshare.net/tonyogrady/an-introduction-to-spiral-dynamics (accessed 1 November 2013).

Op't Eynde, P., de Corte, E. and Verschael, L. (2002) 'Framing Students' Mathematics-Related Beliefs', in Leder, G., Pehkonen, E. and Torner, G. (eds) *Beliefs: A hidden variable in mathematical education*, Dordrecht: Kluwer Academic, pp. 13–38.

Palmer, P.J. (1998) *The Courage to Teach: Exploring the inner landscape of a teacher's life*, San Francisco: Jossey Bass.

Perrault, C. (2010) *The Complete Fairytales*, Oxford: Oxford University Press.

Petriglieri, G. (2010) 'Respected Marginality: Time to make the most of it', keynote at International Transactional Analysis Conference, Montreal, August.

Pickett, L. (1986) 'The Integrative Classroom', *Transactional Analysis Journal*, 16: 241–6.

Pratt, K., and Mbaligontsi, M. (2014) 'Transactional Analysis Transforms Community Care Workers in South Africa', *Transactional Analysis Journal*, 44: 53–67.

Propp, V. (1928) *Morphologie du Conte*; trans. L. Scott (1968) *Morphology of the Folktale*, Austin, TX: University of Texas.

Ramond, C. (2011) *Grandir: Éducation et analyse transactionelle*, Paris: La Méridienne.

—— (1994) 'Don't Change: A cultural injunction', *Transactional Analysis Journal*, 24: 220–1

Resnick, I.B. (1987) *Education and Learning to Think*, Washington: National Academy.

Robinson, K. (2006), 'Ken Robinson Says Schools Kill Creativity', Online. Available at: www.youtube.com/watch?v=NRnToFZQQP4 (accessed 2 March 2014).

Rodriguez, R.F. (1983) 'A Comparison of Teacher Teaching Style with Student Learning Style through the Use of Transactional Analysis', *Dissertation Abstracts International*, 43(11), 350I A.

Rogers, C.R. (1969) *Freedom to Learn: A view of what education might become*, Columbus: Merrill.

—— (1973) *Becoming Partners: Marriage and its alternatives*, London: Constable.

Rosewell, N. (2003) 'I'm OK, My School's OK', *Emotional Literacy UPDATE* (2).

Russell, S. (2009) 'Behaviour Wall: Working together towards behaviour solutions', Online. Available at: www.behaviourwall.com (accessed 3 March 2014).

Salters, D. (2006) 'Separateness and Belonging in the Dance of Life', *ITA News*, 26 August, 1, 3–7

—— (2011) 'Transactional Analysis and Spiral Dynamics', *Transactional Analysis Journal*, 41: 265–76.

Schiff, J. *et al.* (1975) *The Cathexis Reader: Transactional analysis treatment of psychosis*, New York: Harper and Row.

Schmid, B. (1990) 'Persoenlichkeits-Coaching: Beratung fuer die Person in ihrer Organizations- Berufs- und Privatwelt', Online document. Available at: www.coaching-magazin.de/artikel/schmid_bernd_-_persoenlichkeitscoaching.doc (accessed 3 March 2015).

—— (1994) 'Transactional Analysis and Social Roles', in G. Mohr and T. Steinert (ed.) *Growth and Change for Organizations: Transactional analysis new developments 1995–2006*, Pleasonton, USA: ITAA, pp. 32–61.

—— (2008) 'The Role Concept of Transactional Analysis and Other Approaches to Personality, Encounter, and Cocreativity for all Professional Fields', *Transactional Analysis Journal*, 38: 17–30.

Schmukler, D. and Friedman, M. (1988) 'The Developmental Function of Play and its Relevance for Transactional Analysis', *Transactional Analysis Journal*, 18: 80–8.

Schunk, D.H. (2004) *Learning Theories; An educational perspective*, New York: Englewood Cliffs.

Schunk, D.H. and Lilly, M.V. (1984) 'Sex Differences in Self-Efficacy and Attribution: Influence of performance feedback', *Journal of Early Adolescence* 4: 203–13.

Schwerdtfeger, A. (2008) *Was hält Lehrer gesund im Beruf*, Unpublished Presentation.

Seligman M. (1995) *The Optimistic Child: Proven program to safeguard children from depression and build lifelong resilience*, New York: Houghton Mifflin.

—— 'Positive Psychology, Positive Prevention and Positive Therapy', in C.R. Snyder and S.J. Lopez (eds) (2002) *The Handbook of Positive Psychology*, New York: Oxford University Press, pp. 3–12.

Shaull, R. (1984) 'Foreword', in P. Freire, trans. M. Bergman-Ross *Pedagogy of the Oppressed*, London: Penguin, pp. 11–16.

Sichem V. (1991) 'Le Multicontrat en Thérapie d'Enfants', *Actualité en Analyse Transactionnelle*, 60: 147–51.

Siety, A. (2003) *Matematica, mio Terrore*, Milano: Salani.

Sills, C. (2003) 'Role Lock: When the whole group plays a game', *Transactional Analysis Journal*, 33: 214–27.

—— (2006) 'Contracts and Contract Making', in C. Sills (ed.) *Contracts in Counselling and Psychotherapy*, London: Sage, pp. 11–35.

Sills, C. and Mazzetti, M. (2009) 'The Comparative Script System: A tool for developing supervisors', *Transactional Analysis Journal*, 39: 305–14.

Sondheim S. (1987) *Into the Woods*, New York: RCA Victor/Rilting Music.

Steiner, C. (1971) 'The Stroke Economy', *Transactional Analysis Journal*, 1: 9–15.

—— (1974) *Scripts People Live: Transactional analysis of life scripts*, New York: Grove.

—— (1996) 'Emotional Literacy Training' *Transactional Analysis Journal*, 26(1).

—— (2005) *L'ABC des émotions*, Paris: Interéditions.

Stern, J. (2012) *Loneliness and Solitude in Education: How to value individuality and create an enstatic school*, Oxford: Peter Lang.

Stewart, I. and Joines, V. (1987) *TA Today: A new introduction to transactional analysis*, Nottingham: Lifespace.

Stewart, I. and Joines, V. (2012, 2nd edn) *TA Today: A new introduction to transactional analysis*, Melton Mowbray, UK: Lifespace.

Summers, G., Tudor, K. (2000) 'Cocreative Transactional Analysis', *Transactional Analysis Journal*, 30: 23–40.

TAPACY, TA Proficiency Award for Children and Young People, Online. Available at: www.instdta.org/ta-proficiency-awards.html (accessed 3 March 2015).

Temple, S. (1996) 'Non-directive Counselling in Schools', in K. Jones and T. Charlton (eds) *Overcoming Learning and Behaviour Difficulties: Partnership with pupils*, London: Routledge, pp. 81–91.

—— (1999a) 'Teaching with TA', *ITA News*, 54.

—— (1999b) 'Functional Fluency for Educational Transactional Analysts', *Transactional Analysis Journal*, 29: 164–74.

—— (2000) 'A Way of Teaching Life Positions', *The Script*, 30(5).

—— (2004) 'Update on the Functional Fluency Model in Education', *Transactional Analysis Journal*, 34: 224–32.

—— (2005) 'Teachers are Young People's Leaders', *Emotional Literacy Update*, 20: 10–11.

—— (2008a) 'Philosophy, Principles and Practice', Unpublished workshop material.

—— (2008b) 'Bringing Up the Child', in K. Tudor (ed.) *The Adult is Parent to the Child: Transactional analysis with children and young people*, Lyme Regis, UK: Russell House, pp. 217–27.

Thayer-Bacon, B.J. (2004) 'Personal and Social Relations in Education', in C. Bingham and A.M. Sidorkin (ed.) *No Education Without Relation*, New York: Peter Lang, pp. 165–79.

Tisseron, S. (1999) *Nos Secrets de Famille: Histoire et mode d'emploi*, Paris: Ramsay.

Tobias, S. (1993) *Come Vincere la Paura della Matematica*, Milano: TEA.

Tosi, M.T. (2010) 'The Lived and Narrated Script', in R. Erskine (ed.) *Life Scripts: A transactional analysis of unconscious relational patterns*, London: Karnac, pp. 29–54.

Tough, A. (1971) *The Adult's Learning Projects: A fresh approach to theory and practice in adult learning*, Toronto, ON: Ontario Studies in Education.

Tudor, K. (1991) 'Children's Group: Integrating TA and gestalt perspectives', *Transactional Analysis Journal*, 21: 12–18.

—— (1999) *Group Counselling*, London: Sage.

—— (2003) 'The Neopsyche: The integrating adult ego state', in Sills, C. and Hargaden. H. (ed.) *Key Concepts in Transactional Analysis: Contemporary views*, London: Worth, pp. 201–31.

—— (ed.) (2008) *The Adult is Parent to the Child: Transactional analysis with children and young people*, London: Russell House.

—— (2011) 'Understanding Empathy', *Transactional Analysis Journal*, 41: 39–57.

Tudor, K. and Summers, G. (2014) *Co-creative Transactional Analysis*, London: Karnac.

Turner, V. (1974) *Liminal to Liminoid in Play, Flow and Ritual: An essay in comparative symbology*, Houston, TX: Rice University Studies.

Tutu, D. (1999) *No Future Without Forgiveness: A personal overview of South Africa's Truth and Reconciliation Commission*. New York: Random House.

Ugazio, V. (2013) *Semantic Polarities and Psychopathologies in the Family: Permitted and forbidden stories*, New York: Routledge.

University of Oregon Teaching Effectiveness Program (2010) *The Collaborative Research Model: Student learning teams in undergraduate research*, Online. Available at: http://darkwing. uoregon.edu/~tep/showcase/crmodel/index.html (accessed 3 March 2015).

Verney, V. (2009) 'Mindfulness and the Adult Ego State', *Transactional Analysis Journal*, 39: 247–55.

Williams, K.B. and Williams, J.E. (1980) 'The Assessment of Transactional Analysis Ego-States via the Adjective Checklist', *Journal of Personality Assessment*, 44: 120–9.

Winnicott, D. (2006) *The Family and Individual Development*, Oxford: Routledge.

Woollams, S. (1980) 'Cure!' *Transactional Analysis Journal*, 10: 115–17.

Woollams, S. and Brown, M. (1978) *Transactional Analysis: A modern and comprehensive text of TA theory and practice*, Michigan: Huron Valley Institute.

World Production (2004), *Ahead of the Class*, DVD (2007), London: ITV Studios Entertainment; Online. Available at: www.youtube.com/watch?v=B0SMpe1r3Ik&list=PL eW4p41AujfVFy7eIi6rLK-7rnmtNGrTj (accessed 3 March 2015).

Zimbardo, P. and Gerrig, R. (2004) *Psychologie*, Munich: Pearson.

Žvelc, G., Černetič, M. and Košak, M. (2011) 'Mindfulness-Based Transactional Analysis', *Transactional Analysis Journal*, 41: 241–54.

INDEX